The Design of Protest

The Design of Protest

Choreographing Political Demonstrations in Public Space

Tali Hatuka

University of Texas Press ↭ Austin

Chapter 7 is based, in part, on a paper co-authored with Aysegul Baykan, "Politics and Culture in the Making of Public Space: Taksim Square, 1 May 1977, Istanbul" (*Planning Perspectives*, Vol. 1, Issue 1, 2010, pp. 49–68).

Printed in the United States of America
First edition, 2018

Requests for permission to reproduce material from this work should be sent to:
Permissions
University of Texas Press
P.O. Box 7819
Austin, TX 78713–7819
utpress.utexas.edu/rp-form

♾ The paper used in this book meets the minimum requirements of ANSI/NISO Z39.48–1992 (R1997) (Permanence of Paper).

Design by Tali Hatuka

Library of Congress Cataloging-in-Publication Data

Names: Hatuka, Tali, author.
Title: The design of protest : choreographing political demonstrations in public space / Tali Hatuka.
Description: First edition. | Austin : University of Texas Press, 2018. | Includes bibliographical references and index.
Identifiers: LCCN 2017048974
ISBN 978-1-4773-1576-7 (cloth : alk. paper)
ISBN 978-1-4773-1577-4 (library e-book)
ISBN 978-1-4773-1578-1 (nonlibrary e-book)
Subjects: LCSH: Architecture and society. | Public spaces—Social aspects. | Public spaces—Political aspects. | Demonstrations—Planning. | City planning.
Classification: LCC NA2543.S6 H385 2018 | DDC 720.1/03—dc23
LC record available at https://lccn.loc.gov/2017048974

doi:10.7560/315767

Contents

Preface

A woman wakes up in the morning; she is standing by herself near the window; she puts on her clothes, picks up her bag, locks the door, and walks onto the street. She is supposed to meet some friends who, like her, are frustrated with the current leadership; they want and imagine change. They have been planning this action for a while; their talks and meetings have brought them closer to one another. In these meetings, they have envisioned the event—the routes to be taken, the messages to be presented, the boards to be designed, the flags to be hung. Debates are part of this dynamic, and much of their time is spent negotiating ideas and strategies among themselves. New members are joining, while others have decided to quit. The woman hopes that the action will be a success—that other people will take a risk and join them in realizing their vision.

This abstract description of dissent embodies the idea of protest presented in this book—a planned event in a space that is envisioned in the minds of its organizers, who seek to publicly challenge the political distance between those who rule and those who are ruled. To be sure, the meaning of the term "protest" implies different things in different places; however, despite these differences, similarities can be found between diverse events that are taking place worldwide. This search for similarities in the ways in which change is configured or realized has been the key driver in this project. Conceptually, this search was influenced by Elias Canetti's *Crowds and Power*, particularly his ideas on distance and mass assemblies, as well as by two more contemporary works, "The Power of Distance" by Diane Davis, who writes about citizens' distance from the state, and "Construal-Level Theory of Psychological Distance" by Nira Liberman and Yaacov Trope, who explore the concept of cognitive distance and the ways in which individuals perceive particular events. I found these three works, though extremely different, to be particularly useful in examining the dynamics of protests and their spatial manifestations.

Attempting to figure out the process of planning a protest meant traveling from one city to another to interview different activists, some of whom are still emotionally "living" a moment that occurred years or even decades ago. Attending protests in different parts of the world, I was always an "outsider," even when the actions took place in my homeland. As an architect and a planner, I decided to focus on and analyze the event's formal attributes rather than its ideological or political messages. I saw the value in exploring the physical manifestations of citizenship, viewing them as spatial rituals. Through this exploration and related discussions, I began to realize that with the increased democratization and global urbanization of the twenty-first century, protests, as communication tools and a means for change, are not vanishing; they are instead becoming more popular. In part, this increased popularity stems from increased competition over resources and rights, where protests seem to be not only vital tools for concretizing grievances but also a means of creating temporary, yet tangible, communities in cities.

Indeed, competition and contestation are not foreign to me. Living in the Middle East, in Israel—a conflicted zone, where the concept of space is both dynamic and contested—makes me constantly reflect on the fragility and temporality of power, beliefs, and territories. This habitus not only piqued my curiosity but also created some limits in terms of exploring this topic and, in that sense, relating to protests in different parts of the world; the book's perspective is predominantly Western. Thus, I would like to see this exploration as the beginning of a wider discussion on the dynamics between protests and physical spaces.

ORGANIZATION OF THE BOOK

The book has three parts: "Planning Protests," "Spatial Choreographies," and "Continuum." Part I, "Planning Protests," is about the ways in which protesters envision their actions and plan them. In strategizing about how best to act in a particular context, many parameters should be considered. Thus, part I is a broad inquiry into the design of protests in public spaces. It is abstract in its approach, with each of its chapters suggesting general categorization of a particular dimension of the protest-planning process. The discussion is incremental, and the ideas presented in this part should be viewed as building upon one another.

Chapter 1, "Challenging Distance," introduces the book's key premises and the lens through which protests are explored. Chapter 2, "Choosing a Place," focuses on how distance is manifested in space and its role in event planning. Because no ideal space exists for political action, the dialogue between the people and those in power might take place anywhere. Thus, the key question is not only where a particular action occurs but also what types of opportunities does a particular place offer to communicate an ideology? How does setting influence the development of temporary relationships on a mass level? In exploring these questions, "Choosing a Place" provides a set of abstract, temporary categorizations for public spaces and offers a general overview of the dynamics between political events and places. Chapter 3, "Enhancing the Impact," is about distance and distanciation and about the ability of activists to project their message beyond the event's geographical boundaries. More specifically, it examines the ways in which actors employ various spatial spheres and organizing principles to enhance their messages and claims. Tracking the ways in which actors operate reveals a sophisticated and multifaceted configuration of dissent, which extends beyond the boundaries of the nation-state and questions of national identity, thereby pressing us to abandon notions of resistance that assume that a subject stands vis-à-vis the established state's structure of power. Part I closes with chapter 4, "Bargaining Power," which discusses protests as bargaining processes regarding the appropriation of city spaces. Over the long history of civil protest, organizers have frequently struck bargains with authorities and police in advance. Negotiations between organizers, demonstrators, authorities, and police, both before and during the event, put limits on all parties and increase the predictability of encounters during demonstrations. The state's power to permit and limit citizens' tactics is still relevant today when addressing the relationships between activists and regimes, whether they are democratic or not.

Part II, "Spatial Choreographies," is about the specific spatial and temporal dimensions of protests. It investigates specific events' detailed designs, not only as aesthetic manifestations but also as tactics. Tactics, argues de Certeau in *The Practice of Everyday Life* (xix), depend on timing and opportunities that must be seized. However, tactics are not the "victories of the 'weak' over the 'strong' (whether the strength be that of the powerful people or the violence of things or of an imposed order, etc.)." Instead, they concern the clever implementation of the protest's planning strategy. Clearly, tactics cannot be exactly replicated (even by the same activists), but they can definitely inspire other protesters. The unfixed nature of a protest's design is its strength, allowing activists to contextualize their ideas and actions.

"Spatial Choreographies" addresses the dynamics between temporalities and their spatial attributes. They are microanalyses of events that focus on the dynamics between the body and physical settings, between the protest's social dynamics and ritual components (e.g., marching, gathering, and singing), dress code, and schedule (i.e., the timing and duration of the event). Chapter 5, "Staging the Action," provides an introduction to these features, presenting the dramaturgical attributes of three key spatial protest prototypes: the *spectacle*, the *procession*, and the *place-making*. Under each prototype, one can find extremely diverse spatial choreographies. In addition, although all protests are time-space specific and embedded in a concrete political, historical, and spatial context, some protests can also be viewed as offering a sociopolitical choreography in space that can be found, with alterations, in other contexts.

Chapters 6, 7, and 8 present examples of these spatial choreographies. Chapter 6, "Spectacles," analyzes events, whether large- or small-scale performances, that tend to be well-planned gatherings with particular sensitivity to the physical order or architectural attributes of a space. Chapter 7, "Processions," examines events in which walking or marching figure prominently, placing the protest in the mundane and economic space of the city. Chapter 8, "Place-Making," investigates events that use object(s) in a given setting as the heart of the event. The body in this type of action is secondary to the object, though they are closely linked. All the events analyzed in these chapters are major political actions and key events on a national or international scale from the 1960s to the present day. However, these varied cases do not represent a comprehensive list, nor do they aspire to constitute a complete list. Instead, these events illustrate poignant examples of spatial choreographies.

Methodologically, the analysis of the different sites follows the same key steps and includes the following: (1) archival research on the sites and events in question; (2) physical and architectural analyses of the sites; (3) interviews with key figures in the city (citizens or people from the institution, planners, and decision makers); and (4) interviews with the activists who were involved in the action. The interviews with the activists focused on planning the protest and the use of space and included generic questions about the organization of the protest, the planning process for the event, the use and choice of a particular tactic in a particular place at a particular time, the legality or illegality of the action, policing, and violence.

Part III, "Continuum," reflects on the power to perform protestability in our current times. In the closing chapter of the book, "Performing Protestability," it is suggested that protests do not emerge out of the blue as total surprises. Prior social and political dynamics nurture their emergence, and such dynamics include low-key public actions to which the government or the public does not pay attention. This dynamic of creating and managing protests as social processes is on the rise because it is a very basic tool people can use to temporarily break free of individualist constraints, resist the powers that be, and suggest a collective counterposition. Regarding contemporary cities' politics, this chapter discusses activists' challenges in realizing change and in modifying practices of distance.

ACKNOWLEDGMENTS

Obviously, large research projects need significant support. I am extremely grateful for the generous support of several agencies that made this project possible: the US Fulbright Program, the Marie Curie International Outgoing Fellowships (IOF, FP6), and the Marie Curie International Reintegration Grants (IRG, FP7) of the Commission of the European Communities.

This project has a long history. As a Fulbright and Marie Curie postdoc fellow, I started the project at the Massachusetts Institute of Technology (MIT) in early 2005 and completed it when I returned to Tel Aviv as a faculty member and the head of the Contemporary Urban Design Laboratory. While at MIT, I had the good fortune to meet two professors, Larry Vale and Diane Davis, both of whom hosted and supported my stay and my work; our conversations on the relationships between space and politics significantly contributed to the development of this project. I am also thankful to Larry for his careful reading of the first draft of this book and his important and insightful comments. At MIT, I also met Tunney Lee, whose thoughts and wisdom helped me better understand the dynamics of the 1960s in the United States. I would also like to thank Jim Burr, my editor at the University of Texas Press, and to Fernando Lara and an anonymous reviewer for their useful comments and advice.

An important step in assessing the materials I gathered was the opportunity to display the initial stages of the project at a public exhibition in Compton Gallery at the MIT Museum (Cambridge, Massachusetts) in 2008. This exhibition was the first step in understanding the factors that influence the spatial dynamics of protests. I am grateful to all the people who took part in and helped me with this exhibit, including MIT Museum staff members Gary Van Zante, Laura Knott, and Don Stidsen, and my production assistants Shimon Vitzman, Ty Haber, Shereen Srouji, Marilyn Levine, and Nitin Sawhney. The exhibit has received support from the MIT Department of Urban Studies and Planning, the Council for the Arts at MIT, the Graham Foundation for Advanced Studies in the Fine Arts, and the Israel Lottery Council for the Arts in Tel Aviv.

I did not conduct the empirical study on my own. Language and culture are significant assets when exploring different places. I visited many countries and cities, and, wherever I went, I had assistants who helped me navigate various spaces and political milieus. I would like to thank my research assistants, Fabiola López-Durán, Erhan Berat Findikli, and Helga Egetenmeier, who helped with the field study and data collection. I would like to thank Aysegul Baykan for her tremendous help and intellectual contribution to the study about Taksim Square in Istanbul. Upon returning to Tel Aviv in 2009, I continued exploring local protests in Israel and in the Middle East. The Arab Spring and the Occupy movement in 2011 were opportunities to reflect on what I had collected and written. I would like to thank Miryam Wijler, who traveled with me and collected materials across Israel and the West Bank; her help was invaluable. I would also like to thank my research assistants at the Laboratory of Urban Design, Rachel Bikel, Carmel Hanany, Nathan Prevendar, Alexis Wheeler, and especially Roni Bar, for adjusting the visuals for the formatting of the book.

Over the years that I spent collecting materials, I have attempted to write papers on particular cases, which, in the long run, have contributed to the development of the abstract categorizations presented in this book. Parts or reworked versions of these papers have been edited and integrated into the book: "Politics and Culture in the Making of Public Space: Taksim Square, 1 May 1977, Istanbul" (coauthored with Aysegul Baykan) and "The Challenge of Distance in Designing Civil Protest: The Case of Resurrection City in Washington Mall and the Occupy Movement in Zuccotti Park," both of which appeared in *Planning Perspectives*; "Civilian Consciousness of the Mutable Nature of Borders: The Power of Appearance along a Fragmented Border in Israel/Palestine," which appeared in *Political Geography*; "Transformative Terrains: Counter Hegemonic Tactics of Dissent in Israel," which appeared in *Geopolitics*; and "Negotiating Space: Analyzing Jaffa Protest Form, Intention and Violence, October 27th 1933," which appeared in *Jerusalem Quarterly*.

Most importantly, I want to thank two very dear people with whom I am lucky to be able to discuss my ideas and impressions: Hubert Law Yon, a wonderfully wise reader who has critically assessed an earlier draft of the book and helped me vastly over the years, and my life partner, architect Yoav Meiri, with whom I have discussed my rather raw ideas.

Lastly, when I started this project more than a decade ago, I was puzzled and not exactly sure what I might accomplish. "What can be said about social movements that has not already been said?" Bish Sanyal, a professor at the department of Urban Studies and Planning at MIT, asked me one evening during a dinner at his house. It was 2005, and I was still in the early stages of my work. Back then, I found answering Bish's question difficult. That evening, I remember feeling that maybe everything had already been said. Although I suspected that the issue of geometry and space had not been explored thoroughly, I was hesitant regarding its significance in the decision-making process when planning protests. Today, I am able to say that the geometry of space is a significant dimension in protest design, influencing the dynamics and engagement patterns among participants, with activists often being aware of both the physical geometry of a place and its symbolic meaning. For this and other insights, I would like to thank all the activists and organizations that have opened their doors and shared their thoughts and materials with me. It was a long and inspiring journey, through which I learned about the role of human imagination in configuring and reconfiguring space.

The Design of Protest

PART I

Planning Protests

ATTACK
IRAN
ps

1
Challenging Distance

Previous page: The human motivation to challenge social practices of distance is critical in the process of designing and enacting protests. Shown is a march in London calling for the withdrawal of British troops from Iraq, February 2007. Photo by author.

CHAPTER 1

Challenging Distance

> We are all translators; translation is the common feature in all forms of life, as it is part and parcel of "informatics society" modality of being-in-the-world. Translation is present in every communicative encounter, every dialogue.
>
> Zygmunt Bauman, *In Search of Politics*

Protest is an act of translation—a pejorative act of translation of a particular condition—that is publicly displayed. All human beings can participate in this act of translation, highlighting the existing boundaries and limits of an existing paradigm, and such protest is a basic mode of human progress. As translators who respond to concrete conditions, protesters offer new values and norms with which to organize social life. This ability, nurtured by the will to alter accepted or agreed-upon norms, is protestability. Protestability should be considered an inherent human condition in which the individual distances himself from the agreed-upon social-political structure and paradigms to imagine an alternative future.

The actual act of protesting—of challenging the existing order—is not simple. It is a difficult task during which individuals sometimes waive the protection provided by those in power, whether the church, the state, or public opinion; in doing so, they also relinquish their sense of safety and protection in the world. Surely, conflicting practices and protests are situations in which individuals risk creating instability and, in turn, being isolated and unprotected. Thus, challenging those in power requires the courage to object to their rule and to become exposed. If individuals fear challenging those in power, then their likelihood of objecting is reduced.[1] Indeed, as long as individuals are obedient, following the accepted norms, they are never isolated or misguided. When individuals challenge or disobey the ruler, the former must be punished to return to the good graces of those in power.[2] Obedience has its advantages; it maintains the social order and helps human beings enjoy stability and imagine the day after tomorrow. Under this condition of obedience, individuals become part of the power that they obey, thus empowering themselves.

The individual's compliance with such rules and norms requires a dynamic system of regulations that differentiate between the self and the other, between the private and the public, and between the ruler and the ruled. These differentiations create *distance*—mental distance, spatial distance, or social distance, all of which are maintained through daily practices and driven by cultural norms and political institutions. We nurture the distance and boundaries that define our personal space, where we can keep our secrets and feel safe and confident. Such distance is not so much an object or material artifact; it is more a system of beliefs that contributes to a sense of stability and safety. In the words of Elias Canetti,

> There is nothing that man fears more than the touch of the unknown. He wants to see what is reaching towards him, and to be able to recognize or at least classify it. Man always tends to avoid physical contact with anything strange. . . . All the distances which men create round themselves are dictated by this fear. They shut themselves in houses which no-one may enter, and only there feel some measure of security . . . the repugnance to being touched remains with us when we go about among people; the way we move in a busy street, in restaurants, trains or buses, is governed by it.[3]

Clearly, these distances serve not only as a means of establishing our privacy but also as hierarchies among people and between citizens and the government. In this sense, distance helps establish not only authority but also, to a certain extent, mystery through superficial means.[4] When needed, the government guarantees distance by modifying or tightening regulations and ensuring that boundaries are understood and maintained. Through this ongoing process of maintaining and defining distances, social order is achieved, aggression is suppressed, and an illusion of stability is attained.

Planners and architects play a key role in demarcating distance by defining the geometry of space, a geometry that is a signature not only of lifestyle and capital needs but also of power. By developing city plans and designing buildings, professionals seek to inspire admiration by creating spectacular designs that physically establish hierarchies of status and power. Viewing architecture and planning as cultural artifacts within intricate power geometries does not mean that a building or space has a single meaning; on the contrary, it often contains competing or hidden messages and symbols. As such, space is not only an expression of power but also the means through which power is maintained.[5] Therefore, citizens use space when they seek to *bridge* particular distances and when they hope to establish new coalitions or new political agendas by challenging agreed-upon distances. These "bridging" efforts, which require thinking beyond the present, fuel processes of social and political change. People prefer stability and social order, and they tend to experience themselves in concrete ways; however, as Nira Liberman and Yaacov

Trope suggest, they also "transcend the present and mentally traverse temporal distance, spatial distance, social distance, and hypotheticality."[6]

This human motivation to challenge current practices of distance is critical in the process of enacting and designing civil protests. Through collective claim making, claimants distance themselves from the decisions of regimes (and from powerful groups allied with such regimes). Under these circumstances, offended parties often respond with counterclaims backed by governmental or nongovernmental force.[7] This process is contentious and conflictual, though not necessarily violent, and it is based on demanding and claiming particular things by challenging agreed-upon political, social, spatial, and physical distance. Clearly, not all protests are exactly the same, and not all protesters want to completely dismantle political distance and hierarchy. A correlation exists between the state's distance from its citizens and the activists' goals. As Diane Davis argues, moderate distance is likely to sustain the organizational vigor of social movements and often produces conformist political behaviors, whereby groups compete to participate in the existing state structure and state projects without attempting to reformulate the structure as a whole.[8] Extreme distance between citizens and the state tends to provoke the antagonistic activities of revolutionary movements or the complete rejection of a particular nation-state. In terms of protests, moderate distance might stimulate legal protests, such as boycotts, strikes, and marches, in democratic societies. This type of protest, which may include some illegal dimensions, is likely to sustain the existing order. By contrast, extreme distance tends to inspire violent protests and civil disobedience, including activities that deliberately violate the law to protest injustice.

Moreover, not only the distance between citizens and the state but also the varying distances between people are challenged during protest events. As such, civil protests are also about individuals being in a state of exposure to one another, a condition that allows the creation of collectives and the bridging of social differences, at least temporarily. According to Elias Canetti, during protests, individuals feel that they are transcending the limits of their own persons: "He has the sense of relief, for the distances are removed which used to throw him back on himself and shut him in."[9] Although removing the distance between people may not seem a "difficult task," it is a multifaceted mental task that requires people to suppress their fears, to take risks, and to expose themselves to others and to the unknown.

Thus, a threefold argument is suggested here: (1) to enhance stability and obedience, cultures and powers use distance as a tool to create order and hierarchy; (2) distance is established in planned physical spaces and is maintained through daily practices and regulations that influence the ways in which we communicate; and (3) protests challenge the sociospatial order by defying and disrupting agreed-upon practices of political, social, and spatial distance. The particular ways that protesters choose to challenge practices of distance influence the ways they communicate their ideas and how those ideas materialize in space. This materialization of discontent transforms the rather distant and abstract relationships between people and between the ruler and the people into a concrete physical reality.

This process of modifying practices of distance should be seen in the context of growing civilian consciousness of the "power to" (i.e., capacity to) act, the politics of place, and a place's mutable nature.[10] In this sense, the event (i.e., protest) and place are considered interrelated and cannot be understood in isolation from one another. Protests can occur in other spheres (virtual and private); however, in public spaces, which are considered to belong to the people as a whole, the exposure of grievances can affect or involve the culture of a place and its politics.[11] However, although information and communication technologies (ICTs) have undoubtedly contributed dramatically to the reduction of social distance, what is suggested here is a shift in how people understand social, geographical, and political distance and how they express this understanding in public spaces. Clearly, nothing about the will to protest is new. However, the praxis of protest, its choreography, is constantly changing. Boycotts, civic strikes, civil disobedience, fasting, picketing, and marches are all known tactics being performed differently at different times and in different spaces. It is the choreography and

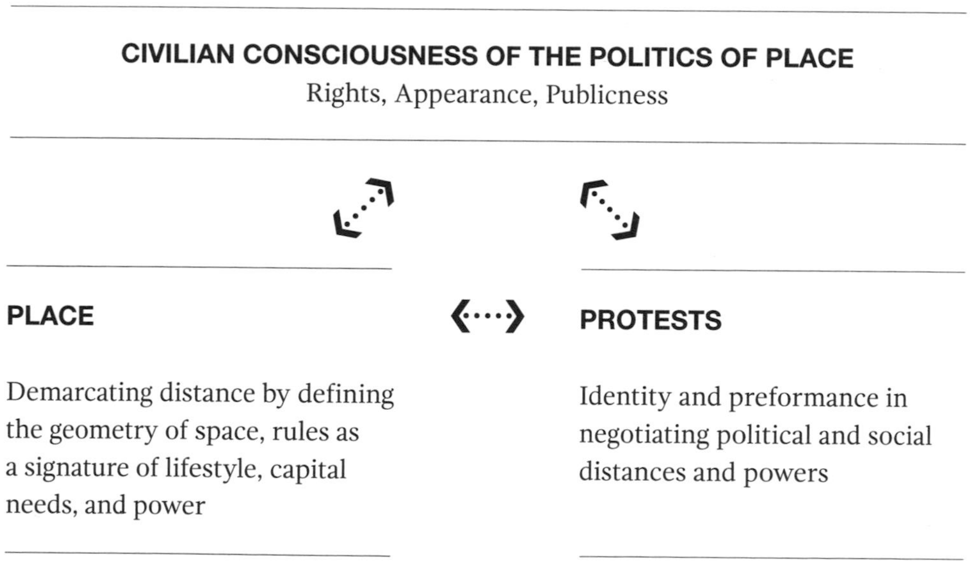

Figure 1.1. Protest and place dynamics.

design of a tactic in a particular context that creates the specificity of the event and opens up new possibilities.

KEEPING DISTANCE IN PUBLIC SPACE

Distance and distanciation are social and political constructs that influence social interactions in public space. Erving Goffman conceptualized the "front" and the "back" to illustrate a fundamental divergence in social activities and distance.[12] For Goffman, the "front" includes the places where we put on public, "on-stage" performances and act out stylized, formal, and socially acceptable activities, whereas the "back" is an area where we are "behind the scenes," where we prepare ourselves for public performances, or where we can relax into less formal modes of behavior. This divide between the public and the private, perceived as two exclusive categories that together appear to account for all elements of life and experience,[13] is one of the great dichotomies in Western thought. The public and the private are understood as opposing but inseparable spheres, and the extension of one necessarily implies the reduced scope of the other. However, the validity of this binary relationship is unclear, especially with the ongoing "privatization" of material spaces and the growing presence of virtual spaces in our lives. Clearly, mobile technology use in public spaces complicates traditional understandings of what it means to be in public by allowing people to bring previously private activities (e.g., chatting, reading, or listening to music) into public spaces.[14] Nevertheless, one of the reasons for maintaining these categories (even in their current blurred configuration) is that they contribute to and maintain the order of social life and reduce conflicts. These categories assist in maintaining distance.

The maintenance of these categories is also apparent in the physicality of spaces. The built environment frames everyday life by offering certain spaces for programmed action while closing off other possibilities. In myriad ways in everyday life, we avoid behaviors and boundaries that we believe will be met with force.[15] However, during protests, these public facilities provide a physical reference for negotiation over competing or hidden messages and symbols.[16] As such, the meanings and manifestations of political distance in places emerge from the meanings that people assign or read into them rather than their actual physicality. This paradoxical consequence, that is, that power depends on those for whom its display was designed, serves the people well. Being aware of this consequence, people use public spaces to communicate their grievances and to challenge agreed-upon practices of distance and, in turn, the legitimacy of the ruling authority.

This task—of challenging agreed-upon practices of distance—is not trivial. The imposition of distance, as dictated by political ideology in public spaces,

Figures 1.2 and 1.3. Planning and architecture have a major influence on the demarcation of social and political distance by defining the geometry of space. Tiananmen Square, Beijing, 2007. Photos by author.

through the definition of social rules and boundaries is intensifying. Critics note that these trends reduce agency and meaningful expression in public spaces.[17] Although public codes can provide a means of balance and stability, these trends also enhance surveillance and control practices, and technology adds another layer to such practices. Viewing contemporary technology as a means of control challenges both the scientific fascination with ICTs and the conclusions of studies that analyze technology's "impact" on society and cities.[18] In particular, this approach offers an alternative to the perspective that celebrates technology as a means through which citizens can have creative input into matters relevant to their interests and concerns.[19] Referring to technology as a means of control, Andrea Brighenti argues, "What the user actually gets is only one actualised possibility (a syntagm) within a larger matrix of possibilities envisaged and foreknown by engineers and programmers (a paradigm). Thus, what the user sees is, in fact, only an epiphenomenon of the matrix."[20] This statement implies a rather gloomy view of freedom, suggesting that nothing unexpected can be produced with new media. Brighenti is not alone; his critical perspective has been adopted by others who have argued that ICTs actually enhance social division and polarization.[21]

These dynamic transformations, which have increased privatization, technological control, and personalization, have been given various names, such as *The Fall of Public Man*,[22] *Bowling Alone*,[23] and *Alone Together*,[24] metaphors that characterize the decline of civic engagement in the public sphere. Undeniably, the private and the personal have taken precedence over the public; private spaces have replaced public gathering spaces; and society has become generally less interested in public matters and more driven by private interests and personal desires. As Zygmunt Bauman writes, there is currently no easy and obvious way to translate private worries into public issues and, conversely, to discern and pinpoint public issues in private troubles. As he further argues, when private agonies and anxieties are translated into public issues, they often are merely publicly displayed rather than becoming public issues.[25] Nevertheless, the wave of worldwide protests in the twenty-first century has shown that people are able to challenge Bauman's argument and that although they usually maintain distance, they sometimes also challenge agreed-upon distances or even violate them. To be sure, this tension between "keeping distance," "challenging distance," and "violating distance" during times of grievance or crisis should be considered an ongoing dialogue between the people and those in power in a particular place. As such, protests can be viewed as challenges to distanciation and disembedding by counteracting tendencies toward reembedding and trust among strangers.[26] These tendencies toward reembedding different parties during protests occur in a concrete place, which has a crucial impact not only on how protests are designed but also on how political distance is challenged.

CHALLENGING DISTANCE DURING PROTESTS

A significant step in challenging agreed-upon distances and communicating protesters' ideas is their materialization and their physical presence in space, that is, their being out there. In this sense, protest actions are prerequisites for the creation of public spaces.[27] Focusing on the physical attributes of protests raises many questions regarding the role of urban form in the organization of protests. As Murray Edelman argues, "Although every act takes place in a setting, we ordinarily take scenes for granted, focusing our attention on actions." However, when political actions are set to take place, a very different practice prevails: "Great pains are taken to call attention to settings."[28] Focusing attention on protest settings demonstrates a conscious effort to manipulate meaning and mass responses during protests or to determine that selected settings are inappropriate for said actions.[29] In examining the spatial planning and design of protests and the dynamics among protests, distance and space are explored, along with their multiple meanings and definitions.

How are protests defined? Finding a single explanation for these phenomena, whose definitions are constantly contested and debated, is difficult.[30] Some scholars regard the act of protest as planned, articulated, and sustained action; others consider it unplanned and inarticulate—even episodic. In current research, protests are perceived as gatherings, campaigns, or movements; others use the term "non violent action" or "collective action." In general, the act of protest is regarded as an instrumental activity that seeks to achieve collective goals. Ralph Turner[31] conceptualized protests as actions that express grievances and indict injustices. According to this perspective, protesters are seemingly unable to directly correct the condition through their efforts; thus, their action is intended to draw attention to grievances, which often provokes ameliorative steps by some target group. For the purpose of this book, the act of protest is regarded as a design, *a planned event in space that is envisioned in the minds of its organizers, who aim to challenge sociospatial distance.* In this sense, the act of protest has two purposes—an external purpose, in which protesters confront a target and thereby enhance the impact of their political message, and an internal purpose, in which protesters confront themselves and, in so doing, intensify the emotional ties and solidarity among participants. Two key challenges exist at the heart of both purposes: the challenge of political distance (i.e., confronting a target) and the challenge of social distance (i.e., intensifying solidarity). To achieve their aims and to overcome these challenges, protesters develop spatial strategies: planned displays through which they use their available means to express their beliefs and ideas.

Similar to the concept of protest, distance also carries multiple meanings. The term "distance" refers to the increased "social space" between different individuals, which allows for greater disembedding of social interactions and, in turn, more freedom.[32] According to George Simmel, social distance is based on social norms that differentiate individuals and groups based on race, ethnicity, age, sex, social class, religion, and nationality. The greater the social distance between individuals and groups, the less they influence each other. From a Marxist perspective, the process of distanciation in modern society has dramatically changed economic thinking toward a logic that is blind to qualitative differences and only cares about quantitative dimensions (i.e., profits). The effect is a weakening of social bonds and increased individuality. This conceptualization of social distance was further expanded by Davis, who suggested that the idea of distance is also important in understanding political distance and, more specifically, citizens' distance from the state.[33] Davis suggested that the distance between citizens and the state (as manifested in practices, procedures, and policies) should be seen in the context of geography, institutions, culture, and class, which have a major effect on the overall patterns, practices, and strategies of collective mobilization.

However, the concept of distance affects not only how we communicate with and approach others or those in power but also how we think about an event, a place, or an idea, which has an impact on whether we view it in abstract or concrete terms.[34] According to Liberman and Trope, distant places, events, or relationships are perceived in abstract terms, which capture the overall essence of situations or objects. If a person is in closer proximity to people, places, or events, he or she will likely think more concretely, focusing on the present in great detail.[35] Furthermore, distance has an enormous impact on how social power is manifested in space. The powerful tend to use social distance to emphasize the differences between themselves and others. Research has demonstrated that those who are aware of the concept of power tend to construe events in a more abstract manner; others, who consider themselves less powerful (or who want to present themselves as such), tend to construct informal and more concrete events.[36] This awareness is also applicable to protests, as activists who perceive themselves as powerful over other participants will tend to construe events in a more abstract manner. Thus, their perceptions of distance are crucial in better understanding how protesters construe distance and how this influences the way they challenge agreed-upon social distance and, in turn, power in physical spaces.

Therefore, as opposed to the focused lens through which the act of protest is examined, the concept of distance is used and explored in multiple ways in this book: (1) *Perceptual*—distance as a means to understand reality and how we think about events and places, which has an impact on whether we view it in abstract or concrete terms. (2) *Political*—distance is the condition of being at variance with, disagreeing with, dissenting from, and disputing those in power. During protests, activists are claiming power and are motivated to hit the streets and challenge the practices of the powerful. (3) *Social*—distance refers to an individual's position (high or low) with respect to others. During protests, the people express their grievances together and thereby challenge agreed-upon or accepted social distance, particularly among participants. (4) *Spatial*—distance refers to the degree of remoteness in any relationship to which spatial terms are transferred or figuratively applied. Spatial distance also refers to the space that lies between any two objects, a condition that defines the order of place and influences daily communication and interactions.

Protests always disrupt political, social, and spatial distance. However, this disruption can take many different shapes and forms. The form of protest is never arbitrary—it is based on the familiarity of the people with a particular space. This familiarity is grounded in daily obedience to an abstract spatial order that the ruler imposes; he or she is being channeled along paths (i.e., streets and roads) and through spaces that are restricted by norms and laws. These daily spaces are the "calculus of force-relationships,"[37] motivated by political power and based on scientific rationality. However, the obedience to these spatial rules is fragile and mutable. People, like the ruler, are also able to think strategically about spaces, and they do so when they grapple with discontent. Henri Lefebvre's writings concerning the relationship between the everyday and modernity discuss the ability of the everyday "spontaneous conscience" to resist the oppression of daily existence. Anthony Giddens perceived everyday practices as a potential challenge to the modern nation-state, whereby the daily routines of skilled participants construct a liberating social order through originality and creativity.[38] Opposing the monotonies and tyrannies of daily life, Michel de Certeau stressed the individual's capacity to manipulate situations and create realms of autonomous action as "networks of anti-discipline."[39] For de Certeau,[40] strategies and tactics alike operate in space and time. Strategy is recognized as being enacted by authority—an institution, a commercial enterprise, or an individual who is part of the dominant order. Strategy manifests itself physically in its site(s) of operations (offices/headquarters) and in products (e.g., laws, language, rituals, commercial goods, literature, art, inventions, and discourse). Unlike strategy, which inherently creates its own autonomous space, a tactic is "a calculated action determined by the absence of a proper locus. . . . The space of a tactic is the space of the other."[41] A tactic is deployed "on and with a terrain imposed on it and organized by the law of a foreign power." An individual who deploys a tactic "must vigilantly make use of the cracks that particular conjunctions open in the surveillance of the proprietary powers. It poaches in them. It creates surprises in them."[42] Tactics are thus actions or events that take advantage of the opportunities offered by gaps within a given strategic system, although the tactician never retains these advantages. Tactics cut across strategic fields, exploiting gaps, to generate novel and inventive outcomes.

This ongoing process constantly shapes and reshapes the dynamics between the state, the city, and the citizens and noncitizens, as well as the formation of space. As James Holston says, "Membership in the State has never been a static identity, given the dynamics of global migrations and national ambitions. Citizenship changes as new members emerge to advance their claims, expanding its reality and, as new

Figures 1.4 and 1.5. Protests challenge the sociospatial order by contesting agreed-upon practices of distance. Shown is a protest against the war in Gaza, Baqa al Gharbiya, Israel, August 1, 2009. Photos by author.

كمبيوتر دانا
وكيل معتمد محمد عويس
טל: 04-6282233 / 052-6734111
كمبيوتر دانا
050-5588469 - 04-6282233

forms of segregation and violence counter these advances, eroding it."[43] Thus, in planning protests, people first temporarily suspend regulations and agreed-upon meanings by thinking about space tactically and in innovative ways and by not following the restrictions of everyday channels. Being prepared for public discontent in advance, the ruler will aspire to channel or restrict the boundaries of dissent by designating particular spaces for protests and by defining legal limits of such action. Thus, the question is not so much what kind of space is needed for protests—or whether governments provide that space—but rather how people reimagine and appropriate the city infrastructure to initiate acts of dissent, what tactics they use to project their messages, and why.

THE DESIGN OF PROTESTS

Planning a protest is a process rather than a single act or decision. This process starts with an assessment of the available resources and the space's physicality, including the evaluation of multiple factors, such as the number of participants, funding, surveillance issues, the scale of the event, the timing, and the type of gathering. However, the physicality of public spaces does not determine exactly how people will interact with one another; it instead suggests the possibilities for or constraints on such interactions. In addition, as protests can take place anywhere, they do not require a particular design but rather a defined spatial choreography that will offer a new reading of the existing and agreed-upon spatial distance. In initiating an act of protest, three key interrelated decisions contribute to the spatial choreography of the event:

Choosing a place for the action. In most cases, participants are highly aware of the political distance manifested in space. Space is often considered a privileged instrument of the authorities, which is used to control social relations among individuals, groups, and classes in a globalized world. Authorities are regarded as a significant actor in a global economic world, one that has enormous power to use social spaces as a means of extending its power and control. In other words, even in an era of intensified globalization, the state continues to play a central role in the struggle over resources. To be sure, there is no ideal space for political actions; dialogue between the people and those in power might take place anywhere. However, different places provide different opportunities in terms of gathering and communicating an ideology. Importantly, the chosen place reflects the ways in which participants view distance and space. Thus, choosing a public space and initiating a related spatial strategy is always an exercise of power in appropriating the right locus from which to see and be seen, "controlling action," "taking over discourse," and being concrete and visible. These activities seek to change the scope of what is seen,[44] which has been dictated by governments, which in turn activate and define the scope of the visible, in other words, what can be seen and, more importantly, by whom.[45]

Deciding on a method to communicate the protest. This decision, or, how to project a message beyond the event's geographical boundaries, reveals quite a bit about the scope of the event, its goals, and its target (e.g., municipal, national, or global powers). Awareness is growing regarding the range of spheres that can be used as tools to organize the form of dissent and as means of challenging power structures. Through this awareness and the use of different spheres, activists transcend dichotomized definitions of power relations (power versus resistance) and configure new "processual" spaces. In this respect, spaces become complex arrays of multiply associated concrete places and virtual spaces of action. These multiple spheres of action are often regarded as an advantage, but they have a critical impact on the question of the event's audience. In other words, the question of method is tightly linked to the target audience. At the end of the day, a protest without a target audience is socially meaningless.

Agreeing about the process of negotiating power and with whom. This decision refers to the negotiations before and after the event with authorities and within the group of activists. Clearly, the government is a strategic player that adjusts its degree of repression in response to past protests to maximize its stability and likclihood of survival. Participants' conceptions of power influence the risks that they are willing to take during the event. Indeed, protests never occur without the risk of violence. However, the question is how the potential for violence is policed, encapsulated in law, and sublimated in design.

These three key interrelated decisions—the choice of place (spatial), the communication method (social), and the conception of power (political)—should be understood in the context of distance and the ways in which protesters understand and perceive such distance. That is, in practice, protests begin by conceptualizing distance and distanciation, which influence and inform social interactions in public spaces.

Spatially, distance is about not only the place's immediate geography—the specific location of the action—but also its influence on other distant locations and viewers. Protesters carefully use spaces to draw media attention, and many protests serve as a staging ground for other activities that seek to reduce physical and ideological distance from other potential actors or venues. Furthermore, activists' awareness of the specificity and accuracy of a place's definition and boundaries also includes an acknowledgment of the space's temporality. This sensitivity to temporality marks a change in the ways in which spaces are perceived during protests; they are seen to represent multiple spheres, trajectories, and histories. In other words, activists have grasped that "for the future to be open, space must be open."[46]

There is no preferable space for protests. However, large organizations tend to initiate megascale events in a focal location, while smaller groups tend to support a dispersed configuration of events, with dissent occurring in multiple venues simultaneously. In addition, protests that tend to be singular and formal often require long-term planning and funding, whereas protests with spatially dispersed configurations might be more immediate, with smaller groups having relative freedom in organizing the event. Unlike megascale protests, which are often authorized actions with prior estimates of participation and growth, the dispersed spatial choreography allows activists to (1) tentatively organize actions on the ground, thereby changing/adding new locations to their map of dissent, and (2) be flexible in terms of activists' participation and growth. In terms of the space's physicality, activists who want to organize megascale protests often (though not always) negotiate with political powers, such as governmental institutions/places, regarding venues, whereas activists who participate in more informal coalitions tend to act in everyday/informal places, generating alternative maps to the geographies of power.[47] Choosing to act in everyday places does not mean that activists operate without order; instead, they have relative flexibility in defining the array of acts, as manifested physically in a specific place.

As a means of enhancing trust, protesters aim to "shrink" agreed-upon *social distance* and differences, at least temporarily. This goal is highly influenced by the ways in which people communicate with each other before and during protests. Indeed, technology has radically changed communication by enhancing the availability of information and by helping create large masses of participants. Communication is also a means of enhancing multiplicity both geographically (e.g., with many cities imitating the same strategy) and ideologically. However, communication also alters the scope of information and the public's ability to absorb it. In other words, it has changed not only the "how" but also the "what," not only the quantitative dimension but also the qualitative meaning of the message. This change has had a tremendous impact on communication practices during protests, which aim to enhance trust and bridge differences among participants.

However, shrinking social distance can be configured in different ways. Participants' ideologies and diverse identities are always at the core of crafting a spatial choreography; thus, activists' approaches to differences have a major impact on the ways in which diverse groups coordinate themselves based on a shared call for change. Again, in a protest that is organized by a large institutionalized organization, major efforts are often made to bridge differences and create coalitions between various groups, including the federal government, religious institutions, and community organizations, to be simultaneously inclusive and unified under a clear vision. This approach is significantly different from the informal approach, which accepts a plurality of actors, visions, and positions.[48] Accepting differences refers to both identity and ideological positioning, with groups limiting and expanding their membership in a way that suits their goals. Either way, an institutionalized organization might aim to reduce distance (and conflicts) by creating a clear structure and vision, while an informal coalition might accept differences (and social distance) as an underlying value, which can assist in expanding the scope and scale of events; however, these differences can also give rise to conflicts among participants or result in a diffuse message. Consequently, in the case of less structured, informal protests' choreographies, one can find key differences in terms of the ways in which they approach distance, difference, and hierarchy, which influence social communication and trust. With more processual protests, participants are able to create bonds and trust, while trust and solidarity are often built on-site (if at all) in cases of more instantaneous coalitions.

Politically, distance is apparent in the decision-making *process* among participants, mirroring the protesters' organizational structure. Events led by institutionalized organizations are often characterized by concentrated leadership, while leadership is diffuse in informal coalitions, often restricting itself to specific goals. While the approval of central leadership is needed for each detail in the institutionalized organization, in informal gatherings and groups, individual cells might operate independently but maintain links to the movement through the circulation of information. These differences affect the concept of political and social distance among actors and, more specifically, the coordination of ideas and messages. As has been previously argued, those who are aware of the concept of power tend to construe events in a more abstract manner; others who consider themselves less empowered (or who want to present themselves as such) tend to construe more informal and concrete events.

THE DESIGN OF PROTEST

Aim	**Key Interrelated Decisions**	**Crafting a Spatial Choreography**
Planning an event that would establish new coalitions or new political agendas by challenging agreed-upon social, spatial, and political distances.	*Spatial*: choice of place *Social*: communication method *Political*: conception of power	**Defining** the dynamics between the body and physical settings, between the protest's social dynamics and ritual components (e.g., marching, gathering, and singing), dress code, and schedule (i.e., the timing and duration of the event)

Figure 1.6. Protest as a planned event in public space.

In sum, the conceptualization of distance affects how a group communicates its message and grievances to the regime and general public. Understanding distance is about examining the "how" as a means of exploring the "what" or the "why" of political action, as distance represents the way in which people see themselves in society's existing power structures and the form of dialogue that they pursue with those in power in a particular time and context.

Evidently, distance is not a static category. Its meanings and implications have evolved throughout human history, and, through this evolution, this concept has changed the ways in which we experience spaces and act in the world. Today, distance is no longer considered "objective," "linear," or "hierarchical"; instead, it is social and political, manifesting itself in the relationships between people and spaces. To be sure, distance and proximity are apparent in every detail of our lives. However, these distances, both the ones that are being imposed on us and the ones we create and nurture, are constructed rather than natural. As such, the process of materializing protestability can be seen to challenge constructed distanciation by developing (temporal) trust among strangers, as trust is what holds people together—"without trust the social contract dissolves."[49]

2

Choosing a Place

Previous page: The square as a public and political forum. The City Hall terrace becomes a stage for speakers and leaders. In this photograph, Prime Minister Golda Meir addresses a mass rally of high school students who are demonstrating against the anti-Zionist UN decision at Kikar Malchei (renamed Rabin Square in 1995) in Tel Aviv, November 13, 1975. Photo by Moshe Milner, National Photograph Collection, Israel.

CHAPTER 2
Choosing a Place

> Public spaces contribute to social integration generally, but do so by strengthening particular connotations of specific spaces. Each such space evokes a number of different meanings, but . . . the meanings of a structure for different people and for different situations complement one another so as to reinforce established inequalities.
>
> Murray Edelman, *From Art to Politics*

When entering a vast square or a grand building, our senses sharpen, and our eyes scan our surroundings, assessing the monumentality of the scene and searching for symbols and messages. These messages and symbols mark social and political status and, thus, distance. Messages appear in the form of sculptures or placards, the scale of buildings, and the geometry of the space—even in the ways in which benches are arranged. This special attention to symbols can be clearly observed in places that are associated with political power, where the use of an admiration strategy, such as a spectacular design, diverts the audience's attention.[1] Political settings are often artificial spaces that are designed to emphasize a departure from a person's daily routine. Massiveness and formality are the most common chords struck in the design of these settings, and they are presented on a scale that focuses constant attention on the differences between everyday life and the events occurring in such places.[2] The architecture in these places, as the seats of government, often symbolically represents power in its purest form, without contradictions or inconsistencies.[3] Although no society is free of contradictions, buildings do not celebrate them—government buildings least of all. As Lawrence Vale puts it, "The sponsors and designers of such public facilities may wish to downplay or transcend these contradictions, or highlight them in a way that reinforces their rule."[4] In addition, these places are not only symbols of power to the people but also reminders to "the functionaries who enter these buildings regularly to exercise authority. For them, the grand scale of the setting in which they make decisions emphasizes their power and their distinction as a class from those who are subject to their

Figures 2.1 and 2.2. Urban form as a symbol of the ruler can be clearly observed in places that are associated with political power, where the use of an admiration strategy diverts the audience's attention. *Top*: The Lincoln Memorial, the Washington Mall, Washington, DC, 2007. *Bottom*: Tiananmen Square, Bejing, 2007. Photos by author.

decisions."[5] These qualities mark the distance between the "common people" and the authorities.

The representation of physical distance, particularly in public spaces, makes these spaces a medium of citizenship, in other words, "a material space and representational forum through which boundaries of citizenship are drawn and redrawn."[6] According to Murray Edelman, "To a pluralist this is an aspect of democracy; to a Marxist it can be false consciousness. In any case, an ongoing society is as inconceivable without the symbolic functions of buildings and spaces as it would be without their physical and technological functions."[7] Indeed, perceived distance affects daily "relations in public" and the negotiation of this distance during civil protests.[8] But, as Erving Goffman notes, social situations vary, and individuals' reactions depend on how much they are obliged to be connected with their surroundings and the social context in which they are embedded.[9] These tensions between distanciation and disembedding, on the one hand, and reembedding and connecting, on the other hand, which are so fundamental in the practice of protests, are critical when choosing a place for such protests.

Therefore, the concept of distance in this chapter does not simply refer to the condition of being at odds with political representatives and the desire to take to the streets and challenge the practices of those in power; it is also about repositioning individuals with respect to one another in a particular place that has a particular meaning. Thus, the underlying premise here is that the place chosen for political action reveals the ways in which actors perceive distance pragmatically and symbolically as a means of both creating social cohesion and realizing change. Therefore, decisions regarding a protest's location cannot be reduced to fitting a particular number of participants in a specific place; instead, these decisions should be considered with regard to the protesters' power to communicate their claims and challenge political distance by manipulating and appropriating spatial forms and symbols.

DEFINING DISTANCE THROUGH FORMS AND SYMBOLS

The urban form is a dynamic contextual and spatial category that changed dramatically over the course of the twentieth century. Generally speaking, the enclosed social spaces that once provided opportunities for interactions in traditional cities have often been replaced with urban structures that are dominated by movement through space, which affords fewer interactions. Urban blocks, defined by squares and streets, have been replaced with freestanding buildings located in amorphous spaces. The layout of the city has been converted from integrated small-scale street grids into a road network that surrounds segregated and insular enclaves.[10] This paradigm is also apparent in the design of public buildings. Prior to the modern period, only a few building types (e.g., churches and town halls) were used as a means of

Figure 2.3. Form and symbolism: March on Washington for Jobs and Freedom. The crowd surrounded the Reflecting Pool and continued to the Washington Monument, Washington, DC, August 28, 1963. Photo by Warren Leffler, Library of Congress.

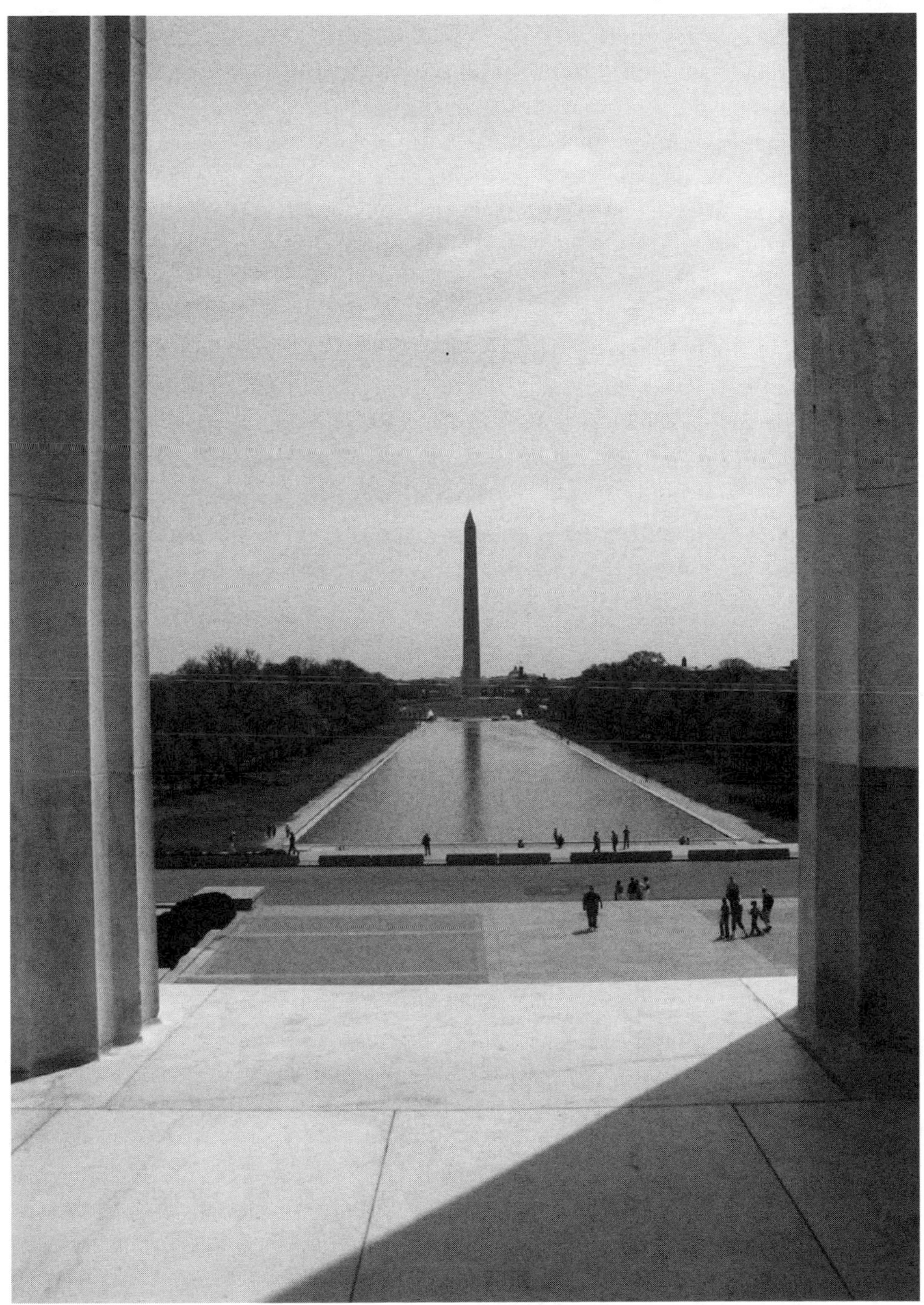

Figure 2.4. The Reflecting Pool on the Washington Mall, Washington, DC, 2007. Photo by author.

distinction; in the modern era, "objects" have multiplied across the urban landscape.[11] These changes in urban design (i.e., block patterns, street layouts, building heights, size and scale) are considered signs of lifestyle changes and the expansion of capital needs; many scholars view these changes as part of a process that has contributed to the reduction of social spaces.[12] Furthermore, scholars have argued that the low density and automobile-scale segregation of the typical twentieth-century city has severely affected the practice of collective action, in contrast to the dense, small-scale city of the nineteenth century, which was a particularly effective communication medium for protests.[13] In other words, the physical distance between locations and the sheer size of spaces have contributed to the spatial abstractness, which, in turn, has influenced social dynamics.

Political power players tend to use urban forms as a means of influencing social norms and behaviors and magnifying representations of their power. However, the representation of social and political distance in space does not necessarily project a single social or political meaning; instead, it provides a physical reference for negotiating between competing or hidden messages and symbols. Thus, a place's meaning does not emerge from its physicality; it instead emerges from the meaning(s) that people derive from it. Aware of their power to interpret the symbolic attributes of particular places and, in turn, to challenge political distance, protesters often use places to add to or modify their meanings, at least temporarily. The protesters' underlying rationale is that symbolic signs have arbitrary relationships with specific objects and that they are constructed through social and cultural systems. As a result, when society changes, the significance of its symbols changes.[14] Hence, though physical forms clearly have an impact on human behavior, human action can also modify the forms and meanings of various places. The configurations of some public spaces are quite important, but "it matters more what democratic performances are conducted within them, and thus what symbolic associations are built up over time."[15] In other words, the physical (i.e., size, topography, and furniture) and symbolic attributes of a place are only important in terms of how they are used and interpreted. Therefore, urban form and symbolism are interlinked and evolve through an ongoing process of interpretation and negotiation. As Edelman notes, "The conspicuousness of public structures, together with their emptiness of explicit meaning, enables them to serve as symbolic reaffirmations of many levels of perceptions and beliefs."[16]

Concisely, two related key points should be emphasized. First, public spaces represent the social and political distance of a particular society in a particular space at a particular time. This distance influences a space's level of abstractness or concreteness. Second, protesters manipulate this distance in their quest to redirect an accepted ideology by renewing or familiarizing themselves with the beliefs of a given ideology. Furthermore, the place chosen for their actions not only indicates their approach to reducing distance but also influences the dynamics among the participants themselves. These points raise the following key questions: If different public spaces represent different concepts of physical or social distance, what types of opportunities do they offer during protests? How does the physicality of space influence the dynamics of protests? For example, does an abstract space that projects hierarchy imply the same dynamics during protests as a commercial street does? The following section attempts to answer these questions by mapping public space typologies to better understand the conceptualization of distance in protest design.

PUBLIC SPACE PROTOTYPES AND PROTEST CULTURES

Context plays a key role in planning protests, which makes describing public spaces in universal terms nearly impossible. However, mapping key urban typologies that have received significant attention from architects and town planners—the square, the street, and the park—serves as a first step in revealing the relationship between distance and the sociospatial engagements that occur during protests. Although these spaces differ substantially from one city to another, exploring their uses, roles, and spatial definitions within a city can help us better comprehend the challenge of overcoming distance during protests (table 2.1).

The Square: Drawing on a Place's Symbolic Characteristics

Defined as a group of buildings arranged around an open space, the *square* affords a high degree of control over an inner space.[17] The typology of the square is apparent in residential developments (with many houses built around central courtyards or atriums),[18] but it gained its reputation as a space for large-scale social gatherings and as a holy place (e.g., the agora, the forum, and the mosque courtyard). Today, the secular "civic" square, around which government and cultural buildings are located, is the modern equivalent of a holy place. These civic squares incorporate architectural elements (e.g., scale, symmetry, monumental buildings, and symbolic icons) to position individuals within a meaningful social hierarchy that promulgates implicit power relationships. These physical and design characteristics, including the unique relationships between the landscape and the built space, play a major role in the organization of protests. Thus, protests that take place in a square, which is a pause or extension within the city's network, tend to generate engagement that uses or challenges a space's defined (symbolic/physical) distance. The enclosed space increases the sense of ritual and solidarity and helps challenge the social distance among participants. Furthermore, central squares tend to signify a locus of power; thus, using them for action is a means of communicating with the ruling power(s) or challenging the distance between the people and the ruling power(s).

Public Spaces: Prototypes and Protest Dynamic

	Square	Street	Park
Use	Meeting place	Traffic/movement channel	Recreation
Key value/ concern	Symbolic	Functional	Leisure
Spatial definition	A pause within the city network	The city network	An isolated, enclosed pause within the city network
Protest dynamic	Static congregations, challenged symbols displayed in space, enclosure that increases sense of ritual and solidarity	Dynamic marching, crowd's growth, enhancing impact by affecting accidental viewers, paralyzing city's network	Large-scale events, festival-oriented, minimal interference in the daily dynamic of the city
Distance	Enclosed space increases the sense of ritual and solidarity and assists in challenging social distances among participants	Significant in exposing message to distant viewers not participating in the event	An island that might be geographically central but distant from the locus of power or city activities

Table 2.1. Key features of the Square, the Street, and the Park.

Protests that take place in squares tend to be structured events, performances that draw on a place's symbolic characteristics. These focal gatherings are often organized events at which participants abide by an agreed-upon set of activities with known aims and distinct symbolic meanings. The theatrical dimension includes the manipulation of symbols, whether existing (with regard to a place or an ideology) or new ones, which link participants over a discrete time period and help increase social solidarity. However, "focal" or "symbolic" does not necessarily imply a large-scale event; instead, it implies a defined event that often takes place in a formal, institutionalized public square in an attempt to reduce the distance between protesters and the ruling power and to achieve high visibility. The scale of the focal event plays a crucial role in terms of the distance among participants. Small-scale events or rituals create more concrete events, while large-scale events transform event participants into anonymous actors, part of an abstract mass. Although large-scale events are more successful in attracting media attention, they are less successful in challenging the social distance among participants.

The main square in Mexico City (Zócalo), the Bastille Square in Paris, Martyr's Square in Lebanon, Taksim Square in Istanbul, and many others are all public squares that have hosted major protests. The difference is linked to the way activists use and appropriate the symbolic and physical attributes of these renowned spaces. *Theater*, *ritual*, and *reiconization* are different spatial choreographies (see part II of the book); although very different in their aims, each tactic uses squares as a means of reinforcing the political formalization of the space, adding another layer of symbolic meaning.

The Street: Planning Accumulative Dynamics

Distinct from the enclosed space of the square, which is attractive and often monumental due to its size and the arrangement of buildings, the *street* is a functional space that is a product of a settlement's expansion. It provides a framework for the distribution of land and provides access to individual plots.[19] Serving as the socioeconomic veins of the city and as channels for traffic and movement, streets (especially commercial streets) are visually dynamic,[20] bustling public areas for inhabitants and visitors. Political actions that take place along city streets are often more dynamic, with active marching. In this type of action, physical distance is significant (e.g., the length of the path) and symbolic (e.g., exposure to distant viewers who are not participating in the event); street protests halt and paralyze the city's network, enhancing the protest's impact by attracting viewers and passersby. Protests that take place on city streets dismantle the physical distance between participants and actively perform their messages throughout the city (e.g., walking and singing).

The Square: Drawing on a Place's Symbolic Characteristics

Rabin Square, Tel Aviv

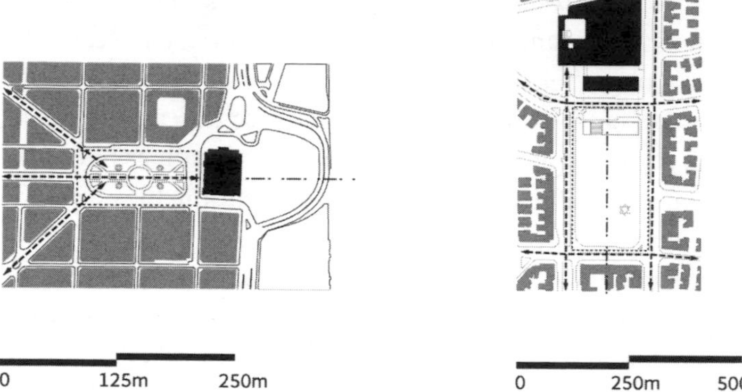

Trafalgar Square, London

Augustusplatz, Leipzig

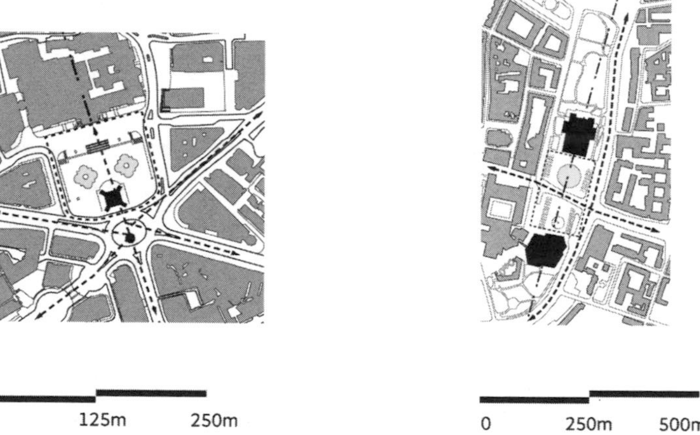

Figure 2.5. Civic squares incorporate architectural elements (e.g., scale, symmetry, monumental buildings, and symbolic icons) to position individuals within a meaningful social hierarchy that promulgates implicit power relationships. Plaza de Mayo, Buenos Aires, 2006; Rabin Square, Tel Aviv, 2010; Trafalgar Square, London, 2007; Augustusplatz, Leipzig, 2007. Illustrations and photos by author.

Plaza de Mayo, Buenos Aires.

Rabin Square, Tel Aviv.

Trafalgar Square, London.

Augustusplatz, Leipzig.

Extending beyond a particular focal point, such as a central square or a monument, this type of protest has a particular logic: its accumulative advantage and its ability to attract participants along the route and to project its message to viewers. The march's route is ideologically meaningful and critical in attracting spectators and additional participants. As such, marching in the main plaza of a city or passing by government buildings might indicate the protesters' intentions to communicate with officials and to challenge or sway their decisions. Marching in residential areas or gathering at nongovernmental venues outside the city center might indicate the group's intention to protest far from the hegemonic powers as a counterpoint to them. The spatiality of the processional gathering varies from vector-shaped (moving from one point to another), to spiraling, to star-shaped processions (moving from multiple points to a focal gathering point). The differences between the spatial forms are related to the scale of appropriation, the scope of the message, and the range of participants, with spiraling and star-shaped processions being able to simultaneously extend the event's geographical boundaries and appropriate different parts of the city.

"Taking to the streets" is a spatial strategy that includes many different connected routes across a city. Unlike protests that take place in central squares, processions are named according to their goals, as was the case in Pakistan's Azadi March to overthrow Prime Minister Nawaz Sharif in 2014[21] and the Peruvians' campaign to overthrow the dictator Alberto Fujimori (the March of the Four Directions) in 2000.[22] However, in most cases, attention is given to the spatial configuration of the event as a whole. The most common form of procession is the vector form, which starts at one point and ends at another, often a central gathering place in the city.

Clearly, streets or routes (as opposed to squares or parks) exist in all cities. During protests, a shift occurs in the ways in which streets or routes are used; the target-oriented movement of the individual is replaced with a target-oriented movement of a collective mass. This shift is a powerful statement about distanciation and disembedding. However, marches can take very different forms, and they often manifest themselves in the social structure of the event. Thus, although all can be regarded as processions, *target*, *conjoining*, *synchronicity*, and *elasticity* choreographies are spatially very different (see part II). The common element of these choreographies is the rather blurred manifestations of hierarchal power differentiation among participants and the limited play with existing representations, though protesters might pass by significant symbolic icons of the ruling power.

The Park: Creating a Constrained Island of Dissent

Unlike the street and the square, the *urban park* is a relatively recent development that emerged in the nineteenth century because of the allocation of royal lands for public use in Europe and the creation of nonutilitarian, landscaped urban areas with woodlands and pastures, which were designated for public recreation.[23] Owned and maintained by the local government, the urban park, with varying uses and on different scales, exists as a modern typology in cities worldwide. As a piece of nature in the midst of a bustling city, the park offers unique conditions for protests. Protests that take place in parks are often large-scale activities and festive events, in which the parks' enclosed, detached nature creates minimal interference in the daily dynamics of the city. Political action in parks tends to be less threatening to the government authority and less disruptive to the economy. The beauty of nature, its loose spatial boundaries, and its recreational character often challenge organizers in communicating their message. Choosing a park for collective action is about creating "an island" of dissent, an island that might be geographically central but distant from the locus of power. However, its key advantage is that it can support long-term events such as camping.

Over the last decade, camping or occupying public parks has become a popular strategy among protesters. In most cases, the encampment includes an array of tents with the infrastructure provided at the site (i.e., water and electricity), and (if funded and needed) additional facilities (e.g., kitchens and toilets) are used to support the daily lives of the protesters. For example, NATO protesters opened a peace camp at Tredegar Park in Newport, Wales, in August 2014; environmentalists protested at Gezi Park in Istanbul to prevent its demolition in May 2013; and the Occupy movement spread rapidly in 2011. All these demonstrations have used this tactic to realize change by creating an "island" of dissent. Parks have two advantages: flexibility and infrastructure. These advantages allow (1) the development of a new physical manifestation that suits the activists' needs and ideas, and (2) the event's resiliency in stretching over a significant period of time. As such, parks allow a range of spatial choreographies, from the more radical and planned, such as *city design*, to the more immediate, such as *narrative* (part II). However, irrespective of the spatial choreography chosen, parks are often spacious pauses in the urban fabric—distinctly bounded, enclosed entities. These particular features might present challenges in the quest for political change.

The spatial features of the square, street, and park and the opportunities they provide for protest events cannot be detached from narration. Protesters respond, contribute, negate, or change the story of a place, which has evolved in the collective memory of a society. The physicality of a place and memory should be seen as mutually constitutive.

To be sure, the key spatial typologies explored—the square, the street, and the park—are abstractions. They provide a general glimpse of the opportunities a particular spatial typology may offer. Moreover, in exploring the spatiality of protest, it is impossible to examine city spaces in a vacuum, separate from the buildings surrounding them, which also mark political distance and hold significant meanings. Public institutions (e.g., government buildings), transit hubs, private consumption spaces (e.g., malls), labor facilities (e.g., factories), and their adjacent public spaces often become sites or even targets of contestation. In some cases, as part of the protest's performance and the message's purpose, the design of a collective action may carry a meaning that runs counter to the representation of the building or institution. Furthermore, most protests do not follow a pure form; instead, they use diverse spaces to develop their strategies (e.g., marching through the streets and congregating in a square in front of a government building).

In addition, the outlined typologies are not apparent in all cultures; in some cities, protests may primarily occur in the streets and in informal public spaces (open spaces that allow large gatherings).[24] Thus, particular attention should be paid to the social rules and cultural traditions of a society, which affect the accessibility of public spaces. The laws that govern public spaces and the use of regulations to define distance and its adjustment during protests (often through negotiation and permits from authorities) amplify contextual differences.

CHANGING THE NARRATION OF SPACE

The discussion of the role and power of symbolic meaning and collective memory in making change is associated with the debate surrounding historical narration, the ways in which it is constructed, and those who construct it. The unsettled conventions of historical narration have led to the contemporary perception of memory as a function of social power, a social expression of contextual settings. For example, the French sociologist Maurice Halbwachs argued that memory is not a matter of reflecting on the properties of the subjective mind; instead, memory is a question of how minds work together in society and how their operations are structured by social arrangements.[25] Halbwachs proposed that social groups—families, religious cults, political organizations, and other communities—develop strategies to maintain their images of the past through places, monuments, and rituals of commemoration.[26] In this sense, the physicality of space plays a crucial role in constructing memories and reminders of a group's social power.

Halbwachs's theory was rediscovered during the 1970s and 1980s with the expansion of collective memory studies. These studies became the debris of lost or oppressed identities, with scholars and citizens engaged in excavating the genealogy of these identities. This conceptual shift changed the role of collective memory and citizens' engagement with places. As a result, collective memory became an elastic material that is often remodeled, distorted, and thus unreliable as a guide to the realities of the past. Furthermore, in many cases, memory became a consumable product, experienced in place. In other words, memory became significant not for its true representation but as a proxy for social, political, and cultural power and influence.

The critical thought on the interlinked relationships between memory and politics has also significantly influenced the practice of architecture and planning. Parallel to and in association with the discourse on collective memory, a shift has occurred in the citizen's role in the construction of places. Citizenship has been perceived not only as membership in a polity but also as a reminder of the right to participate in the public sphere. With the turn of the twenty-first century, these trends have been developed and enforced, with governments focusing on enhancing civil participation and civil engagement as a tool that reinforces democratic legitimacy and power. This approach has significantly changed the citizen's role in the production of place—until the 1960s, the citizen was a passive subject in the process of planning. Today, the citizen is viewed as an active agent who participates in the development of the built environment.

The adoption of this participatory approach should also be considered in the context of the failure to realize some type of utopia in the twentieth century,[27] resulting in the disassociation of planning from the promise of utopia. This postmodern opposition to utopian projects champions everyday life and celebrates civil society.[28] Since the 1960s, planning and architecture have focused on the "here and now," objecting to all utopian concepts. Thus, planning and architecture adopted a dynamic framework influenced by a pragmatic approach to creating new visions,[29] which has affected the relationships between the professional, the citizen, and the state. The citizen became a reference point, a player, and an individual participating in the process of place-making. This approach became part of the general agenda of inclusiveness and civic engagement that governments promoted.

Most importantly, these discourses—collective memory (in social sciences) and citizenship (in architecture and planning)—are similar in their approach to time and space. Both are rooted in presentism—a counterpoint to the historicist idea of "progress," which resulted in the destruction of past ways of living and dominated thinking about historical time during the modern age.[30] Advocates of presentism negate this destruction and forgetting by offering interpretations of the past that arguably contribute to morally responsible, critical perspectives of the present. Adopting presentism implies that history is no longer conceived as a grand narrative or continuity that has informed the understanding of historical time in the modern age. Everyone can contribute to the historical narrative, at any given point of time and place.

With the growing significance and influence of these discourses, cities became the concrete spheres of negotiation over narratives. The physicality of places and the ability to experience them in daily life became more significant than historical textbooks. Moreover, citizens had the opportunity to negate or challenge a place's symbols, memories, and images as conceived by professionals. This acknowledgment of the mutable nature of memory defined new (and complex) relationships between place, narratives, and spatial practices in cities worldwide.

Continuity	Reconstruction	Negation
accepting the legacy of place and communicating with it by adding an additional layer	adding to narration, adding what has been "lost," or emphasizing neglected parts	replacing existing narration or symbols, renaming, creating new elements

Figure 2.6. Choosing a strategy for changing space's narration.

These discursive changes also transformed the memory map of the city into a means of social struggle, a means of power. As a result, multiple synchronic maps that are layered on top of one another in an endless process of production are being created in cities. This approach to the memory and narration of place raises conflicting voices; some argue that memory has become a business, while others claim that it is a way of reimagining a place.

Clearly, narration is fundamental to any collective action, and a major task of activists is to build a narrative that would best link the space's narration and their politics. In addressing this task, three key approaches can be identified: *continuity*, *reconstruction*, and *negation*. Each of these strategies approaches space, physicality, and civil participation in a different way, resulting in a different approach to the existing narration of place. First, *continuity* is adopted by protesters who accept the legacy of a place and communicate with that place by adding another layer to the place's narration. Using this approach affects the performance of protest (part II), with a tendency toward agreed-upon or known spatial choreographies. Second, and different from continuity, *reconstruction* is the approach being held in reserve from the existing narration; this approach aims to reconstruct the meaning of space with what has been lost, adding missing components or emphasizing neglected parts. Third, and the most radical approach, is *negation*. This approach implies the total disruption of a place's narration, resulting in the destruction or replacement of existing symbols, renaming, or the creation of new elements.

Many public spaces have been modified after protests. Such modifications frequently involve renaming places (e.g., Rabin Square in Tel Aviv and Augustusplatz in Leipzig), redesigning a particular object to memorialize a protest (e.g., marking the circle of the Mothers of Plaza de Mayo in Buenos Aires), or destroying objects. Therefore, although narrations may be physically manifested in stone and concrete, they are all replaceable; this impermanence is a constant reminder that every act of memory carries a dimension of betrayal and forgetting.[31]

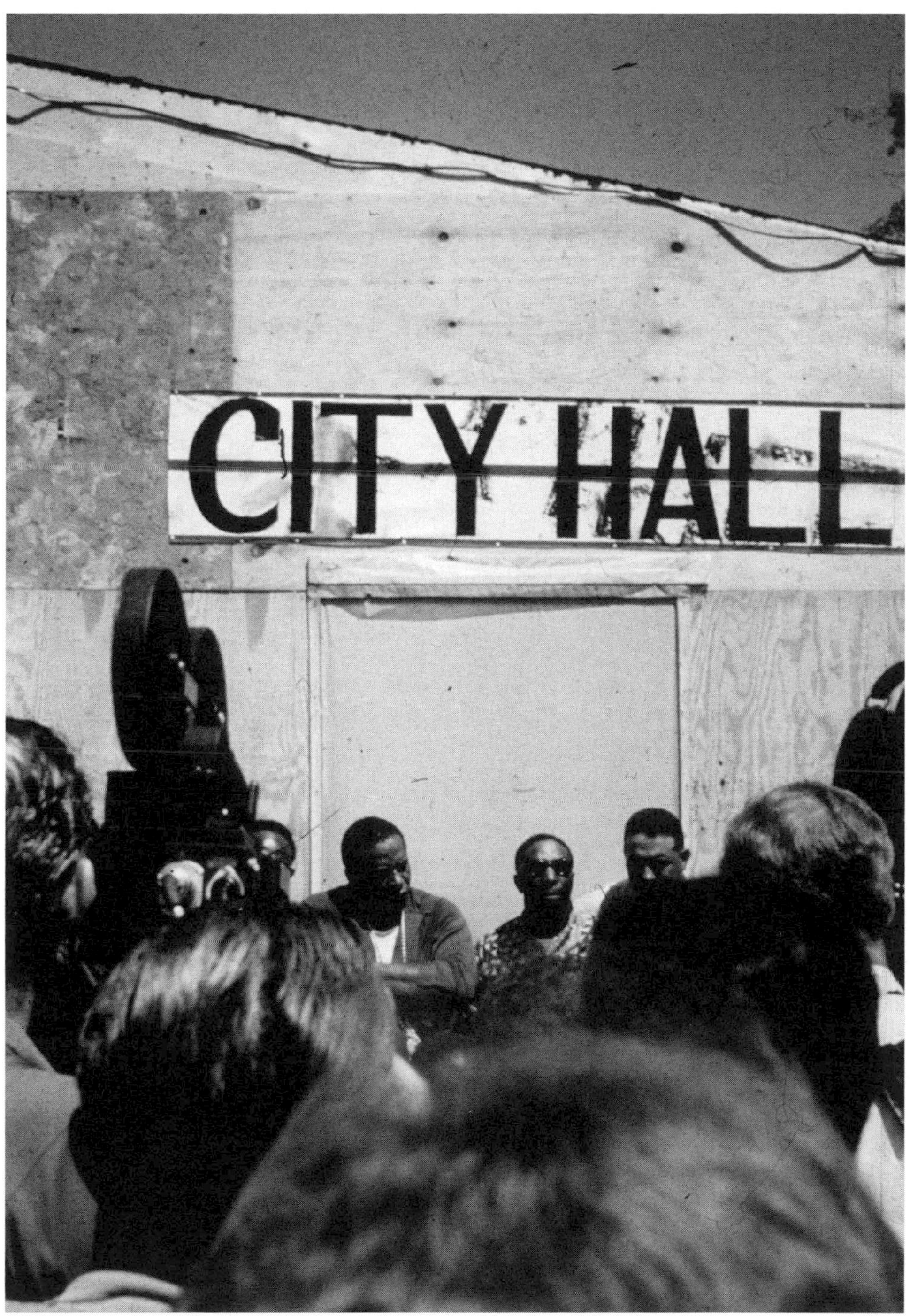

Figure 2.7. Public spaces become public when they are not only "mapped" by sovereign powers but also constituted by civic practices, debates, and social conflicts. Space of Gathering (The "City Hall"), Resurrection City, Washington Mall, Washington, DC, 1968. Photo by Tunney Lee.

CHOOSING A PLACE, APPROPRIATING THE RIGHT LOCUS

Although scholars conceptualize public space differently,[32] they tend to agree that the current concept of "publicness" should be understood through the ascendancy of a market-based paradigm and the provision of public goods.[33] Studies have shown that as a result of the reduced size and scope of the state, urban development has been transferred to the private sector.[34] However, beyond the processes surrounding the privatization of publicness, changes in the social nature of public spaces have been acknowledged, in part due to feminist and gay liberation movements, immigrant movements, and wider access to media and television.[35] In particular, with the massive growth of cities, public spaces have arguably become more impersonal and transient, playing a functional and symbolic role at best.[36] Technology contributes another layer to these changes, which alters the dynamics of encounters and their various forms. On the one hand, these changes turn public spaces into venues that are surveyed and controlled by the authorities; on the other, they enhance the flexible use of personal devices by individuals. In fact, the reliance of cities on technology has made them inseparable because of their codependent development and evolution.

Yet, as has been argued in this chapter, public spaces become public (or "spheres") when (and inasmuch as) they are not only "mapped" by sovereign powers (including supranational organizations) or imposed by economic forces (the "automatic domination of the market") "but also 'used' and 'instituted' (or constituted) by civic practices, debates, forms of representations, and social conflicts."[36] Thus, by definition, every public space is a political space, but not every political space is a public space.

Moreover, any public space represents temporary and fragile sociopolitical order and narration. A society may be attached to this order (for a short while or for a longer period of time), but meanings are constantly changing. These changes must be agreed upon or accepted by the public to avoid conflicts; an order or meaning that is not accepted by the public will expand political distances and encourage ongoing dissent and conflicts.

Finally, mapping the relationship between a public space's physical attributes, its narration, and the event provides understanding of the possibilities and constraints of a mass political public dynamic. Indeed, protest can take place anywhere—in a backyard or in a central location—as much depends on the way protesters' interpret the politics of space and its manifested distances. Thus, it does not require a designated space, but it does require a place that would provide an opportunity to challenge existing agreed-upon distances.

3

Enhancing the Impact

Previous page: Communicating a message to distant venues, actors employ various spatial spheres and organizing principles to enhance their messages and claims. Shown is a march in London calling for the withdrawal of British troops from Iraq, February 2007. Photo by author.

CHAPTER 3
Enhancing the Impact

> Thinking the spatial in a particular way can shake the manner in which certain political questions are formulated, can contribute to political arguments already under way, and—most deeply—can be an essential element in the imaginative structure which enables in the first place an opening up to the very sphere of the political.
>
> Doreen Massey, *For Space*

Doreen Massey's quotation above pinpoints one of the primary features of protests—the use of imagination to "think the spatial." To examine how space and boundaries are defined and to imaginatively envision new demarcations and structures, an individual cannot work within the conventional hegemonic boundaries of space or discourse. Instead, one must approach these tasks as an exploratory project, an expression of the desire for dialogue, and a call for a revised concept of space. This focus on reimagining space is at the core of numerous recent protests worldwide, challenging us with the ongoing and ever-specific project of protest practices through which society will be configured.[1]

Thinking the spatial, particularly the ways in which the protest's message travels, is key to understanding how contemporary dissent relates to the concept of distance. In this sense, distance is not only about the distance between dissent and the locus of power or the physical distance between participants but also about the action's influence on distant places and viewers. Many protests currently serve as staging grounds for other activities that aim to reduce physical and ideological distance from other potential actors or venues. This aim seems more feasible today with the ICT revolution, which blurs the boundaries between physical and virtual spaces. Indeed, ICTs have changed the ways in which we approach distanciation, but they have rearranged social groups into new configurations rather than eliminating social distance. This change and the role of ICTs in protests dramatically influence the ways in which people relate and communicate with one another during protests. In addition, to a certain extent, ICTs arguably involve the simultaneous reduction and enhancement of distance.

In communicating their messages, contemporary protesters utilize various spatial spheres and organizing principles. Tracking the ways in which protesters act reveals and multifaceted configuration of dissent, which extends beyond the boundaries of the nation-state and questions of national identity, thus pressing us to abandon notions of resistance that assume that a subject stands vis-à-vis the established state's structure of power.[2] Instead, to better understand the spatial choreography of dissent, this chapter explores a range of *spheres* (physical, geographical, and virtual) that are supported by four key principles—difference, decentralization, multiplicity, and informal order—through which protesters define newly imagined, at times concrete spaces. Unlike protest rituals led by the dominant political parties or activist groups, the more recent forms of dissent occur in parallel spheres, thereby constructing a social platform that challenges bounded politics by using imagination and space to create new possibilities. In essence, this platform, which advances discursive change, is based on a flexible strategy that tolerates various forms of action and conflicted positioning and that allows activists to modify its character based on what is actually happening on the ground.

In illuminating these ideas, the focus here is on Israeli groups of activists, but the discussion is not context specific, as the key principles of this choreography of dissent can be found, with modifications, in different protests worldwide—in both democratic and nondemocratic regimes. The elasticity of these principles and their configuration as an open system support activists by broadcasting their messages and reducing the distance between spaces and people worldwide.[3] In abstract terms, contemporary dissent arguably offers a new way of thinking about space and social relations that departs from the structural (often bounded and hierarchical) system of political power and enhances a diffused, flexible system.

PROTEST AS THE JUXTAPOSITION OF SPHERES

Space matters.[4] Space concerns not only power relations but also the needs, demands, and actions of protest movements.[5] This perspective challenges the structural analysis of power that tends to assume that no spaces exist outside of power.[6] Adopting this perspective helps capture the dynamism and contradictions in contemporary acts of dissent and the process through which actors organize and articulate symbols, scripts, and performances to craft their dissent.[7] The notion of dynamism relates to a twofold process: a group's structural dynamic, which enables growth and adaptation to change, and an action's spatial dynamic, which works through various spheres in calling for change. This dynamic requires sophistication and careful planning in organizing a dissent action and social tolerance among members to achieve the framework above. Thus, defining the (loose) boundaries of dissent is one of the activists' creative tasks in crafting dissent, and it significantly influences (1) the social dynamic among activists, (2) the political/ideological message, and (3) the imagined future.

The key characteristics of contemporary dissent work concurrently through different spheres of action: the physical, the geographical, and the virtual, whereby parallelism enhances the scale of the event. Although many activist groups are active on the web, physical space is still an important sphere in which to challenge the sociospatial order. To enhance a protest's spatial-concrete impact, activists also often plan to cover a wide geographical area by creating multiple events simultaneously. Geographical spread and multiple settings also provide the ideological means through which activists can create an alternative vision (e.g., social or political) to the one crafted by a central power. Finally, the virtual sphere is significant in terms of both reaching remote viewers/supporters (by taking advantage of ICTs) and crafting and spreading the event among participants. The virtual sphere is a critical player in a protest's production of symbols and strategies; it influences political decision making and public opinion, thus serving as a decisive participant in the protest. The virtual sphere is a means through which activists communicate among themselves, fuel the Web's need for a steady supply of spectacular images and stories, and gain the attention of more spectators with the assistance of the media.

However, instead of viewing these spheres in isolation, we should regard them as related and connected, as a dynamic array that is influenced by the social relations between activists and the scale of the event.[8] Furthermore, this dynamic array dictates the particular character of dissent. First and foremost, it requires the dismissal of a rigid social structure or a totalizing political vision, the adoption of flexibility as a means of responding to unexpected happenings (physical and virtual), and tolerance of the actors' varied identities. More specifically, this array of actions implies four underlying principles:

(1) *Difference*. The demise of a totalizing vision of change has forced contemporary movements to accept a plurality of actors, visions, and instruments for social transformation as part of the nature of dissent. Accepting difference refers both to identity and to ideological positioning, with groups limiting and expanding their membership in ways that suit their goals. Either way, difference as an underlying value not only assists in expanding the scope and scale of events but also may give rise to conflicts among participants. In many cases, difference leads to pragmatism in the way that dissent is performed and organized, often including a basic set of symbols and ideas that creates a sort of unified image and message while affording flexibility for differences. Plurality and difference also make decision making and the handling of multiple variable problems difficult, which often results in sociospatial decentralization.

(2) *Decentralization*. Difference, plurality, and the ways in which actors are recruited to the act of dissent can result in spatial and organizational decentralization.

Figures 3.1 and 3.2. Space matters and informs not only power relations but also the needs, demands, and actions of protest movements. *Above*: A Friday demonstration against the Israeli occupation of Nabi Saleh, in Nabi Saleh, April 20, 2011. *Right*: A Friday demonstration against the Israeli occupation of Sheikh Jarach, East Jerusalem, March 11, 2011. Photos by Chen Misgav.

Leadership is not concentrated but diffused, often restricting itself to specific goals. In some cases, individual cells operate entirely independently from the rest of the movement, although they maintain links to the larger movement through the circulation of information and persons.[9] Embedded in everyday life and responding to ongoing changes, this complex and multifaceted structure does not fold because of communication and virtual exchange, which different groups use to different degrees. Virtual exchange is used as an information tool, not only passing information from one unit to another but also serving as a mechanism that creates patterns of communication and behavioral codes, bringing a degree of homogeneity to the whole. In other words, these groups resemble an amorphous nebula of vague shapes with variable densities.[10] The principle of decentralization is also spatial, contributing to dissent's geographic spread or polycentric gatherings, which are based on the concept of a network. In essence, a polycentric event comprises multiple cells of action that occur simultaneously. In most cases, each cell acts with relative autonomy. This flexibility can enhance the scale of the event and its ability to grow (through the emergence of new cells; figure 3.3).

(3) *Multiplicity*. The organizational structure of activist groups has translated into a new spatial and geographical logic. Instead of a megascale event in a city center, many actions take place in multiple venues simultaneously. Each act is organized by its respective local group, which is entitled to relative freedom in planning the event. This strategy allows activists to (1) tentatively set up actions on the ground, thus changing/adding new locations to their map of dissent; (2) be flexible in terms of activists' participation and growth; and (3) maintain differences while decreasing conflicts among participants. In many cases, the spatial spread of dissent mirrors the internal order of the groups' organization, which has produced not only conflicted actors but also a segmented, reticular, and multifaceted structure of power. Multiplicity also implies waiving the option of protesting near or at governmental institutions and choosing instead to act in informal places, generating alternative maps to the geographies of power.

(4) *Informal order*. Choosing to act in everyday places does not mean that activists operate without order; they instead have relative flexibility in defining the array of the acts themselves, as manifested physically in specific places. The order of dissent responds to the physicality of places, which includes a setting's topography, boundaries, traffic movements, and building use (i.e., government buildings, commercial buildings, and residential buildings). These physical factors are all considered, thereby influencing the planning of actions, making dissent time-space specific. In addition, different from the geographic and virtual dynamics and the flexibility of growth, the local order of dissent (i.e., the performative components) is more stable. This stability is very much needed, as the order of the dissent and its ritual components represent how participants see themselves and how they want to be seen. In other words, this representation has significant symbolic meaning,

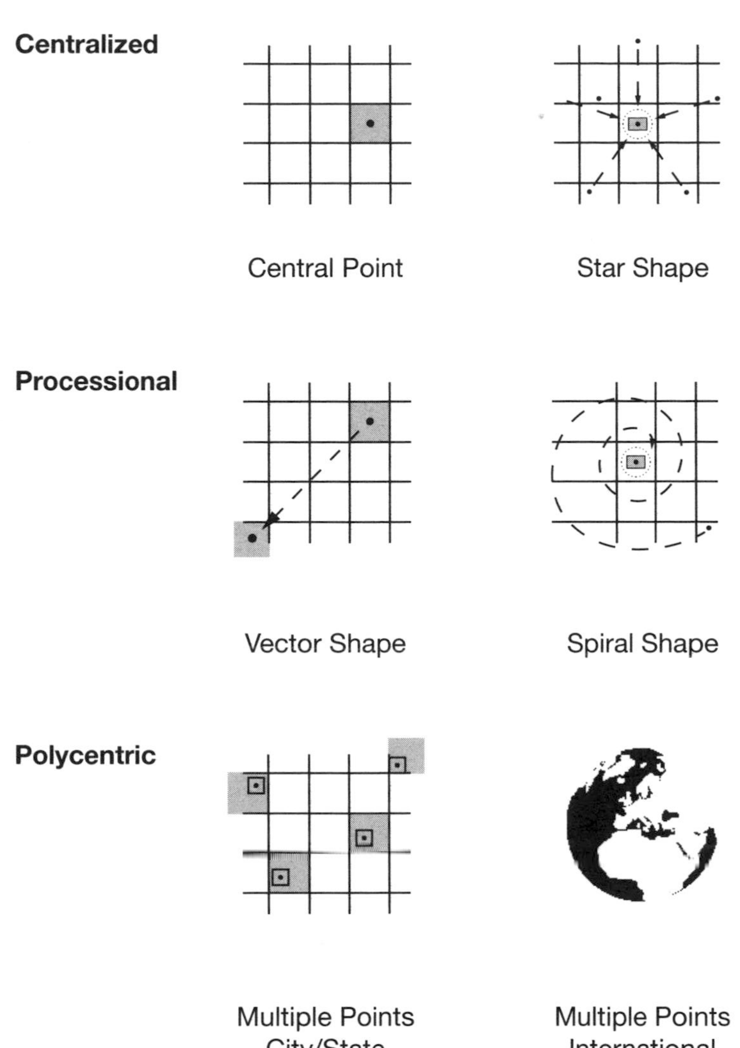

Figure 3.3. Centralized and decentralized forms of protest. Focusing on a protest's spatial dimension, it is possible to identify three key types of gatherings: centralized, processional, and polycentric. These categories refer mainly to an event's spatial manifestation and do not necessarily relate to the number of participants involved. However, difference, plurality, and the way actors are recruited to the act of dissent can result in spatial and organizational decentralization.

both internally—in creating a temporal unity—and externally—in projecting the message clearly.[11]

In sum, when practiced by a diverse set of actors, dissent is an opportunity to challenge the discourse by defining an open space for transformative purposes. However, contemporary dissent is unique because it occurs in multiple platforms and across various spheres simultaneously (see figure 3.4). The spatial and functional juxtaposition of spheres and the ways in which this relationship contributes to a space's future configuration matter.

Enhancing the Impact: Framework for Action

Protests	‹···›	Spheres of Action	‹···›	Principles
Multifaceted imaginative actions, spatially based with a reflexive role of subject taking conscious decisions regarding his/her contribution		• Virtual • Geographical • Physical		• Difference • Decentralization • Multiplicity • Informal order

Figure 3.4. Spheres of action and key principles of protests.

In exploring these ideas, three activist groups in Israel are analyzed: Women in Black (WIB), Machsom Watch (MW), and Anarchists against the Wall (AATW). Perceiving power as a means of spatial control, these groups primarily aim to challenge the legitimacy of the state's violent actions, viewing them as an occupation mechanism that guarantees hegemonic ideas about the spaces that are associated with nationalism and national identity. However, the motivation for choosing these groups—which have emerged from within the political boundaries of the state and been affected by its actions and policies—is not their (similar) ideological stances but their creativity in crafting new spatial geographies of dissent by employing novel practices of protest that depart from the hegemonic traditional protest rituals that occur in central Israel. WIB situates its protests at key physical junctions in Israel; MW monitors checkpoints on the West Bank; and AATW mainly protests at the separation wall itself, joining the Palestinian protests in their villages. Although these strategies may seem quite different, the analysis exposes parallel structural principles.[12] All three groups resist state violence and the occupation of Palestinian lands, but each group uses a different sociospatial strategy. Despite these strategic differences, these groups employ a similar model of action, even though their activities challenge political distance in different ways and represent different methods of establishing a dialogue with the ruler, in this case the state.

THE SEARCH FOR ALTERNATIVE FORMS OF PROTEST

Early one morning, while driving to a 4:00 a.m. MW shift at checkpoints in the West Bank, one activist commented to other passengers, "I realize that we have left the occupied territories to the settlers. And why is that? Because we thought that beyond the '67 line is occupied territory and we should not go there as occupiers. But now we realize that we should cross the green line," adding ironically, "and not protest as a 'lefty' activist of the Peace Now movement in Rabin Square in Tel Aviv."[13] Many contemporary activists have noted this irony, viewing both Rabin Square (the central square) in Tel Aviv and the Peace Now (PN) movement as hegemonic and anachronistic, thereby challenging both the structural and the ideological character of dissent.

The structural turn marks a departure from the traditional mode of political protests in Rabin Square that have been organized by PN, which was established in 1978. PN is associated with political parties, such as Meretz and the left-wing Labor Party, which have access to social capital and power.[14] This movement aims to appeal to as wide a segment of the population as possible, without committing to operate according to a predetermined strategy. Hence, the movement encourages and calls for the participation of people of different political party affiliations in its rallies, and it has even organized some joint demonstrations with the Labor Party and other parties on the political left. The second related turn is ideological. The PN movement's demonstrations carefully maintain their moderate and patriotic ideological image; for instance, all slogans and placards are approved in advance by the organizers, and unapproved ones are often removed.[15] The acts usually take place in the center of Israel—far from the occupied territories.

This turn should also be seen in the context of the geopolitical dynamic along the borders of Israel and Palestine. Historically, the borders of the Israeli state were established in the 1949 armistice agreements between Israel and its Arab neighbors. These borders came to be known as the Green Line after the 1967 war and Israel's occupation of additional territories, and they stopped functioning as the border between two sovereign entities (Israel and Jordan). From the Israeli perspective, the character and manifestation of the Green Line has been dynamic, shifting from an approach that supports separation (1937–1967) to an approach that advocates territorial inclusion with no political rights for the occupied Palestinian population (1967 to mid-1990s) and then returning to an approach that again fosters separation (since the Oslo agreements signed in 1993).[16]

With the escalation of the conflict in October 2000—the events known as the Second Intifada (the second Palestinian uprising against Israeli occupation)—and Israel's repressive, violent response to it, the conception of a physical border in the form of a separation wall emerged.[17] Creating a "new political geography," the wall further contributed to the unjust conditions under which most of the West Bank territory and resources are controlled by Israeli citizens. Palestinians, lacking real sovereignty, only have limited self-governance in restricted areas.[18] Furthermore, the Israeli practices of control along the wall restrict the movement of Palestinians and Israelis who reside in the West Bank, and they have created multiple installments and reference points along the border, including the Green Line (as an imagined line with historical and symbolic importance), the separation wall, an array of checkpoints, and the legal system that separates Israeli citizens from Palestinian inhabitants. Although all these practices significantly affect Palestinians' daily lives and rights (or lack thereof), the wall and the checkpoints are the most conspicuous physical embodiments of Israeli sociopolitical control.

The reality of Israel's occupation and contemporary control practices is the moral point of departure for the three groups examined. Believing in their transformative capacities to intervene in a given set of events and to alter them somewhat, WIB, MW, and AATW have created new avenues for opposition that aim to create a discursive shift with regard to state violence and to critically address the mechanisms through which the state regulates violence.[19]

THE MANIFOLD SPATIALITIES OF PROTESTS

Generally, WIB, MW, and AATW are negotiating the geography of citizenship and the law. Bound up in the regulation of the nation-state, space and citizenship in Israel and Palestine have been structured through a legal hierarchy of rights. The law determines who is allowed to do what under particular conditions and in specific locations. In addition, because legislation involves the creation of a power structure, it is also an immediate manifestation of violence. Thus, by addressing occupation and state violence, groups are negotiating the jurisdiction that separates both territories and types of people, regarding the law as a discursive body.[20] However, each group practices different forms of action and different modes of orientation (i.e., positioning vis-à-vis the state), which are also manifested in the spaces chosen for their acts of dissent. Mapping the groups' spheres of action reveals some similarities: (1) All the groups hope to receive global attention. Thus, they all use ICTs, though to varying degrees and with different levels of expertise (and WIB formed in the 1980s before the spread of ICTs); (2) the three groups share a similar geographic strategy, spreading action across multiple venues; and (3) concretely, all three groups participate in weekly events in informal settings, and they particularly focus on the choice of place and its influence on their practices and performances. Notably, they all choose key spatial typologies in which to organize their multiple simultaneous acts: junctions, checkpoints, and the wall (see figure 3.5 and map 3.1). The following analysis is divided into two sections: the first presents each group and discusses the spheres of their actions, and the second addresses the underlying shared principles of their actions.

Junctions: Enhancing Israeli Awareness of State Violence

Triggered by the outbreak of the First Intifada (1987),[21] WIB was formed by a small group of Jerusalemite women. Started as a weekly vigil of women dressed in black, the organization soon became a *national* network of some thirty vigils throughout Israel.[22] At its peak, the Jerusalem vigil—the largest—was estimated to include approximately 350–400 activists,[23] with a steep decline occurring after the Gulf War (1990–1991) and the Oslo Accords (1993). Today, only four vigils are active: in Jerusalem, Haifa, Tel Aviv, and Gan Shmuel, with 8–15 female participants each.[24] The vigils occur at the same spot every Friday between 1 and 2 p.m., with participants wearing black to symbolize their mourning for the tragedies of both Israelis and Palestinians and carrying signs with the slogan "Stop the Occupation" in three languages (Hebrew, English, and Arabic).[25] In the early years, verbal assaults and physical violence characterized the dynamics between vigil participants and the crowd, which also influenced the group's strategy.[26] Today, threats have dissipated, though these women still suffer from verbal attacks,[27] and two police officers regularly attend the Jerusalem vigil.

In terms of its mode of orientation vis-à-vis the state and society, WIB seeks to raise public awareness among Jewish Israelis about the occupation in the West Bank and the humanitarian situation in the Gaza Strip. Although participants hold different political views, they are united in their resistance to Israeli occupation, as is evident in their statement in a leaflet from 1991: "We are women who hold different political convictions, but the call to 'Stop the Occupation' unites us."[28] They aim to convince Israelis that "what happens to the Palestinians is their problem and our problem, and it's hurting us."[29] However, the pain is ideological rather than personal; thus, comparing themselves to the Mothers of the Plaza de Mayo, these activists note the differences between the two groups: "We have a different

The Geographical Spread of Dissent

1. Vigil locations (based on their activities in May 1990).
2. Checkpoints visited by Machsom Watch (based on a map sent by the group that represents the general activity in the years 2001–2010. Changes of activity are influenced by day-to-day events and political decisions, Oct. 2010).
3. Actions of Anarchists against the Wall based on data from AATW website, Oct. 2010.

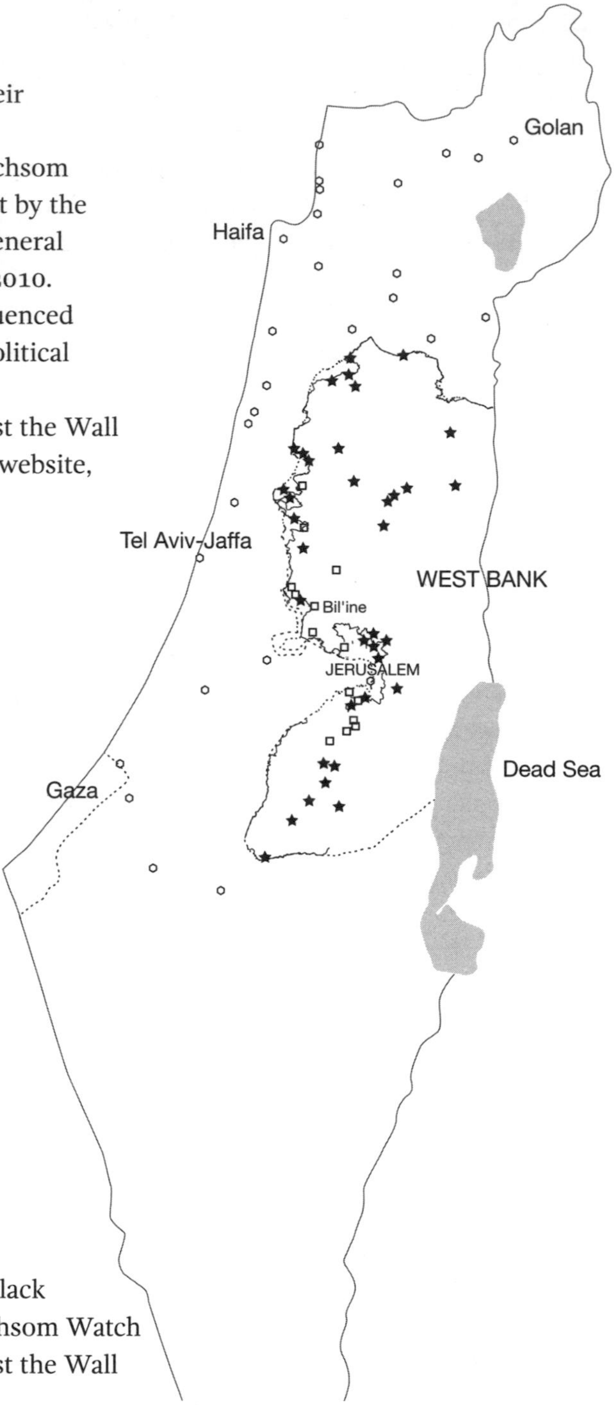

□ Vigil locations, Women in Black
○ Checkpoints visited by Machsom Watch
★ Actions of Anarchists against the Wall

Map 3.1. The geographical spread of dissent: WIB, MW, and AATW

Figure 3.5. *From top to bottom:* A Tel Aviv vigil, November 2008; an early-morning shift with Machsom Watch, December 28, 2009; and dissent in Bil'in. Photos by author.

reality: the mothers of the Plaza de Mayo are talking about their own children, a very, very personal thing for them; we are talking in general about the situation in Palestine."[30] Fighting against Israeli occupation, these activists do not have direct contact with Palestinian women.

For WIB, place matters, and their vigils take place at traffic junctions. These sites are not loci of power but rather "regular" places. Place matters; however, during acts of dissent, the activists do not modify the chosen location in any way. On the contrary, their strategy is to create a distinction between the hectic and colorful dynamics of these places, on the one hand, and their acts, on the other. By standing in silence and wearing black, they stand out in the landscape. The essence of this approach is replicated in different ways nationwide, and the map of the vigil locations (see figure 6.17) shows the many sites of these coordinated acts, which are all located within Israel's boundaries before the 1967 war. The decision to hold these vigils across Israel, on the one hand, and to position them within the boundaries of the Green Line, on the other, related to the activists' orientation toward or targeting of the Jewish population in Israel. These two spheres—the physical and geographical—are the group's focus. However, the global scale of these acts is also apparent, though not so much in terms of the use of ICTs or a deliberate goal of WIB. Instead, their strategy has been adopted and spread internationally—a formula for action that has been used in Spain, Italy, Croatia, Bosnia, and India, among other locations. Therefore, the global scale of this movement is an outcome rather than a means to an end.

In terms of communication, the activists who participated in the first vigils in 1988 maintained contact with interested parties via general media exposure and word of mouth among friends.[31] Growth was spontaneous and flexible, and in situations that required decision making, participants used paper handouts that were distributed during shifts. For communication among participants, WIB has also used faxes and, more recently, a Facebook group. The decision to create the Facebook page took place in a meeting held on March 13, 2010, in Jaffa. The thirty participants who arrived were not in full agreement regarding this tool, as most of them did not use Facebook; thus, the 190 members of the Facebook group do not represent all the activists involved in the movement. In addition, though their strategy was successfully "exported" worldwide, WIB does not have an independent website; rather, it has a page on the (Israeli) "Coalition of Women for Peace" website, and a description of its early activities appears on the international website of WIB.

Far removed from the mainstream of a society, though simultaneously part of it, WIB aims to recruit those in the crowds and to change the discourse from within. In other words, actors seek to operate in proximity to the people, with whom they want to interact. This proximity to the crowd can be best achieved in everyday places and informal spaces, in contrast to the symbolic spaces associated with the power of the regime.

Checkpoints: A Critical Approach to the System of State Violence

Triggered by the Second Intifada (October 2000),[32] MW (checkpoint watch)[33] is a volunteer organization of women who monitor Israeli checkpoints in the West Bank. A few women from Jerusalem, after newspaper reports about the violation of basic human rights, decided to observe what was happening at the checkpoints, which inspired this initiative. The first volunteers were drafted from WIB, and—because they felt that "they can do more and what they do is not enough"[34]—they started monitoring the Bethlehem checkpoint in February 2001. Over time, the growth of the organization led to the monitoring of checkpoints across the West Bank. At the height of their activities, MW included three hundred to four hundred activists, who operated in shifts seven days a week. Two to five volunteers work each shift, traveling in a car between checkpoints and writing a summary report on the activities taking place there.

MW defines itself as a "volunteer organization of Israeli women who are peace activists from all sectors of society. We oppose the Israeli occupation in the area known as the West Bank, we oppose the appropriation of Palestinian land and the denial of Palestinian human rights. We support the right of Palestinians to move freely in their land and oppose the checkpoints which severely restrict Palestinian daily life."[35] Although volunteers have various political views, they are united in their resistance to Israeli occupation, as they state in the declaration above. Their activities are oriented toward assuring human rights by maintaining contact with officers in the Civil Administration (an arm of the military that is responsible for controlling Palestinian civil affairs in the West Bank) and other army officials.[36] Activists perceive gender as highly significant in maintaining nonviolent dissent, and participants believe that women are better able to approach both the soldiers and the Palestinians to secure human rights. As Hagar Kotef and Merav Amir explain, "These sexist presuppositions, which are common to many other societies, especially nationalistic and militaristic ones, place women in an external position vis-à-vis the political domain."[37]

MW's strategy and aim to expose the Israelis' suppression of Palestinians at checkpoints have affected its decision to focus on the geographical spread of checkpoints and to report their findings to the international community. On a local scale, MW marks a shift in protest strategies, moving dissent from city junctions to these checkpoints, where "occupation is taking place."[38] MW activists do not leave any mark on the places they visit. In this sense, place matters only because of its association with repression. When the army decides to close or abandon a checkpoint, it is also removed from the activists' driving route. Geographically, this dissent reflects time and space and requires constant attention to international diplomatic efforts, national policies, and actions. Different from WIB, which uses physical junctions to create the network of places that are chosen by activists, the point of departure here is a network of checkpoints that are dictated by the central government. During MW shifts, activists drive through the West Bank or Palestinian villages, where the checkpoints are considered temporary and, at times, unfixed.

Virtual spaces complement this dynamic reality and strategy and represent channels through which the group can disseminate its findings. MW's active website (in English and Hebrew)[39] is part of its dissent strategy; it contains reports uploaded at the end of each shift, a list of checkpoints, images, and movies.[40] In addition to the site, the group has a Facebook page[41] that coordinates members and assists with communication. According to MW, the website is designed to illuminate and emphasize incidents and events at Israel Defense Forces (IDF) checkpoints in the occupied territories about which the public should be informed. For the most part, these events are not reported in the conventional media.

MW seeks to challenge practices of distance, which are engineered by the state, by creating a body that monitors the state and its representatives (i.e., the army). Activists aim to interact with the soldiers and their commanders at checkpoints, where repression is taking place. These sites are geographically distant from the daily life in city centers and, in turn, are perceived as abstract. Therefore, MW aims to concretize these sites.

The Wall: Confronting the Army while Expropriating Palestinian Land

AATW is a group of Israeli activists that formed in 2003 after the establishment of the separation wall. The group calls itself a nonviolent action group, following other international solidarity organizations in the West Bank,[42] and its activities are coordinated with the Palestinian villages' local committees, who lead protests against the separation wall.[43] These activists are aware of their privileged status as Israelis, and they seek to use this advantageous position as a "tool for solidarity" with Palestinians. As they declare, "It is the duty of Israeli citizens to resist immoral policies and actions carried out in our name. We believe that it is possible to do more than demonstrate inside Israel or participate in humanitarian relief actions. Israeli apartheid and occupation isn't going to end by itself—it will end when it becomes ungovernable and unmanageable. It is time to physically oppose the bulldozers, the army and the occupation."[44]

Although it operates in various villages,[45] the group is well known for its involvement in the Palestinian struggle in the village of Bil'in. The protest in Bil'in started in February 2005 as construction began on the wall near the village,[46] and it continues today as a regular Friday ritual that Israelis, international activists, and locals attend. Participants fall within many age groups, though most participants are younger.[47] As established by the Palestinians, weekly demonstrations in Bil'in and other locations strategically begin at approximately 1:00 p.m. after the Friday prayer. Israeli activists come alone or in private carpools from Tel Aviv. Starting near the mosque, the demonstrators march together down the village streets and through the agriculture fields toward the gate of the separation wall. The gate is where the activists meet the Israeli army. After the activists request that the gate be opened, the army declares that the demonstration is illegal. At this point, tensions escalate on both sides, with the army firing tear gas and the Palestinians throwing stones. An hour or two later, if nothing unusual happens, the protest ends. Both Palestinian and Israeli antiwall demonstrators are often arrested and prosecuted.

For AATW, all spheres matter. Place is *key*, and dissent often includes symbolic actions, including demonstrators who chain themselves to olive trees (symbols of both peace and the longevity of Palestinian ownership of the land) or lock themselves inside an iron cage (the literalization of their captivity and powerlessness) as a way of impeding the construction of the wall. Other demonstrations are more conceptual, including those in which demonstrators wear black viper dolls around their necks to symbolize the suffocation that the wall causes.[48] This strategy of reappropriating place is being replicated in nuanced ways in other places along the wall. The aim is to confront all places where immoral policies and actions are carried out. Importantly, the spread and variety of local protests along the wall and regional protests are affected by what is happening on the ground. In that respect, the group focuses on both the local and the international community.

As with MW, virtual spaces are key tools in acts of dissent, and activists maintain a website where they regularly upload videos, photos, and textual reports (in English) after each week's Friday demonstrations. However, while MW focuses more on the situation and human rights overall and its role in exposing the reality on the ground, the AATW Facebook page is more concerned with documenting the protests and their outcomes (e.g., arrests and violations of human rights). In May 2010, the group created a Facebook page rather than a Facebook group, which gives them more control over membership. Through Facebook, members can coordinate their arrivals for the demonstrations and can also update each other regarding other events and calls for actions against state violence.[49]

Extremely distant from the political perceptions of mainstream Israeli society (the regime and the people) because of their goal (i.e., protesting against the wall) and collaboration with the Palestinians, who are considered the enemy by the mainstream, this group seeks to confront the army and to challenge physical and political distance by expressing their opposition at places where injustice and repression are actually occurring. In this case, actors feel extremely removed from the state's ideas and policies.

THE UNDERLYING PRINCIPLES OF THE GROUPS' PROTESTS

Clearly, the three groups presented here have created new and different geographies of opposition, generating alternative sociospatial readings to understand the geographies of domination in Israel and Palestine (table 3.1). However, these groups are similar in terms of how they use the different spheres, which contributes to the performance and character of their protests. How does this juxtaposition affect the management of the protest? Does it influence the profiles of the actors who participate in the action, the decision-making processes, or the order of the event? Engaging with these questions, the analysis reveals that the three groups share similar and interrelated organizational principles. These key principles assist in bridging the ideological gaps among participants, bypassing conflicts and coordinating the action in the various spheres.

› Spheres of Action	**Women in Black**	**Machsom Watch**	**Anarchists against the Wall**
› Physical	Performing in place. Traffic junctions with varied access/ exposure to pedestrian crowd.	Monitoring place. Checkpoints in the West Bank/ along the Green Line.	Reappropriating place in Palestinian villages.
› Geographical	Creating a net of vigils. Action duplicated, with nuances.	Multiple shifts of dynamic driving' routes along the Green Line.	Action duplicated, with nuances along the wall.
› Virtual	Limited use of ICTs, international adoption of strategy.	Use of virtual sphere for exposure and awareness.	Use of virtual for exposure and awareness.

Table 3.1. Comparative Analysis: WIB, MW, and AATW. When WIB started (1989), ICT use and the internet were not as common or accessible as they are today. Nevertheless, these women established a network that challenged injustice before the availability of such electronic means. They accomplished an unusual achievement, "exporting" their ways of dissenting to different places and contexts across the globe where they were successfully applied.

Difference

At first glance, comparing the profiles of the groups' activists, we find two very different groups. In the case of WIB and MW, the activists are Israeli women (ages fifty–eighty) from relatively homogeneous socioeconomic backgrounds, who have participated in different nonviolent organizations for many years (as early as 1987). However, to become a member of each group, one must fit two eligibility criteria related to gender and nationality/civilian identity. The activists' female identities are regarded as critical and powerful. Some members believe that women are capable of approaching the checkpoint without provoking antagonistic responses, which helps them maintain *nonviolent* acts of dissent, while others stress a political feminist agenda; all agree that female identity is imperative.[50] On the other hand, the AATW is a heterogeneous group in terms of age, gender, and national identity, and its members collaborate with Palestinian villagers (all men) and international activists, thereby crossing national and discursive boundaries. However, these three groups share a *tolerance* toward different political positions within their groups and toward new initiatives. Arguments are unavoidable, and, from its earliest days, WIB frequently argued about what their protest signs should represent: "Some of the women were very much . . . to the center of the political map, and others were more to the left, and they finally decided on just the hand that says 'Stop the Occupation' (Dai La'Kibush)."[51] Both WIB and MW activists are generally allowed to initiate activities independently, and they frequently do so.[52] This relative "openness" allows volunteers to simultaneously have diverse political views and unite in their general resistance to Israeli occupation.

Gender clearly affects the dynamic between actors and soldiers, especially when comparing WIB's and MW's activities with those of AATW, which tend to end in violence. Unlike WIB and MW, which use female identity as a tool of power, AATW approaches national identity as a tool of power, as something to be enacted. AATW activists—like MW activists—are Israelis who use their privileged national identity to support Palestinians, seeing their citizenship as an important asset in their struggle.[53] Their status is especially important in softening Israeli soldiers' responses to Palestinian activists. According to the activists' testimonies, soldiers act differently when Israeli citizens are present, which explains why the latter's presence is so valuable.[54] Therefore, for AATW, differences are addressed in multiple ways, both in terms of participants' diverse identities and positioning and the arguments that arise because of these differences. In all three cases, the groups do not define a strict ideological agenda, instead focusing on action, directly protesting against what they perceive to be an intolerable reality. This focus, as well as the structure of their activities, enables the groups to encourage participation among diverse activists who sometimes have conflicting political agendas.

Decentralization

When examining how the groups are organized, we observe that they function as networks with diffuse power relations. Each WIB vigil is absolutely autonomous, and its participants are able to determine the time, place, and composition of the shift and are responsible for placards and signage. In annual meetings, WIB members hold general discussions about the situation on the ground and members' new initiatives. This diffuse structure is based on the personal relationships within each vigil group, which enhances members' commitment to smaller groups. In the case of MW, this diffuse configuration is further enhanced. Although they are assisted by a secretarial body (with no power to make decisions), a regional shift coordinator, and a website manager, the two to three members on each shift are free to decide how they organize that shift. Similar to WIB, MW holds general meetings approximately every three months, making decisions based on the vote of those in attendance. Daily contact among activists is maintained through a mailing list. Likewise, AATW does not define itself as a formal organization, nor does it function as one; instead, it is a dynamic group. Activists make decisions in a nonhierarchical manner during periodic meetings. Membership is dynamic and in constant flux, though some of the group's founders are still active.[55] Thus, members voluntarily take on important tasks, such as organizing transportation from central Israel to the demonstrations and communicating with the media, and these responsibilities may change from time to time. Furthermore, activists are welcome to initiate new forms of protest.[56]

Thus, in all three groups, decentralization is a means through which the activists can not only maintain differences but also grow (and shrink) with minimal management. Overall, decentralization enhances (1) flexibility with regard to the action's design and location; (2) personal will and voice within the team; and (3) an elastic organizational structure, which helps activists avoid caring for and maintaining a rigid, hierarchical, and expensive management structure. However, this lack of control may result in contradictory outcomes; it may not only enhance growth but also result in decreasing the number of participants if they find that the group's agenda is insufficiently defined or ineffective.

Multiplicity

Spatially, all groups choose *key typological places* of dissent, which contribute to their identities and the terrain's configuration. Even when they shift from one location to another, they choose similar types of places. Waiving the option to protest near or at government institutions, they generate alternative maps for the geographies of domination. More specifically, addressing the state's political boundaries (or lack thereof), we also see how dissent is moving east—a shift that marks activists' acknowledgment of the need to act where daily violence takes place.

The maps of these actions, either within Israel's boundaries or along its borders, challenge colonization by illuminating places that are unnoticed by and concealed from the general public. WIB stands at traffic junctions in Israel (within the 1967 borders), with varying levels of access/exposure to Israeli pedestrians. MW stands at checkpoints in the West Bank and along the Green Line, demonstrating in locations where human rights are disregarded. Neither group attempts to redefine or challenge the existing spatial boundaries, but in choosing particular places and target audiences, they challenge discursive boundaries. However, in the case of AATW, which protests in Palestinian villages where land has been expropriated, activists challenge both spatial and discursive boundaries and the mechanisms of the state. Most of the violence and arrests occur in these locations. In the case of WIB, vigils spontaneously emerged in different places in the early 1990s, and although many vigils later became inactive, the performance of the other vigils was not affected. The same is true for MW. The map of checkpoints is dynamic, affected by both foreign and national policies; in the case of AATW, the map is also influenced by Palestinian decisions regarding the protests' location, which depends on what is happening on the ground and what changes have occurred in the ongoing construction of the wall. In sum, this particular strategy allows activists to design shifts and routes dynamically.

Beyond identity and flexibility, multiplicity also contributes to the activists' message; it should be seen for its plurality, taking many forms in different places, and thereby be relevant to various audiences. In this sense, multiplicity is not only a pragmatic means of enhancing the message's impact but also a means of highlighting the far reach of the message due to its relevance to a large portion of society.

Informal Order

As opposed to the spatial dynamic, the order of dissent (i.e., the performative components) is more stable. As knowledgeable participants who are highly aware of their strengths and limitations, activists in all groups have created consistent patterns of action in concrete places: WIB silently stands with signs during its weekly vigil every Friday from 1:00 to 2:00 p.m. MW watches checkpoints in two shifts each day, seven days a week. AATW joins the Palestinian demonstrators weekly, every Friday at 1:00 p.m.; they start their march near the village mosque and walk with Palestinian flags to the gate of the wall, yelling slogans in their encounters with soldiers. The traffic junction, the checkpoint, and the fence/wall in Bil'in are all places. Indeed, because these acts occur in real, concrete places, the dissent is effective and draws ample local and international attention.

In all cases, the body plays a significant role in personalizing the struggle. In WIB, the body is marked and not taken for granted; the body is the message—knowledge is performed and communicated through the protesting body. In their black clothing, WIB activists project images that confound existing cultural codes and thus become more difficult to tolerate because they challenge the daily appearance of secular women.[57] In MW, the body's detection and assaults on mobility are the subject of dissent. Challenging gender boundaries by monitoring the regulators of checkpoints (soldiers and private security companies), MW activists seek to make their protests personal by sharing stories about and experiences with the body of the other, the Palestinian. In the case of AATW, the body is part of the performative dimension of dissent (e.g., chaining themselves to olive trees or wearing particular outfits to symbolize the suffocating effect of the wall).[58] Using this creativity to gain media coverage, activists seek to *personalize* their struggles and to *fill* the place with evidence of its Palestinian landowners.[59] Furthermore, the bodies of Israeli protesters are also used as human shields for the Palestinians who protest alongside them in confrontations with Israeli soldiers, who often use tear gas and other means to disperse protests. Thus, different from its roles as a symbolic reminder for WIB and the normative reminder for MW, the body is a living reminder of wounds, deaths, and losses in the case of AATW.

Overall, the principles described here are related as components in a complex array of spheres in which place and space are complementary parts rather than opposites. In other words, the dynamic relationships among all these spheres help groups reduce social distance by creating alternative spatialities. These alternative spatialities have been achieved by addressing space both as a mechanism for creating meaning and interpreting social realities and as a device for negotiating between the state and citizens. In addition, as has been shown, although these different groups respond to the same grievance (i.e., occupation and violence), each group responds differently, crafting its own spatial-discursive method. WIB focuses on creating a discursive change within Israeli society, while MW and AATW challenge the mechanisms of the state by confronting its violent acts on the ground (i.e., the repression at checkpoints and the construction of the wall)—a difference that is also apparent in their target audiences. MW addresses Israeli society and decision makers (attempting to realize change from within); AATW addresses the army's actions and speaks to the international community and the Palestinians (as an act of solidarity). Thus, this mode of action, with its key generative principles and spheres, is flexible enough to allow the creation of distinct dissent strategies spatially (by choosing location of dissent, its physicality, and its materiality), socially (by establishing a dynamic of alternative social relations between authorities and activists), and politically (by challenging the patterns of institutions that stabilize a place's spatial and social dimensions).

REIMAGINING SOCIOSPATIAL DISTANCE

The protests and actions presented here exemplify a major shift in the ways citizens perceive physical, geographical, and social distances, which have affected how they take to the streets. Contemporary protests do not look for a unified group in terms of political ideas. Instead, protesters reflect various perspectives and positions and act in different spaces and locations. A protest can be a mass gathering of different groups that unite under a general slogan. Although different groups now unite to support a common cause, they often maintain their identities (and their social distance) throughout the protest. Furthermore, a protest's ability to spread its message and increase its numbers relies on its capacity not only to unite groups but also to blend a multitude of media, leaders, and viewpoints in a complex way. As such, the organizational structure of protests resembles a web rather than a strict hierarchy, which contributes to the widespread dissemination of different protests in different places. In the second decade of the twenty-first century, this spirit characterized the Arab Spring and New York's Occupy Wall Street—protests that were based on informal leadership and a multitude of voices.

Contemporary protests are also characterized by elastic boundaries between the public and the private and between the personal and the collective, modifying the ritual dimension of traditional human communications. In this sense, mobile phones have dramatically affected protests' action, with users imagining themselves to be capable of communicating with and beyond the crowd, as argued by Vicente Rafael:

> Unlike computer users, cell phone owners are mobile, immersed in the crowd, yet able to communicate beyond it. Texting provides them with a way out of their surroundings. Thanks to the cell phone, they need not be present to others around them. Even when they are part of a socially defined group—say, commuters or mourners—cell phone users are always somewhere else, receiving and transmitting messages from beyond their physical location.[60]

However, as Stephen Graham suggests, "tactic knowledge," which is often developed in trusting, face-to-face interactions, is gradually shrinking.[61] As Amin and Thrift have warned, technology "must not be allowed to take us unaware."[62] This warning is particularly relevant for protests, as their impact is tied to the ability to develop trust and reduce social distance among participants.

Finally, the importance of this array of spheres, both as a tool for organizing the form of dissent and as a means of challenging geometries of power, is increasingly gaining recognition among protesters. Through the employment of different spheres, activists transcend any dichotomized definitions of power relations (power versus resistance) and configure new "processual" spaces. Yet, in our current world, the configuration of "processual" spaces is monitored and surveyed. Nothing escapes the gaze of authorities. Paradoxically, as our daily realities are recorded and enhanced by cameras and controlling forces, sometimes surveillance supports acts of dissent and increases their exposure. Activists have adjusted to monitoring, making it a source of strength. Moreover, the gaze of controlling practices (of the police and the army) enhances the sense of safety among participants. In this way, surveillance also serves the protesters.

4
Bargaining Power

Previous page: Local institutional features (e.g., police organizations), the nature of the judiciary, legal codes, and constitutional rights play important roles in defining the opportunities for and constraints on protest policing. A steel-helmeted police riot squad goes into action against Arab rioters outside Government House, Jaffa, October 27, 1933. Photo by Kluger Zoltan, National Photo Collection, Israel.

CHAPTER 4

Bargaining Power

> Every regime empowers agents—police, troops, headmen, posses, sheriffs, and others—to monitor, contain, and on occasion repress collective claim making. Some of the agents are violent specialists, and most others have violent specialists under their command. These agents always have some means of collective coercion at their disposal and always enjoy some discretion in the use of those means. In one common sequence, claimants challenge repressive agents, occupy forbidden premises, attack symbolically significant objects, or seize property; then agents reply with force. Because variants on that sequence occur frequently, when repressive agents are at hand they actually perform the great bulk of the killing and wounding that occurs in public violence.
>
> Charles Tilly, *The Politics of Collective Violence*

Power is rarely given. It can be claimed, negotiated, and, in extreme cases, taken. Power gained through acts of protest has the potential to yield new political rights. This process of claim making to achieve rights is often seen in the context of what has been loosely referred to as "identity politics," which consists of struggles for legitimation and recognition. These struggles "take place within boundaries, across boundaries, over placement and around character of boundaries, and about relations between people sharing a common answer to the question 'Who are you?' on one side and other political actors, including agents of government, on the other."[1] Following this rationale and in addressing the question of power in protests, three interrelated dimensions are of importance: tactics, context, and identity. First, *tactics*, or the ways actions are displayed and dramatized,[2] define the degree of an act's publicness in a place and its impact on the public at large (asking the question of where and how to act). The particular physicality of the space and how the actors perceive their scope of power are two factors that highly influence the tactics of an action. Second, the particularity of the space comes into play in terms of how actors define *the context of power* (What is the lens through which protesters see the state/civil rights?) and how actors do or do not challenge current state apparatuses, "inside/outside division,"[3] and address the included-excluded binary. Defining these tasks requires in-depth knowledge of rights and laws, both local and international. The third dimension, *identity* (How do protesters see themselves?), is how actors appear, communicate, and define their identity vis-à-vis the appearance of the sovereign (i.e., new identities, disassociation from national identity, etc.). Notably, these rather flexible dimensions—tactics, context, and identity—allow people to initiate new (informal) definitions vis-à-vis the rather formal relationships and contract between the inhabitant and the regime.

This initiation of new (informal) definitions plays a central role in the creation, escalation, and protraction of conflicts between protesters and authorities. This contentious politics is affected by not only current nationalistic trends but also by a civilian consciousness of the politics of place, particularly its mutable nature. As has been argued, nowadays citizens do not take their capacity to act (the power *to*) for granted, nor do they conceive of control practices (the power *over*) as primary; rather, they see these forms of power as two sides of the same coin.[4] Stating this differently, the ongoing contract between the state and the individual is perceived as negotiable. Overall, citizenship is perceived as a sociospatial concept that limits and allows individuals to perform physical and legal actions, thereby playing a significant cultural-ideological role in which geopolicy and culture intersect to establish a national identity.[5] In contemporary times, perceiving the city or the state as an arena for citizens is clearly impossible; it is instead perceived as a forum for contesting different types of inhabitants, including foreigners, refugees, and migrant workers, who might not be citizens.[6]

That is why struggles motivated by identity politics cannot be reduced to the local or national sphere. Numerous protests are nourished by the geopolitical, cultural, and economic conditions that exacerbate urban alienation, increase the marginality of immigrant groups, fuel youth gangs, and drive illegal activity, making urban landscapes sites of social exclusion and revanchism—all of which have fueled (sometimes violent) acts of dissent. Examples of such conditions include the riots in Los Angeles in 1992; the riots in the Paris suburbs in 2005; the events in Israel in October 2000; and the upheavals and protests from 2010 to 2012 in Tunisia, Egypt, Syria, Libya, and elsewhere (which have come to be associated with the "Arab Spring"). These protests contest not only symbols, infrastructures, and resources but also the meaning of citizenship in urban centers.[7] Such protest events represent a relatively recent phenomenon; from a historical perspective, prior to the American Revolution and the French Revolution, struggles or protests in which citizens demanded their rights rarely occurred. People remained loyal to religious and cultural traditions; in most cases, they undertook collective action on behalf of such traditions, though only if their rights were violated.[8]

The meaning of citizenship in urban centers is also a contested issue in academic discourse, with thinkers suggesting different positions based on the liberal, communitarian, social democratic, immigrant and multicultural, nationalistic, and feminist models.[9] Each of these positions differs in its views of the relationships between citizenship, rights, practices, and ideas of the "common good," consequently resulting in diverse definitions. For example, John Rawls proposes identifying justice with the idea of "fairness" and prioritizing rights over goods; some call for reform within social institutions to accommodate the cultural distinctiveness of multiple ethnic groups within a single state; and Iris Marion Young proposes shifting the focus from a search for commonality (and, as a result, bypassing diversity) to making the public sphere truly representative of both individuals and groups.[10] These examples portray the scope of citizenship in providing a common status for individuals—helping integrate members of society, on the one hand, and excluding nonmembers, on the other. However, while citizenship and territorial borders both function in relation to the sovereign state, territorial borders do not always mark the borders of citizenship.[11] Contemporary concepts such as "being political," cosmopolitanism, and denationalized citizenship suggest new venues in which to address the relationships between contemporary life and citizenship.[12]

CIVILIAN CONSCIOUSNESS OF THE POLITICS OF PLACE
Rights, Appearance, Publicness

TACTIC: ENHANCING PUBLICNESS	⟷	**CONTEXT: BUILDING [ON] RIGHTS**	⟷	**IDENTITY: CONSCIOUS APPEARANCE**
Where and how to act? Defining an action's strategy, scale, and location.		Why do we act and for whom? Scale of reform suggested, and the way it does or does not challenge inside/outside divisions.		How do we see ourselves? Defining identity vis-à-vis formal national definitions.

Figure 4.1. Claiming power: tactic, context, identity.

From a sociocultural perspective, citizenship (as a manifestation of civil rights) and protests can be seen as related concepts, both expressed in practices of performance and materialization.[13] Indeed, citizenship ties people to a place in different ways, but this tool also frames civil society in a particular space, fixing the conditions and basic rules of all associational activity (including political activity) and daily life. Yet, this fixation of conditions and rules in a place is temporal and thus undergoing constant modifications.[14] This double character of change and fixedness of citizenship implies change on a daily basis but also suggests that both spaces and citizenship are performative,[15] even theatrical, concepts that are crafted by humans and are, in turn, adaptable and challengeable. Therefore, new rights can make the possession and wielding of previous rights more effective, and the accession of such rights can either remove or build new fences between groups.

Undeniably, during protests, which are regarded as conflictual and threatening, this heterogeneous (or more loose) framework of residency often collapses and division is reerected between the citizens of the territorial nation-state and other inhabitants (immigrants). Discrimination during protests is often determined by the degree of disparity between the city's dense and heterogeneous lived spaces and the nation as an idealized construct.[16] The vulnerability of noncitizens during protests has become a major concern in contemporary cities and protests. For example, such vulnerability was reported at the Women's March on Washington (WMW) on January 21, 2017, a day after the inauguration of the 45th president of the United States. Aiming to protect immigrants, organizers recruited a legal observation team, mainly law students, legal workers, and lawyers who volunteered and received training and direction from the National Lawyers Guild for the march. Law enforcement officials were committed to not making any arrests of undocumented immigrants who were participating in the march, and a law team was available at the event.

Thus, central to planning protests, as a form of contentious politics, is the question of control over both the design of the event and its dynamic, including the protections of participants. The aim (in most cases) of both protesters and the authorities is to minimize the gap between the planned and the unpredictable.

CONTROLLING THE EVENTS

Each country (and sometimes different cities within the same country) controls or polices protests in different ways. Local institutional features (e.g., police departments), the nature of the judiciary, legal codes, and constitutional rights "play an important role in defining the opportunities for and constraints on protest policing, as they set the conditions for the actual protest policing strategies."[17] In particular, the "rootedness" of a democratic culture seems to have an important impact on the reactions of elites to emergent challengers, and vice versa.[18] The dynamics of protests—and their potential to harm people or damage objects or institutions—not only depend on protesters but also on the regime. In addressing the regime, Charles Tilly suggests two parameters associated with the regime that affect the character and intensity of collective violence during protests: *governmental capacity* and *democracy*. "The first means the extent [to] which governmental agents control resources, activities and populations within governmental territory"; based on the law, this capacity may range from very little control to ample, nearly absolute control.[19] Democracy implies the extent to which members of the population under the government's jurisdiction maintain unrestricted and equal relations with government agents, exercise collective control over government personnel and resources, and enjoy protection from arbitrary action by government agents. Clearly, democratic regimes with high governmental capacities will create the most space for claim making and participation (e.g., Germany or Britain).[20]

These two parameters also influence the distance between the people and the state. As argued by Diane Davis, "Some citizens or groups of citizens are more distanced from the state than others, and it is the extent of citizens' distance from the state that explains their likelihood of joining social movements, the strategies they are likely to pursue, the meaning they attribute to movement activism, and even the identities enshrined in these collective actions."[21] Distance from state institutions triggers alienation, which nurtures protests. But the sense of distance from state institutions is not a sudden event and does not imply that people who participate in protests are isolated. On the contrary, Anthony Oberschall has shown that personal networks and contacts play a major role in the recruitment of activists, and people who are well positioned and integrated into collective city life are seemingly more likely to participate in popular protests than those who are socially isolated, atomized, and uprooted.[22] Individuals choose to participate in mass movements against a particular regime if the distance between the movement's demands and the policies of the incumbent regime exceeds an individual-specific critical level. As Susanne Lohmann argues, the regime indirectly controls the emergence of protest movements because if it implements political reforms, it can shift its policies toward those demanded by its opponents and thereby reduce the size and strength of the opposition. However, there is a level of mass turnout, a revolutionary threshold, beyond which reform attempts are futile and the regime collapses. This revolutionary threshold endangers the regime's survival.[23] Thus, the regime should be perceived as a strategic player that adjusts the degree of repression in response to past events to maximize its change of survival.[24]

Importantly, the fear of the unexpected does not only apply to the authorities. The unforeseen number of participants and the threat of sudden disorder or violence increase anxiety among both protesters and authorities. A protester's greatest fear is a loss of control, which may result in violence. Violent political action attempts to maximize relatively insubstantial resources, but it exposes activists to the possible costs of such behavior (i.e., death, loss of freedom, and physical injury). Moreover, violence that is not state inflicted is often considered criminal, as part of the state's differentiation between "orderly" violence and violence that threatens order. These complex relationships between violence and order have emerged, in part, in time with the modern state's attempts to dictate what qualifies as legitimate violence and what does not. Undeniably, violence is rooted in the state's actions and the assumption that its citizens are willing to fight (and die) for the regime. In other words, the state is constructed through violence, which maintains its sovereignty. Even when a state seems peaceful (internally and externally), physical violence is still a tool that the state uses—which is made permissible by its citizens. However, protesters do not necessarily aim to commit violent acts; they instead rely on the effect of the implicit threat of such violence. Therefore, protests may be perceived as strategies through which groups of people simultaneously manipulate others' fears of disorder and violence and protect themselves from paying the potentially extreme costs of using such strategies.

The anxiety and fear among participants and the authorities can be reduced by (a) explicitly declaring the intention to resolve any conflict without violence; (b) taking many precautions to demonstrate that intention; and (c) preparing to suffer—or even sacrifice lives if need be—rather than inflict suffering on others while holding to their beliefs.[25] The core principle underlying nonviolent action is "Thou shalt not kill," which can be found in religious and philosophical texts. This ethical departure point for protests is regarded not only as an approach that seeks to "humanize" the revolution's goals—but also as a way of resolving conflict within the existing democratic system.[26] Mohandas Gandhi and Martin Luther King Jr. were prominent advocates of this principle, and their movements have demonstrated that nonviolence can be developed as a coherent strategy of change.

Developing and implementing a nonviolent strategy is a process that includes both choosing a method and developing a preliminary dialogue with the authorities. This dialogue is dynamic and influenced by the intent and methods adopted by protesters, with different methods implying different types of negotiations. Gene Sharp classifies protest methods into six clusters: (1) protest and persuasion, (2) social noncooperation, (3) economic noncooperation and boycotts, (4) economic noncooperation (i.e., the strike), (5) political noncooperation, and (6) nonviolent intervention.[27] As new methods are constantly emerging in response to geopolitical conditions, communication technologies, and the contemporary wave of transnational immigration, Sharp's list may seem incomplete, but his classification helps highlight the methods that have a direct effect on the physicality of space. In particular, persuasion and intervention are categories that can be physically expressed.

NEGOTIATING POWER

The threat of violence can never be eliminated from protests, since protests threaten power. As a consequence, throughout history, "states and legal systems attempt to manage and limit the ways in which methods are used."[28] Yet protest is a dynamic practice, with new methods constantly emerging, and with new rules and new laws also being defined to limit the use of space in the name of social order. The question pertains not only to when and why violence erupts during protests but also to how the potential for violence is policed, encapsulated in law, and sublimated by design. According to Don Mitchell, the key dilemmas are how order can be maintained in the face of the demand for public spaces for acts of dissent, and how speech rights, which are deemed necessary for the production of truth, can be protected through the imposition of order?[29] The solution in democratic regimes is establishing agreed-upon spatial distances while allowing for freedom of speech. This approach shifts the control over speech itself to the space in which said speech occurs. This shift makes space a key factor in the process of planning protests and the immediate materiality during the process of negotiation (if it takes place) between the regime and the protesters prior to or after the event (in the case of unpermitted protests).

Figure 4.2. Women's March on Washington, January 21, 2017. Mobilus In Mobili, CC'BY'2.0, Flickr.

Defining laws of conduct in public spaces aims to increase control and order. Public space "engenders fears, [and] fears derive from the sense of public space as uncontrolled space, as a space in which civilization is exceptionally fragile."[30] Whether violent or nonviolent, protests are a type of public conversation, irrespective of the potential brutality or one-sidedness of that conversation. This conversation or claim making in public space starts with the negotiation of the event's spatiality.[31]

Negotiating the Shape of the Event

Negotiation is about power and the ability to create a strategy that will best fit the performance of public claim making. During protests, the temporary occupation of a particular space challenges the rules, laws, and social codes that govern that space. The negotiations between organizers, demonstrators, authorities, and police, both before and during the event, place limitations on all parties and increase the predictability of encounters over the course of such protests.[32] Furthermore, protest policing is sensitive to the pressures of the various actors involved. The purpose of negotiating is to increase the "known" variables, including the following:

1. The scale of the protest and the estimated scope of participation on local and global levels, if relevant. Scale also relates to the organizations involved and their internal coordination on behalf of protesters. This variable concerns the size of a place and the number of people that it can host (the scale of place), thereby influencing whether the protest takes place at a local, national, or global level (the scale of protest), as well as their interrelationships.
2. The spatial logic of action (a centralized event, multiple events, or something in between. The spatial logic of the event is also associated with issues of control over the event, regime surveillance, and participant safety.
3. An agreed-upon use of spatiality (the routes to be taken and the places to be occupied). The insistence on a particular form of protest or place is linked to the role of spectators, media attention, and the overall impact. The use of spatiality will affect the dynamic between bodies and the setting (i.e., a spectacle, a procession, place-making, or some combination). In this context, the decision should define the location (i.e., an institutional space such as a civic square, a place of leisure such as a park, or the city streets), and the scope of the appropriation of space (e.g., the installation of a stage, microphones, flags, posters, and new icons. Timing is also important (e.g., whether the event is held during the day or the night, whether the protest is long or short, and whether the protest is a repeated or one-time event).

In response to these parameters, political parties, interest groups, and movement organizations express their preferences with regard to protest policing, often influencing policymakers directly. The means of control may vary from highly controlled (by the regime and by protesters) gatherings that ensure participant safety and solidarity to loose events with minimal monitoring. The agreement over the means of control (if achieved) might enhance the trust among stakeholders, which, in turn, might have an effect on the event itself. In democratic regimes, protesters tend to come to an agreement with authorities, sometimes even publicizing the bargaining process through the media as a way of swaying public opinion and enhancing the visibility of the event.[33] However, in nondemocratic regimes, a large share of protests are expected to be forbidden; thus, event planning is often concealed.

Negotiation may also take place after the event regarding the end of the protest. This form of negotiation specifically applies to protests that occupy space for longer periods of time and those that have not obtained permission a priori. In democratic regimes, such negotiations have taken place in tent cities built in prime locations during the Occupy movement of September 2011 or during protests in Israel in summer (July–August) 2011. In these cases, negotiations regarding the disbanding of the protest (permits had not been given in either case) took place during the event. In these situations, protests might result in broken negotiations.

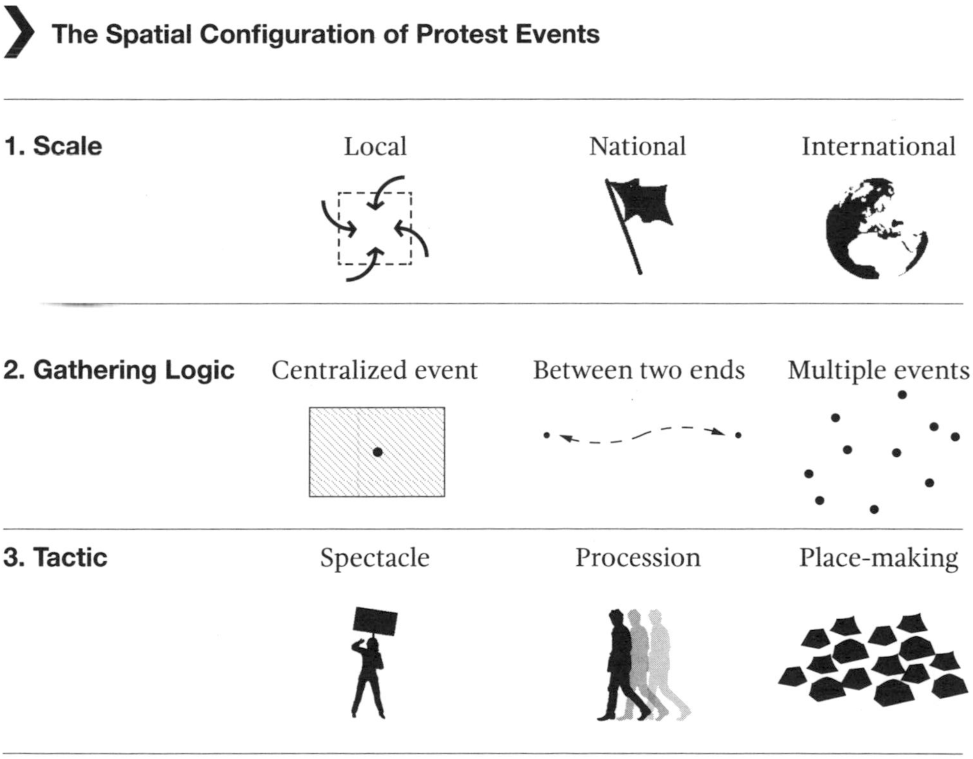

The Spatial Configuration of Protest Events

1. Scale	Local	National	International
2. Gathering Logic	Centralized event	Between two ends	Multiple events
3. Tactic	Spectacle	Procession	Place-making

Figure 4.3. Negotiating the "known" variables.

Broken Negotiations and the Eruption of Violence

As defined by Charles Tilly, broken negotiations are conditions in which "collective action generates resistance or rivalry to which one or more parties respond by actions that damage persons and/or objects."[34] As he further argues, broken negotiations are significant because they occur over the course of an organized social process that is not intrinsically violent. In that context, even when the use of spatiality, the scale of the event, and the means of control have been agreed upon, and even when protests are meticulously planned, fear of the unexpected remains, which might lead to broken negotiations. Numerous parameters might have an impact on this dynamic:

1. The unexpected use of spatiality (e.g., the routes taken and places occupied are not as planned). The agreed-upon layout is fragmented because of uncoordinated scale (more people than expected), timing (the start or end time has changed), misinformation, and disorder.
2. Unexpected scale—the growth of the event exceeds the scale of the spaces designated for the event, resulting in a violation of social order, which might lead to disproportionate reactions by the police.
3. Scattered violence—participants respond to obstacles, challenges, or restraints via damaging acts; attacks on symbolic objects or places and assaults by government agents. In particular, there may be unexpected destruction of representational objects that symbolize hierarchy that is no longer recognized—a violation that represents the invalidity of socially established and visible distances.
4. Unexpected individual aggression—"individual" refers to a single or several actors engaging in destructive interactions with one another. During protests, individual aggression is hard to predict and can quickly escalate into major collective violence. Thus, in many cases, protest organizers deal with this matter by recruiting agents who are responsible for event security. This internal effort is further supported by the police and other institutional forces.

These unexpected dynamics threaten the regime, which, in turn, might increase the use of power against protesters. Governments (mainly democratic ones) rely on the assumption that only orderly rational discourse can be held in public, and violent dissent is considered to be a transgression of the boundaries of appropriate behavior in public spaces. The government regards violence during protests as an attack on established boundaries and distances (physical and symbolic). From the perspective of the protesters, violence is also problematic in terms of public opinion, though it sometimes encourages conformity with the political system. This tension between negotiating distance—bargaining with authorities over the form of protest—and violating distance—breaking this negotiation process—can be observed in dissent in different parts of the world that ended in violence.

For example, the protests in Taksim Gezi Park in 2013 initially contested the urban development plan for the park. The Gezi resistance "had a clear urban agenda to reclaim the right to the city of ordinary citizens who rely on the use value in the city and place it over the right to the city of capitalists, developers and their allies who recast the city as a locus of exchange value and capital accumulation." This resistance ended in a violent eviction of the sit-in protest in the park, which resulted in numerous protests and strikes regarding freedom of speech. The "brutal response intensified over the next days and weeks, while the resistance amplified and spread over Istanbul, to other cities in Turkey, and in the world. The protests took place in various peaceful ways, yet the government always resorted to political violence in response, leaving 7 dead, thousands injured and millions worried about the direction of democracy in Turkey."[35]

Another example can be seen in student protests in the United Kingdom in November and December 2010. The demonstrations were largely led by students who were opposed to a proposed increase in the tuition fee cap, which they considered detrimental to higher education. The first march took place on November 10 and involved thousands of students marching in central London, who ended up attacking and occupying the headquarters of the Conservative Party. After this violent event (which divided the movement), other events also resulted in clashes between the police and protesters. As Bart Cammaerts argues, "The spectacle of symbolic damage enacted by the protesters exposed the exuberant passion and anger of the student protesters concerning political choices made by democratically elected representatives against their interests." In the end, the campaign did not achieve its goal, as these government reforms passed, and the public viewed these protests as highly controversial events. However, as Cammaerts argues, the "use of the logic of damage should foremost be seen as a communicative act of resistance and the result of the lack of channels of communication between those taking a political decision and those directly affected by the decision."[36]

Broken negotiations, which often result in violence, are a hotly contested issue, and some perceive them as an essential step in the implementation of change. As Don Mitchell argues, despite the claims of those who seek to protect the status quo in the name of social order, violence might promote justice or expand civil rights:

> The seeming irrationality of violence—"acting without argument or speech and without counting the consequences"—becomes a *rational* means for redressing the *irrationality* of injustice, for withdrawing consent from an order that does not deserve to be legitimated. Violence thus has a (contested) normative aspect.[37]

In sum, violence is rooted in protests as pejorative acts of opposition to the ruling parties. Forming a spatial "dialogue," protesters voice collective grievances that express and embody an oppositional consciousness against the dominant system. This oppositional consciousness fosters a sense of efficacy and promotes the belief that acting collectively can realize change, but fears of the unexpected remain.

DISPUTED CODES

Bargaining process, broken negotiations, and fear of the unexpected that ends in violence is not a new dynamic,[38] as can be seen in the protest that took place in 1933 in Jaffa. Although the political and historical context of the 1933 protest in Palestine is particular, the analysis of the march's broken negotiations is one example of many that reveal the relationship between participation, space, and political distance. The site of the protest was Clock Tower Square, where the British headquarters and government offices were located beginning in 1917; this space thus housed the civic, cultural, commercial, and religious activities of the Palestinian Arab community and British government offices, which required increased surveillance in the area. In the early twentieth century, Jaffa was a conglomeration of ethnic and religious communities, and Clock Tower Square, a civic and commercial center, also served the city's Palestinian Jewish community and the Jewish neighborhoods beyond it.[39] However, by the 1930s, it was no longer the locus of the Palestinian Jewish community. The parallel development of these two communities and Jewish demands for autonomy contributed to the British Mandate for Palestine's decision to separate Tel Aviv from Jaffa.[40] The existence of two entities also implied separate civic arenas. For the Palestinian Arab community, the civic locus was Jaffa, particularly Clock Tower Square. For the Jewish community, there was no distinct locus of civic activity; protests took place in different locations across Tel Aviv.[41]

Many grassroots protests by Palestinian Arabs against the Zionist Project took place in Palestine prior to Israel's establishment as a state. Palestinian Arab political resistance intensified as a result of Jewish immigration to Palestine and Great Britain's pro-Zionist policy, as evidenced by the Balfour Declaration of 1917 and calls for a Jewish homeland in Palestine.[42] This resistance initially aimed to force Britain, which had gained mandatory control of Palestine at the end of World War II after the collapse of the Ottoman Empire, to halt Jewish immigration; prohibit the transfer of Arab lands to Jews; and establish an independent, representative national government in Palestine.[43] During the first event in October 1933, the Palestinian Arab[44] executive committee proclaimed a "general strike," which implied the cessation of business, the closing of shops, and the suspension of public transport. The committee sought to hold a demonstration in Jerusalem, which would move from the gate of the Holy Mosque to the Holy Sepulcher, then march to Jaffa Road via Sweiqat Allon and continue to the general post office and the Damascus Gate, where members of the Arab Executive would deliver speeches to the demonstrators. Planning this political procession challenged the 1929 government's prohibition of political protests in Jerusalem.[45] However, against the government's will, the protest took place in Jerusalem and ended in violence. According to reports:

> At about 12:20 p.m. the people left the mosque. The crowd was then estimated by one witness at between six and seven thousand . . . it was anticipated that the crowd would leave the city by the Jaffa gate and attempt to reach the government offices by the route outside the city wall, which would have been in accordance with the resolution of the Arab Executive issued on October 8, but just before reaching the Jaffa Gate, the crowd turned to the right and took a shorter route inside the walls of the Old City towards the New Gate. . . . The District superintendent of Police, after calling upon the crowd to go back and disperse and blowing a whistle, ordered a baton charge.[46]

Much has been written about British policy regarding Jewish immigration and the resistance of Palestinian Arabs during the time of the British Mandate for Palestine.[47] In these writings, the events are portrayed as riots, a clash between the regime and citizens, but they fail to consider the complex dynamics created by the spatial dimension of the act and its cultural meaning. From the report above, the event's turning point is seemingly attributable to an unexpected initiative to change the procession's route. Could the ensuing violence have been avoided if the people had followed the expected route? This question is particularly interesting because these events practically repeat themselves two weeks later in Jaffa. Among the various events of 1933, the procession in Jaffa's central square provides us with significant details about the process of negotiation along the procession route, allowing us to understand the clash between the regime and citizens as a contest over space and its control.

Bargaining: The Shape of the Event

The Palestinian Arab executive leadership in Jerusalem proposed the demonstration in Jaffa.[48] The march's route, as designed by the Committee of the Muslim-Christian Association and the Executive Committee of the Palestine Youth Congress in Jaffa, would start at the mosque, continue through adjacent streets, and end at the bandstand on King George Avenue (map 4.1). The route was not approved by the High Commissioner, and, on October 24, the District Commissioner suggested receiving a Palestinian Arab delegation from the mosque gate in his offices, situated just across the square. He was prepared to accept a peaceful presentation of grievances,

Map 4.1. The Arab community's first proposed route: (1) The route started at the mosque and went along Ajami Hill (residential area) and then Salahi Road and King George Avenue to the bandstand, where it was to end. The alternative route proposed by the Arabs and accepted by the British: (2) The route started at the mosque and went along Port Road to the government offices, where it was to end. Author's illustration, based on Palestine Survey 1934, National Map Archive, Israel.

Figure 4.4. October 27, Clock Tower Square, Jaffa. Photo from Faraday Collection, Middle-East Centre Archive (MECA), St. Anthony College, Oxford.

but he would not tolerate any defiant public demonstration.[49] The Palestinian Arab leaders rejected his proposal. The British offer to receive a delegation disregarded two key elements of mass demonstrations, namely, the sense of equality that would break down hierarchical representation and the demonstration's focus on inclusion instead of reduction,[50] as would have been the case if a small delegation met with the official. Demonstrations want to engage as many people as possible, and this urge to grow is the foremost attribute of mass protests, which contributes to the creation of an imagined community.[51]

The leaders then proposed an alternative route that would end at the Commissioner's office. This route, which was shorter than the previous one but longer than the first one suggested by the Commissioner, was actually approved by the Commissioner on the government's behalf. The differences between the longer and shorter routes were crucial to the British, who clearly stated that they would regard any procession along the longer route as illegal and would disperse it through police action.[52] Thus, the British were evidently concerned with the length and legality of the routes. However, what were the differences between these routes?

In the original route suggested by the Palestinian Arabs, no direct confrontation with government officials or the police was planned. The march was to start at the mosque, which is considered not only a religious place but also a community arena, and would avoid entering the square. The original route would have gone through residential streets, ending at the King George Avenue bandstand, where speeches would be given. However, the British preferred a shorter route, where the demonstrators' movement from the mosque to the police station had to comply with city ordinances, thereby limiting the spatial form of the march. For large assemblies, as was the case in Jaffa, those in power (e.g., political parties and institutions) often seek to maintain control and order by actually collaborating with activists in the careful selection of spaces of a certain size, scale, and orientation. These highly controlled gatherings benefit participants because their scale enhances the mass's experience of togetherness and solidarity, thereby intensifying their impact.

Audience and Form

The insistence on a particular form of protest is connected to the role of spectators who, though not actively involved, play an important role in protests—either voluntarily or involuntarily.[53] A march attracts spectators with noise, symbols, and physical disruptions in the streets, which also contribute to the impact of an event. The routes that participants use for demonstrations also attract those who are not involved in such events. Thus, the form of a march and its route are critical in attracting spectators. The route proposed by the Palestinian Arab community along residential streets would probably have attracted many spectators, whereas the route suggested by the British officials—through the square with its public buildings—offered no advantage in terms of involving spectators. At most, some viewers might have viewed the protest from roofs or windows, which were mainly occupied by the police.

Furthermore, as envisioned by the Palestinian Arab community, the procession had a dual purpose—not only as an act of protest against the British but also as a way of strengthening the community's shared narrative. These views of the protest—internal (facing themselves) and external (facing a target)—further extended the role of space and its symbolic use. Thus, by choosing to walk along residential streets rather than through a square occupied by British police, Palestinian Arabs aimed to reclaim, or "possess," their daily environment. The practice of "possessing" spaces, even temporarily, whether private or public, is appropriation. When inhabitants possess or repossess spaces of their daily environment, they challenge the established social order that is associated with the dominating powers.

Intention and Form

The bargaining over the form of the protest created a conflict between the Palestinian Arab parties. The younger Palestinian Arabs insisted that the longer route should be taken, while the older ones and the president of the Palestinian Arab Executive in Jerusalem, Musa Kazim Pasha, favored the shorter route.[54] On October 26 and the morning of October 27, meetings were held in Jaffa with leaders of the Palestinian Arab executive council from Jerusalem to decide which route should be taken. However, no decision was reached, which increased the uncertainty and anxiety of the British police, and the disputes became a by-product of the symbolic display of collective purpose and control.

A message was conveyed to the British, warning them not to restrict the activity, and stating that weapons, bombs, sticks, and stones would be used should an attempt be made to disperse the demonstration.[55] This threat lends credence to Canneti's observation that some of the most striking traits of a mass's inner life are feelings of persecution and anger and frustration that are directed against those it defines as enemies.[56] However, the government and police, who failed to understand the codes of the event, also insisted on maintaining control and order: "We are faced with a situation we must tackle with grit and determination so as to assert our authority over those who violate the law, and we must show to all and sundry that we are determined to preserve law and order by every means in our power, as is our bounden duty."[57]

At approximately 11:30 a.m., midday prayers commenced at the mosque. At noon, after prayers, people emerged onto the port road and joined the mass of men and women already assembled there. This confused the police, who assumed that the women were present "solely for the purpose of embarrassing the police . . . to act as a buffer between the mob and the police."[58] The procession began, and a large number of people joined the march from adjacent streets. At the junction where the port road enters Clock Tower Square, Musa Kazim Pasha, the president of the Palestinian Arab Executive, attempted to turn the procession north through the square to the District Commissioner's offices—"to make the procession take the short route."[59] However, according to the report, "extremist" Palestinian Arabs prevented the diversion, and the procession turned south toward Ajami Road (i.e., along the line of the longer route). The authorities' fears were realized. Another unexpected change occurred when, upon reaching Ajami Road, the people turned toward the square to face the police. At this point, the British police confronted an intimidating mass of people descending the slope into the square (map 4.2).

Violence and Form

The images of the demonstrators marching down the hill toward the square confirm that they were talking or clustering in groups. Hence, at this juncture, it is difficult to determine whether descending the hill was intended to shorten the route or to actually confront the police. However, the police clearly interpreted this change of route as a provocation. In the photograph, the mass and the police face one another. Approximately sixty policemen are on foot, armed with batons, and some forty unarmed mounted police form a cordon behind them. Some of the estimated mass of 8,800 were armed with sticks and stones. The photograph clearly shows the formal array of policemen facing the informally clustered mass.

The report states that shouting began. There were calls for violence. Some people shouted "Attack them!" ("Aleihum!") The first police action was a call in Arabic for the mass to disperse, which produced no effect. Officer Faraday, commanding the police force, ordered a charge with batons, and the police on foot rushed at the crowd and forcefully pushed it back up Ajami Road. The road was cleared, and the corners of the two roads running into Clock Tower Square—the port road and Siksik Street—were also cleared. The mass reformed and attacked the police with stones, bottles, and pieces of iron and wood, among other things. The police were ordered to advance again; the mass retreated but then returned. The time was 12:15 p.m. To understand the hostility between this mass and the police, one must consider that a crowd, once formed, tends to grow rapidly, with great power and determination, which are reinforced by outside attacks.[60]

Men with firearms, who had been kept out of sight behind police barricades, were ordered into the square. At the same time, some mounted police rode in from Suq El Khudra and Siksik Street and from Ajami Road. Their horses, slipping on the asphalt, fell down with their riders and created confusion and chaos. The violence and use of firearms continued on both sides, resulting in many casualties and fatalities.

What caused the violence in Jaffa? Could it have been avoided? This march, inspired by grievances against a particular policy, aimed to strengthen the community's shared narrative by forming a spatial "dialogue" between the community and the ruling parties. The path from the mosque—through residential areas, past spectators, and along the avenue—suggested the community's reclamation of its everyday space. By holding the procession in the daily sphere of the Palestinian community, the activists sought to reacknowledge the community sphere—with its institutional buildings and residential areas—as an alternative to the spatial order imposed by the British government with its formal institutions located in the square. However, the buildings did play a role in the event discussed here. They were certainly reference points (e.g., the mosque), but the urban surroundings were more important, as is often the case with processions that encourage the movement's growth.

This act of appropriating daily spaces during protests allows inhabitants to voice collective grievances that express and embody an oppositional consciousness in a system of domination. Oppositional consciousness fosters a sense of efficacy and promotes the belief that acting collectively can realize change. After the protest, one reporter notes that one of the problems in Palestine is the absence of a Hyde Park, a Union Square, or some other plaza that can serve as a traditional forum for the peaceful expression of views,[61] but, in doing so, he misinterprets the codes of protest and their symbolic forms. In other words, Jaffa's public spaces (e.g., the mosque and the bazaar) differ from the public spaces in European and British cities (e.g., squares and parks), with their particular spatial array, laws, and cultural norms. As a social ritual, the procession uniquely combines the urban setting and the cultural codes of collective behavior that are embedded in a particular political context. This overlap differs from one protest to the next and from one sociocultural setting to another. The British officials' misunderstanding of this overlap resulted in a broken process of negotiation.[62]

BETWEEN PREDICTABILITY AND UNCERTAINTY

Even when coordinated with the authorities, protests always cultivate uncertainty on both sides. This destabilization reminds us that uncertainty and improbability are inherited in our social reality—thus fracturing the "social fantasy" held by both the government and its citizens.[63] This fantasy requires some sort of ideological symbolism to conceal the fragility of a state, which could collapse at any moment. But the unknowns always exceed the knowns. Ulrich Beck explains, "Can we know the future we face? The answer of course is, no, we cannot; but yes, we must act 'as if' we do."[64] Culture, religion, rationality, and grand narratives are all means

Map 4.2. Route taken by the protesters. (1) Musa Kazim Pasha attempting to turn the procession northward. (2) The procession advancing along the long route. (3) The crowd turning around and facing the square. Author's illustration, based on Palestine Survey 1934, National Map Archive, Israel.

Figure 4.5. Arab crowd gathers near the Great Mosque in Jaffa in an illegal demonstration against Jewish immigration from Germany, October 27, 1933. Photo by Kluger Zoltan, National Photo Collection, Israel.

of addressing uncertainty and risks. They are social support tools that are used to address the unknown. The role of the contemporary project of the nation-state is to coordinate, administer, and distribute the necessary resources to address these uncertainties, and this coordination is manifested in physical spaces, thereby providing a sense of stability and order. Protests play the opposite role. Protests are about exposing uncertainties and enhancing risks. They are about opening up spatial configurations and imagining the spaces of the (unknown) future.

What is the influence of the physicality of space in violent protests? Can particular spatial choreographies of protest ensure peaceful events? The answers to these questions are complex. The physical and the social must always be understood as mutually constitutive. However, the staging of the action, particularly a protest's spatial choreography; the juxtaposition of people and their appropriation of spaces; and the spaces themselves have a crucial impact on how the protesters design and carry out their action. Broken negotiations can occur in all protests, but they happen more often in elastic, "becoming" strategies that form open-ended protests, with spatial choreographies that are unknown to the organizers and to the government in advance. The only things known in advance are a general idea and an estimation of the rhythm or the intensity among particular objects and entities. The loose configuration of this type of event is the most threatening to those in power.

PART II

Spatial Choreographies

JORGITO

Jueves 31 de

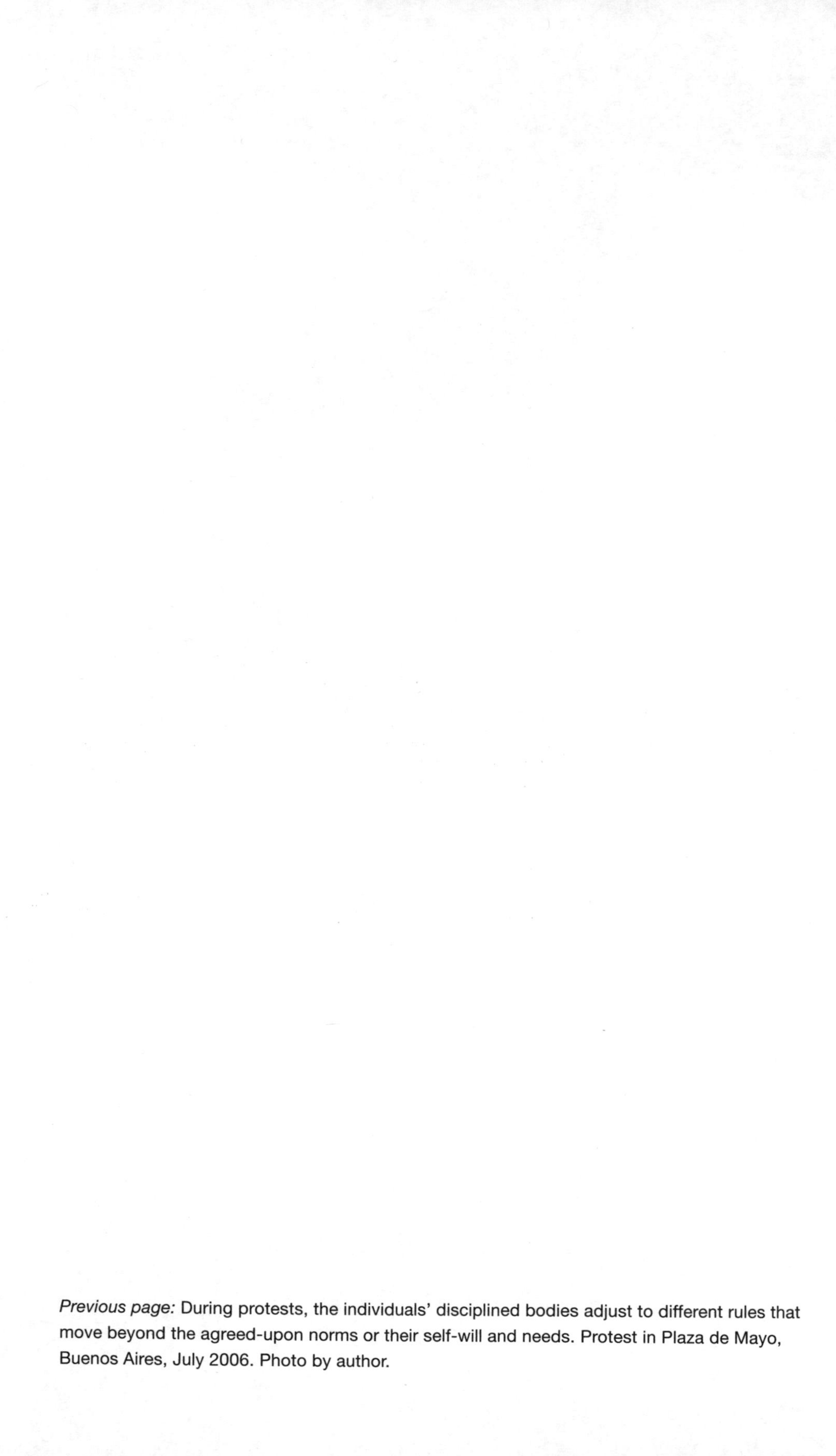

Previous page: During protests, the individuals' disciplined bodies adjust to different rules that move beyond the agreed-upon norms or their self-will and needs. Protest in Plaza de Mayo, Buenos Aires, July 2006. Photo by author.

CHAPTER 5

Staging the Action

> It is the backstage preparation and designing of these contrived environments which aid in the manipulation of political thought and action. Successful design propaganda occurs when the decision to accept an ideology in a political theater is based on an aesthetic fantasy created by stage design, actors and audience rather than the thoughtful analysis of the ideas presented.
>
> James M. Mayo, "Propaganda with Design: Environmental Dramaturgy in the Political Rally"

Our bodies are historical constructs that have been disciplined, regulated, and controlled in an endless circulation of power and knowledge.[1] During everyday life, the body tends to follow norms and spatial rules that are dictated by professionals and policymakers.[2] However, during protests, the individual's disciplined body adjusts to different rules beyond the agreed-upon norms or his or her self-will and needs. The acceptance of these different rules creates a temporal synchronicity of wills and movements, a condition that is simultaneously rousing and terrifying, where "a head is a head, an arm is an arm, and differences between individual heads and arms are irrelevant."[3] Doing the same thing, stomping on the ground or shaking their heads together, the protesters could be regarded as a dancing mass; people move on their own, but the movements are coordinated, close together, and dense. This condition, where people act as one, enhances strong feelings of equality and emancipation—of being part of something bigger than oneself. It is a hypnotic sight.

To be sure, all protests start with the body. During protests, bodies are used for various roles, tasks, and strategies in different places. Referring to a body of protesters, Susan Leigh Foster suggests that whether participants become "the reflexive body sitting at the lunch counter, the campy body lying on Wall Street, or the glocal body blockading Downtown Seattle, they choose to spend their day constructing physical interference, and this engagement with the physical imbues them with a deepened sense of personal agency."[4] In addition, although often taken for granted as something that needs no explanation, the body is the anchor of a physical protest, becoming a "turbulent performative occasion."[5] Public gatherings enable and enact a performativity of embodied agency, in which we own our bodies and struggle for the right to claim our bodies as "ours."[6] This position implies that both bodies and spaces are performative, with no ontological status or fixed characteristics. Therefore, instead of thinking about spaces and places as preexisting sites in which bodily performances occur, we need to examine bodily performances themselves as constituting or reproducing distance, places, and events. In this respect, the body cannot be separated from the event, and it has the crucial power to adjust and modify the setting of a place—as such, the spatial setting and the body should be regarded as mutually constitutive—creating the event's *spatial choreography*.

CRAFTING A SPATIAL CHOREOGRAPHY

The concept of a protest's spatial choreography refers to the intricate juxtaposition of people—and their appropriation of spaces—and spaces themselves. This concept is offered here to reveal how spaces and people interact during protests, exposing the ways in which the protesters design and carry out their action. The protest's spatial choreography plays a dual role: it is a mechanism for constructing meaning and for interpreting social reality, and it is a device for negotiating sociopolitical distance. Clearly, spatial choreography negates the reductionist sociopolitical frameworks that focus motivation, agendas, and outcomes.[7] It conceives of protests as planned acts in which both spaces and bodies are considered evolutionary, with their use implying not only protesters' present perceptions of them but also the ways in which bodies and spaces are imagined. When examining protests through the lens of spatial choreography, attention should be given to four key interrelated topics: design, bodies, hierarchy, and vulnerability.

Design

Spatial choreography entails a design, based on *intentionality and materiality*, in which the body can eliminate everyday distances through collective efforts. In achieving this task, protest organizers often create an intentional scheme of action that aims to define a new (temporary) space. The scheme always follows an order, which juxtaposes two interrelated systems: the order of the assembly and the order of the space. The order of the assembly is based on the use of bod(ies) as a means of concretizing a discourse in material spaces, following ritual performance components (e.g., marching, gathering, and singing), a dress code, and even a schedule (i.e., the timing and duration of the event) that represent how participants see themselves—either as supporters of or protesters against the existing social order—within the culture of their society. The order of the assembly occurs within the arrangement of a space, which is defined by architects and authorities and is regarded as a representation of a particular society's civic identity. The order of the place includes physical components such as the site's topography, boundaries, traffic, and building uses (i.e., governmental, commercial, or residential).

Bodies

How and where bodies are used in space and how they constitute space varies greatly from one event to another. In some protests, the setting is the body itself; in other cases, the setting is the body within the geography of a particular place.

Figure 5.1. All protests start with the body. During protests, bodies are used for various roles, tasks, and strategies in different places. Photos, *clockwise from top left:* London, 2007; London, 2007; Athens, 2007; the National Mall, Washington, DC, 1968. All photos by author, except for bottom left photo by Tunney Lee, Rotch Visual Collections, MIT.

Therefore, the event's choreography has a tremendous effect on physical distances and related social meanings. Distance, rank, and power are seen not only in the spatial array of the event but also in the postures of the varied bodies participating in the event. People can stand, sit, lie, squat, or kneel, and each of these postures—and particularly the change from one posture to another—has a special significance.[8] Standing, for example, connotes being independent and needing no support. People normally stand before they begin to walk or run, and "because standing is thus the antecedent of all motion, a standing man creates an impression of energy which is as yet unused. Standing is the central position from which every other position can be directly reached."[9] As such, many acts of dissent are "standing events," as we ascribe a relatively high degree of tension to this posture. A standing man may do anything, but a sitting man is expected to remain in his seat. This seated position confirms authority, and the longer people remain seated, the more secure they appear. "Sitting" during protests is associated with tactics such as camping, which last a longer period of time. However, sitting is different from sitting on the ground, as the latter implies an acceptance of anything that may happen. Sitting on the ground connotes a lack of needs, and the body is rounded as if it expects nothing from the world.[10] Though rare, some demonstrators lie on the ground during protests. This posture is associated with death or a disarmament, weakness, and fragility, and, when used, it is often part of the message or story that is told to an audience. Importantly, not all protest participants exhibit the same posture or body language. Leaders or key figures may differ, and these variations may represent the dynamics and hierarchies among demonstrators.

Hierarchy

Generally, spatial choreography assumes particular types of interactions among participants. The links between leaders, participants, and viewers during the event are carefully planned, and are expressed through particular physical/spatial relationships. For example, on the one hand, a speaker who stands in the middle of a circular space projects a message that he is part of the crowd and emerges from it; on the other hand, a speaker who stands on an elevated platform at one end of a rectangular space evokes a distinct hierarchy and theatricality. Therefore, during political protests, the "I" does not dissolve into an abstract collectivity; instead, one's "own situation is presented or 'demonstrated' as linked to a patterned social condition."[11] Therefore, during protests, the distances and differences among participants are not completely eliminated. Furthermore, in some cases, dominant participants tend to use social distance to emphasize the differences between themselves and others. In these cases, the protest's spatial choreography will reflect this tendency, and the event will, in turn, be more formal and abstract. In other cases, efforts will be made to create a sense of horizontal relationship dynamics, which will be reflected in the dynamics among participants, who will tend to construct informal and more concrete events. Thus, the protest's choreography creates a political body that does not necessarily dismantle hierarchies or speak with a single voice. The protest's choreography should be considered "an exercise of the popular will, and a way of asserting, in bodily form, one of the most basic presuppositions of democracy, namely that political and public institutions are bound to represent the people."[12]

Vulnerability

During the event, the body is in a precarious position. Protesters expose themselves to risk and pain. Unlike in dance, a protest's spatial choreography does *not* follow the norms and spatial rules. However, protesters are not following a script or stepping outside the quotidian routines of daily life into nonnormative action. Protesters participate in a conscious "perceptive and responsive physicality that, everywhere along the way, deciphers the social and then choreographs an imagined alternative."[13] Consequently, they immediately become exposed to police force and sometimes to physical suffering. Surveillance practices, which are in use in most public spaces, are an integral part of planning any protest. Some of the spatial characteristics are temporarily modified to fit the order of the action, with barriers, blocked routes, and adjusted traffic rules controlling the order of the demonstrators' movement. In addition, the police attempt to maintain this order through additional means of surveillance, such as cameras and secret agents in the crowd, who remain alert to any potential form of violence. However, in many assemblies, direct coordination occurs between the organizers (activists or political powers) and the police. This coordination is often regarded as desirable by both sides, with the organizers regarding it as a means of ensuring safety and the police considering it a means of maintaining civil order. The increased media attention provides additional surveillance, simultaneously controlling events from above and on the ground. This dialectic of the "I"—being not only part of a powerful political body but also exposed and vulnerable—is the working premise of any protest that aims to reconfigure social and political spaces.

In sum, the concept of spatial choreography is about the dynamic between bodies and spaces and about the way this dynamic affects both social and political distances. In abstract terms, it is about the logic behind *how* protests are performed as a means to understand how they function and *what* a particular design enables them to accomplish.[14]

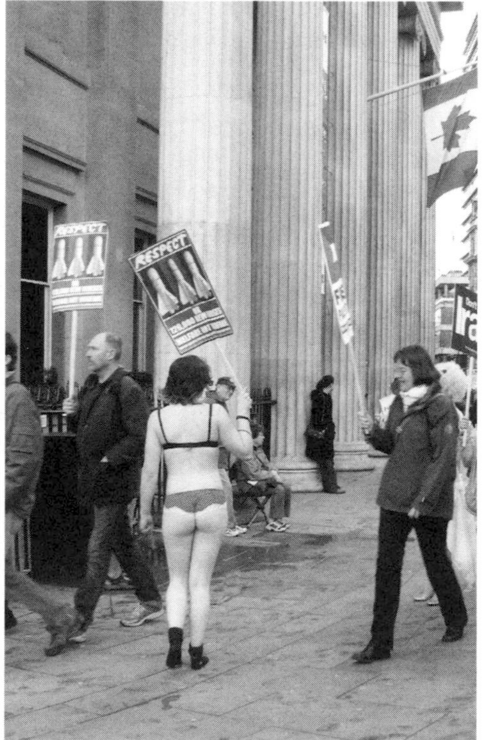

Figure 5.2. Protests start with the body. However, *how* and *where* bodies are used varies greatly. London, 2007. Photos by author.

Figure 5.3. During the event, the body is in a precarious position. Protesters are exposed to police force and, sometimes, physical suffering. *Top:* Falun Gong, Central Bus Station, Tel Aviv, 2013. Photo by Yaira Yasmin. *Bottom:* The piqueteros, central Buenos Aires, 2007. Photos by author.

SPATIAL PROTOTYPES OF ACTIONS: SPECTACLE, PROCESSION, AND PLACE-MAKING

Of the numerous spatial choreographies, three key prototypes of actions—the *spectacle*, the *procession*, and the *place-making*—can be identified. Each of these prototypes generates multiple choreographies, which, in turn, offer different relationships between bodies and settings (see table 5.1).

Although often associated with grand events, the spectacle has no scale; it can be a massive event with many participants or a small event with very few participants. As defined in the *Oxford English Dictionary*, a "spectacle is a specially prepared or arranged display of a more or less public nature, forming an impressive or interesting show or entertainment for those viewing it." In relation to protests, the spectacle refers to a well-planned event, which takes advantage of the physical order and the architectural attributes of a particular space. It often has a focal point, perhaps a stage or a performance that captures the crowd's attention. In some cases, the spectacle is located in a space that is associated with symbolic attributes or with sacred sentiment; in other cases, it appears in an informal space, among the mundane. The actions that fall under this category range from mass gatherings to small group assemblies. However, beyond scale and choreographic differences, the tactics in this category share three key attributes: (1) defined roles for participants, (2) spatial distance between the key actors and the participants or general audience, and (3) a set of agreed-upon symbols that are associated with the event. In the spectacle, the body tends to respond to the choreography set in advance and is thus respectful and obedient. Overall, the spectacle refers to events that are generally well-planned gatherings and are particularly sensitive to the physical order and the architectural attributes of a particular space.

In illustrating the power of the spectacle, three diverse choreographies are analyzed. The *theater* is a choreography that is designed to place the individual in a meaningful social hierarchy. It is based on three key features: hierarchical relationships, planned displays, and a captured audience. These features will be further examined through an event that took place on November 4, 1995: a political rally in Tel Aviv's Rabin Square. Another choreography, the *ritual*, is based on the notion of repetition, not only over time (i.e., repeating the same thing over and over again) but also in the way that the act is physically performed in space and the way that the motivation behind the act reveals itself through varied symbols. In addition to being based on the notion of repetition, this choreography is also based on the assigned roles given or taken by participants and the creation of a bounded space, as seen in the case of the Mothers of the Plaza de Mayo in Buenos Aires. Importantly, the spectacle does not necessarily take place in formal spaces; it might also occur in mundane, informal spaces, as in the case of Women in Black (WIB) in Tel Aviv.

WIB's choreography, *bareness*, is characterized by its spatial informality, reserved communication, and physical vulnerability.

The major difference between spectacles' choreographies is their approach to social and spatial distance. The theater separates the audience from the leadership. In these types of protests, activists often create event-spaces that preserve and sometimes further increase the distance between participants and leaders. The ritual choreography, similar to the theater, is based on an agreed-upon choreography of the body, which organizers establish in advance as a means of creating unity and clarifying their message. However, the ritual's is based on repetition, on performing the same act again and again, that not only helps project a memorable spatial message but also enhances the familiarity and trust among participants. The most extreme choreography, in its approach to the crowds, is bareness. Being ideologically distant from mainstream society (the government and the people), this spatial choreography keeps its distance from the crowd and the government, thereby sacrificing its opportunity for growth but gaining control over its actions and messages.

In contrast with the spectacle, the *procession* has a straightforward definition, referring to the actions "of a body of people going or marching along in orderly succession in a formal or ceremonial way, festive occasion, or demonstration" (*Oxford English Dictionary*). However, even when carefully planned, processions are loosely organized in nature. Processions essentially make use of the most primal form of human locomotion on land, that is, walking. This simple act of protesters putting one foot in front of the other produces magnified rhythms of sound, creating a dynamic performance that enhances social bonding. The site of the procession is a mundane space, an economic space; if used, symbols during these protests are held by the participants themselves. Processions sometimes pass by institutional buildings or spaces, referring more to their secondary identities as representations of power and locations of other remembered events or spaces than to their primary identities, which are derived from public use. The body is constantly responding to the movement of other bodies that surround it, which is the most significant constituent of the event. The body is the core of the procession's composition, dictating its rhythm and density, which influences the distance between participants. As such, the physical distance between participants is not defined a priori; it is dynamic and often unforeseen, dictated by the pace of this dense movement. Overall, spatial choreographies associated with processions share three key attributes: (1) they focus on the body and its movement; (2) the people carry the symbols of the protest, which are closed and concrete; and (3) they are informal and dynamic events. Thus, with minimal control over the participating body/bodies, processions entail significant uncertainties for both organizers and regimes.

In examining events that are based on marching as a key feature, and in placing the protest in a mundane space (i.e., the economic space), various spatial

The Dynamic between Body and Setting

	Body	Setting	Distance
Spectacle	Respectful. Relative control of body(ies), rhythm dictated by the pace of ritual.	Emphasis on the stage, use of symbolic attributes, tends to be fixed.	Coordinated, defined.
Procession	Flexible, responds to adjacent bodies, minimum control of body(ies), rhythm dictated by the pace of movement.	Attention to the body, informal, dynamic, symbols held by the people.	Dynamic, changeable.
Place-Making	Respond to the object. Relative control of body(ies), rhythm dictated by practices associated with the object in place.	Emphasis on the assembly of an object(s) symbols built in place.	Mediated by objects.

Table 5.1. Body, Setting, Distance, and Spatial Array in Varied Types of Action.

Spatial Array

Stage

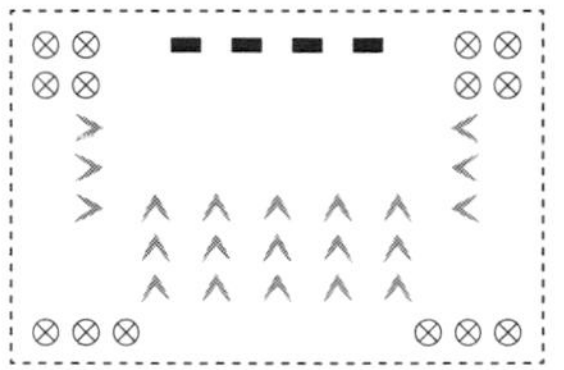

Informal

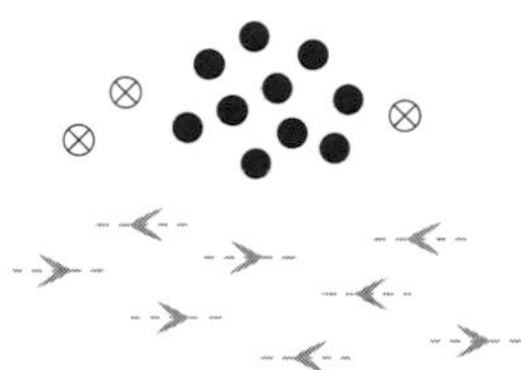

Planned

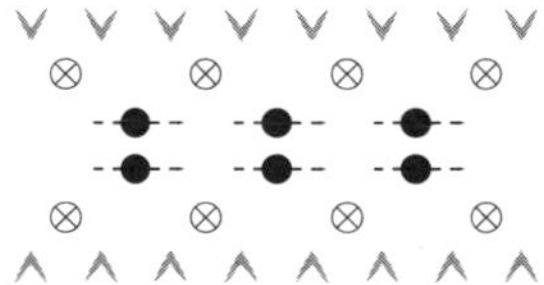

Spontaneous

Formal

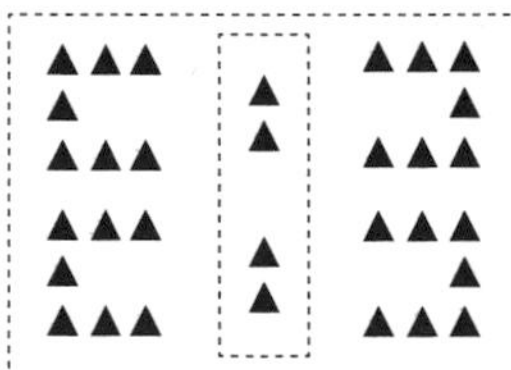

Elastic

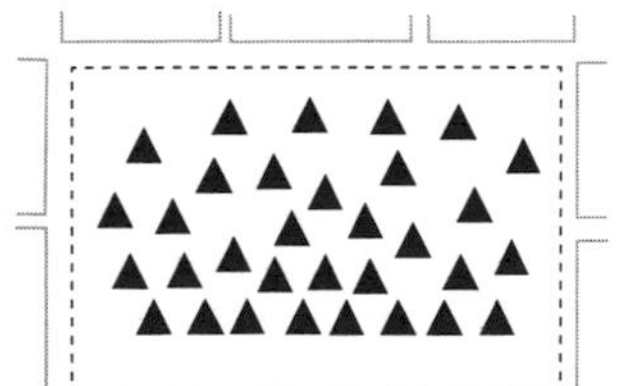

Viewers · Protesters · Speakers · Security · Object · Boundary

choreographies are discussed. The first choreography, the *target*, is a well-coordinated performance at the city scale. The Target is about "conquering the city" by reclaiming the streets, with several processions ending simultaneously at a defined, known, and symbolic space. The use of the Target choreography can be observed in the case of a demonstration in Istanbul's Taksim Square on May 1, 1977. Another spatial choreography, *conjoining*, aims to create a sequence of movement in the form of a ring in a city's historical core or other places where this form is spatially feasible. However, conjoining is a choreography that requires density, and this type of spatial reclamation can be observed in a protest held in Leipzig on October 9, 1989. A more contemporary protest configuration, *synchronicity*, involves shrinking geographic and ideological distance by producing an orchestrated transnational procession with simultaneous rhythms that is based on a network of national movements. A distinct example of this type of event is the protest against the invasion of Iraq on February 15, 2003, which simultaneously took place in many locations worldwide. The fourth example, *elasticity*, perceives space itself as a process, and, similar to a protest, space is conceived as a verb rather than a noun. This choreography is about becoming, with space regarded as a continuum, and, if assigned, roles are temporary. The elastic protest can take place anywhere; for example, a protest in Caracas took place along the Francisco Fajardo highway on April 11, 2002.

With regard to processions, distance is perceived in vastly different ways. In the target choreography, the concept of distance is primarily associated with physical and geographical meanings that refer to remoteness or the degree of remoteness in any relationship to which spatial terms are transferred or figuratively applied. Conjoining, similar to target choreography, is based not only on physical multiplicity but also on social variety and coordinated dynamics among various groups and locations in the city. A related choreography on an international scale is synchronicity, which is based on worldwide sociodemographic diversity as a means of creating a responsive "global alliance" against a particular political climate. Lastly, with elasticity, distance is not a category being defined a priori. Distance between participants and space is not fixed but lived.

The third prototype, *place-making*, involves changing a place's physicality and meaning through the use of objects or other means over a period of time. The object(s) are often the heart of the event; the object's form, spatial location, or spread has symbolic meaning. In this type of action, the body is secondary to the object, but the two are closely related. The object's creation and survival rely on the body. Pitching tents, building sheds, and erecting statues are all place-making acts, which vary in terms of practices and efforts. Clearly, the place-making spatial choreography requires preparation and adequate infrastructure. Rhythm is mediated by the object, with the body relating and responding to the object. The power of this type of action lies in its desire and ability to suggest an alternative symbolic setting to an existing social order. The questions of control and certainty in the occupation of spaces vary, but they relate to how an action is framed in advance by its political leadership. Being so central, the object has a major influence on the ways in which the distance between participants is defined and enacted. In other words, place-making actions focus on the erection of an object and its resilience as a means of defining a new place. The body relates and responds to the object, and distance is mediated by the object.

Place-making involves events that use objects in a given setting as the heart of the event, and, although the human body is secondary to the object, the two are closely related. Three actions are further discussed. *Reiconization* is a choreography that aims to achieve radical change or to leave a mark on the collective memory by creating a memorable icon and displaying it publicly. A central locus, symbolic appropriation, and image supremacy characterize these types of events, as can be observed in the case of Beijing's Tiananmen Square on June 4, 1989. Another very different spatial choreography is *city design*, which aims to challenge the ruler in his playground. City design displays power through territorial claiming by creating a holistic spatial system, as observed in the establishment of Resurrection City on the National Mall in Washington, DC, in 1968. The third example in this category is the *narrative*, an event designed to enhance feelings of empathy by telling a simple or even generic story that is popular and easy to digest. The narrative is perceived to be generated by "the people" and often uses an illustrative object. Simplicity is needed for the accumulative nature of these types of events, as has been observed in the Occupy movement of 2011, focusing on Zuccotti Park in New York.

The concept of distance also includes the relationships of protesters—that is, embracing or negating—with the objects added to particular spaces. In the case of reiconization spatial choreography, distance plays a crucial role in both the meaning of the icon as developed by the protesters (i.e., the extent to which the icon challenges the ruler's ideas), and the ways in which the icon is perceived by those in power. City design, based on imagining a new event-place, offers a new definition of social and physical distances. Because physical and social distance is mediated by the object, varied city-design plans will create different configurations of distance. The narrative choreography aims to reduce the social distance between participants and to enhance the growth of the movement by increasing empathetic feelings through the telling of a simple or even generic story that is popular and easy to digest. Paradoxically, the more universal/global the participants' claims are and the more they are able to reduce social and geographical distances, the greater the distance between protesters and governments.

In addition, although these spatial choreography protests are time-space specific and embedded in a concrete political, historical, and spatial context, their attributes can also be seen to offer a sociopolitical choreography in space that can be found, with major or minor alterations, in other contexts. "Borrowing" a particular choreography always requires adjustments with regard to culture and place,

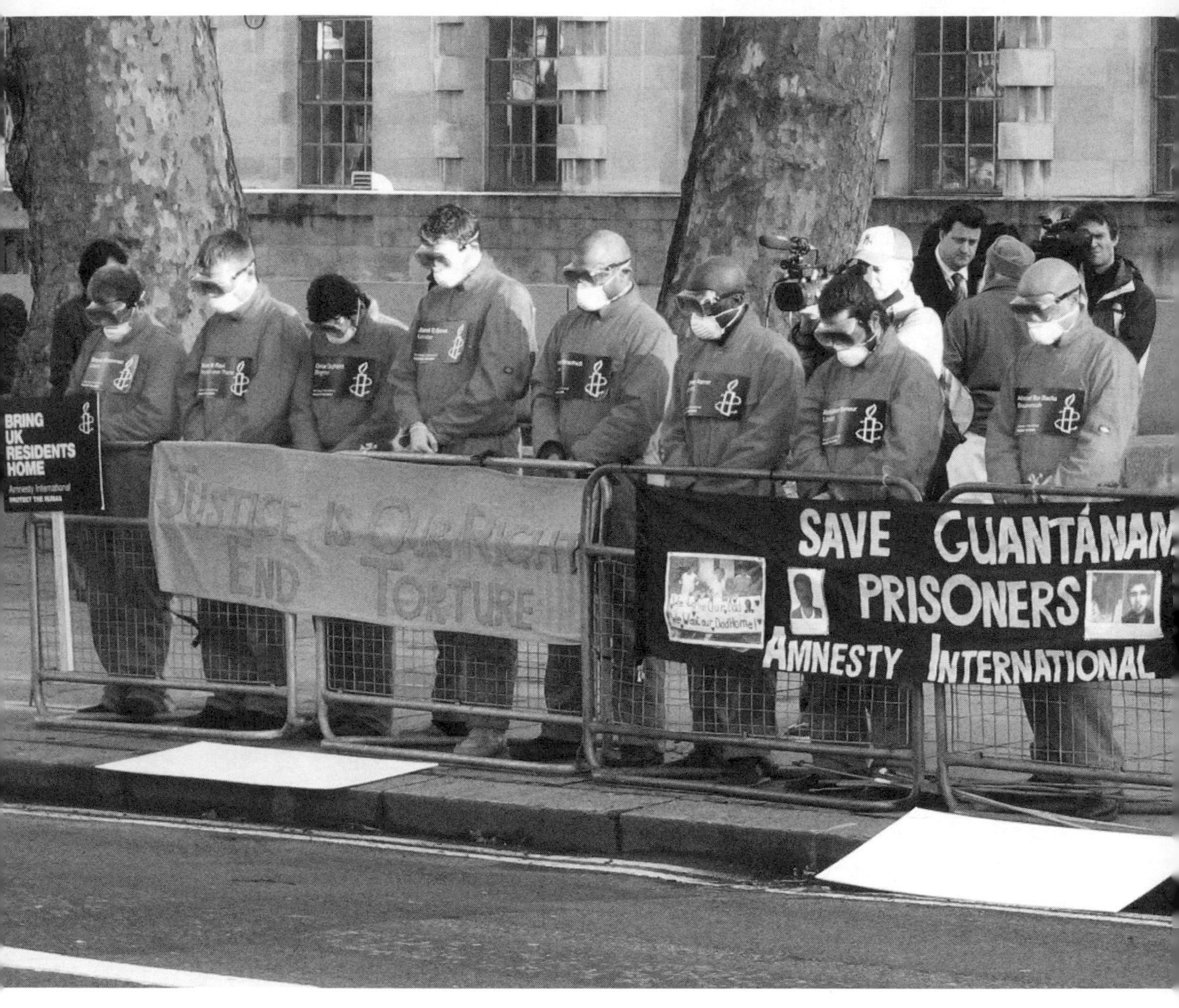

BRING
UK
RESIDENTS
HOME
Amnesty International
END TORTURE
SAVE GUANTÁNAM
PRISONERS
AMNESTY INTERNATIONAL

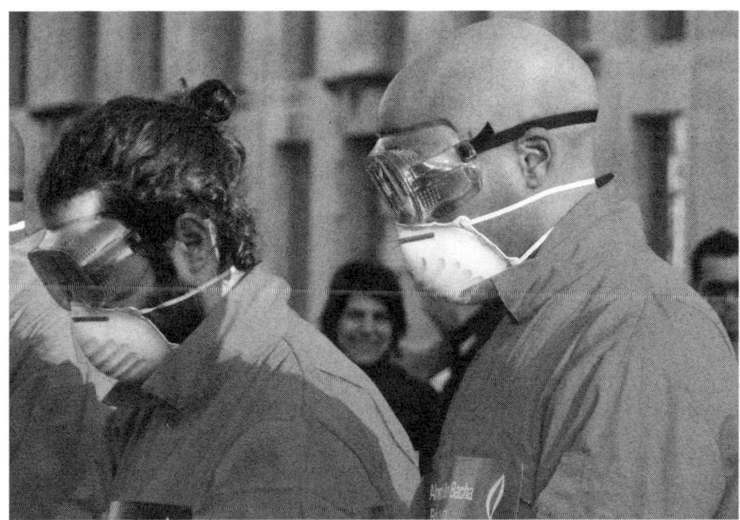

Figure 5.4. Spectacles range from mass gatherings to small group assemblies. However, beyond scale and choreographic differences, the tactics in this category share three key attributes: (1) defined roles for participants, (2) clear spatial distance between the leaders and participants, and (3) a set of agreed-upon symbols associated with the event. Shown are dissenters in London calling for prisoners to be saved from the Guantánamo Bay detention camp by Amnesty International, February 2007. Photos by author.

which opens numerous possibilities and repertoires. In this sense, a protest's choreography (even when used by the same group in the same place) is never static. Moreover, each of these spatial choreographies has advantages and disadvantages. However, decisions regarding how to design the event and which spatial choreography to use in a particular place relate to many additional factors, particularly to issues such as accessibility, the law governing a particular place, cultural norms, and concrete and symbolic goals. In that sense, protest choreographies are often developed over time, and they are evolutionary.

DOES A WINNING SPATIAL CHOREOGRAPHY EXIST?

There is no winning spatial choreography in the making of change. There is space; there are people; and there are cultural distances that define political hierarchies, social orders, and physical representations. Indeed, all spatial choreographies juxtapose the social, political, and spatial; but each approaches this juxtaposition differently. In general terms, it is possible to argue that the less conformist choreographies are more challenging in terms of political distance. Positioning the various choreographies in a spectrum, theater and synchronicity are at the more conventional end, and elasticity, city design, and narrative occupy the less conventional end. In addition, choreographies that evolve over time are more successful in challenging social distances and in developing trust among participants. Here, the strategies based on ad hoc dynamics, such as theater and elasticity, can be placed at one end, and ritual, bareness, and conjoining, based on close familiarity and trust, can be placed at the other. Some choreographies, particularly the one associated with place-making, such as city design, narrative, and reiconization, can be placed somewhere in the middle, as these choreographies are based on occupying sites for a period of time and trust that often evolves over time. Finally, challenging spatial distance is about offering new readings of or even reconstructing space in a way that does not comply with existing norms. The most radical approaches are city design, reiconization, ritual, conjoining, and elasticity, which not only offer the negation of the existing narrative but also suggest an unexpected appropriation or a new way to construct and construe space. In this sense, theater and synchronicity are the less innovative choreographies in terms of offering alternative interpretations of the meanings associated with the place.

Certainly, each society lives with agreed-upon distances and hierarchies until the people decide to challenge them to forge new futures. This process of acknowledging the limits of accepted distances and developing new proximities and coalitions is a process that evolves over time; the event and its foci do not emerge out of the blue; they are instead nurtured by prior social and political dynamics. The process of performing protest and dissent is thus not only "taking to the streets" but also a

Figure 5.5. Place-making involves changing a place's physicality and meaning by using objects or other means over a period of time. Rothschild Boulevard, Tel Aviv, the Tent Protest, June 2011. Photos by Yaira Yasmin.

creative task that "transgress[es] the symbolic order and mark[s] a shift to a new situation that can no longer be thought of in terms of the old symbolic framings."[15] In other words, a significant step in communicating protesters' ideas is suggesting new meanings in particular spaces. This process of crafting a spatial choreography is a creative task that brings an idea into physical existence. In this sense, protest actions are prerequisites for the creation of public spaces.[16]

Finally, the concept of spatial choreography is based on the premise that activists plan events with awareness of their power, the space in question, and the distances they need to challenge and bridge. In that sense, distance, as both a contextual and a universal category, influences how we comprehend and act in the world. Although the quest for change always occurs within a particular context, if successful, it travels and sometimes loses its original meanings.

SPECTACLE

Theater
Rabin Square, Tel Aviv

- Hierarchical Relationships
- Planned Display
- Captured Audience

Ritual
Plaza de Mayo, Buenos Aires

- Assigned Role
- Bounded Space
- Repetitiveness

Bareness | King George/Ben Zion Crossroads, Tel Aviv

- Physical Vulnerability
- Spatial Informality
- Reserved Communication

PROCESSION

Target
Taksim Square, Istanbul

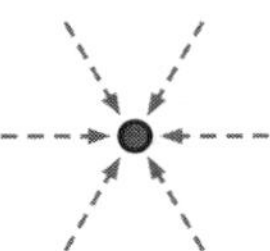

- Assigned Roles
- Symbolic Reclaiming
- Coordinated Performance

Conjoining
Augustusplatz, Leipzig

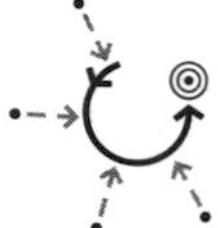

- Planned Sequence
- Spatial Reclaiming
- Concretizing Alliance

Synchronicity
Worldwide

- Orchestrated Spectacle
- Geographic Shrinkage
- Simultaneous Rhythm

Elasticity | Autopista Francisco Fajardo, Caracas

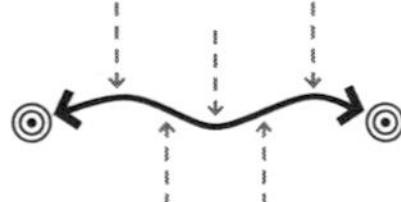

- Becoming
- Space as Continuum
- Temporal Rules

PLACE-MAKING

Reiconization
Tiananmen Square, Beijing

- Central Locus
- Symbolic Appropriation
- Image Supremacy

City Design | National Mall, Washington, DC

- Power Display
- Territorial Claiming
- Holistic System

Narrative
Zuccotti Park, New York

Of the people,
by the people,
for the people

- Of the People
- Illustrative Object
- Accumulative Story

Figure 5.6. Key attributes of spatial choreographies. Illustration by author.

6
Spectacles

Previous page: The spectacle tends to be a well-planned event, which takes advantage of the physical order or the architectural attributes of a particular space. Right-wing supporters protest in Jerusalem's Zion Square against the Israeli government's policy. Photo by Ohayon Avi, National Photo Collection, Israel.

THEATER | TEL AVIV, RABIN SQUARE, NOVEMBER 4, 1995

> We looked for a central place, a place which would fit masses of people; a place which in terms of transportation is accessible . . . a place where in the surroundings you can concentrate many vehicles and so on. But also a place that has defined symbolic meaning, and this square already had a symbolic meaning . . . its name was Kings of Israel Square. It also carried symbolic meaning, as many assemblies took place there . . . that attracted a huge audience . . . there isn't another place of this size.
>
> Eli Eshet, September 3, 2010

Protests designed as theater position the individual within a *meaningful social hierarchy*. In these actions, architectural aesthetics are often used to emphasize symbolic meaning by integrating vistas and perspectives that promulgate the power relationships that are implicit in the square, as the theater and the agora did in Athens.[1] Richard Sennett points to two visual rules that dominate the [Greek] theater, namely, the speaker's exposure to the audience and the dynamic configuration between the speaker as an active agent and the audience as observers. When used in a protest, these rules define the *hierarchical relationships* between the leaders and the audience, which often are further emphasized by barriers or even designated spaces for the leadership and the audience, thereby creating two parallel but related social dynamics: those who act on the stage and those who are present in the space as listeners or active participants. Furthermore, as in a theater, participants are a *captive audience* and are often recruited in advance. Their mere presence supports the show taking place on stage. In these types of protests, the participants tend to be "stagnant crowds,"[2] in other words, a rather passive audience that is aware of "the play" that they are about to see and of the actors who are about to perform. Spontaneous reactions to the performance are limited. This dynamic and distant relationship between the leaders and the audience is maintained throughout the event.

Spatially, theatrical protests tend to use spaces that are designed to be populated by the masses. In everyday life, these types of spaces are constant spatial reminders of the social and political distance between the citizen and the authority. The distinctive geometry and physical proportions that characterize these types of spaces, along with the rules, laws, and social codes that govern them, project power and monumentality and help enhance the pathos of the event. Thus, in protests designed as theaters, the physical space plays a major role in defining this dynamic. In the case of a mass congregation, activists or rulers use the spatial architectural features to transform the individual into an anonymous participant, part of an abstract crowd that is considered a unified entity. Sometimes, the desired setting for the participants makes use of the physical attributes of a space without modifying them; in other cases, the site is customized through additional means, such as the installation of a stage, microphones, flags, and posters, which reinforce the visual and textual symbols of the place. Either way, the desired number of spectators is more or less known in advance, and the trajectory of the event is relatively fixed. However, although the theater is a seemingly rigid spatial choreography, its power should not be underestimated. Familiarity with the event's "format" helps reduce fear and anxiety among participants and maintain their presence throughout the whole performance.

The visual-aesthetic aspect is central in these types of actions. Aesthetics assist in attracting the participants' attention and focus. Practically, this aspect involves the development of a sense of rhyme or pattern for the event as a whole. Similarly, the repetition of visual and vocal elements (within the same event or in relation to past events) also contributes to the rhythm of the action as a whole. Therefore, just as in a real theater, the show is produced by grouping elements to create emphasis, direction, and effect. A well-planned "theatrical" protest will aim to achieve harmony between the physical and the sociopolitical, between the order of space and the rhythm of the event.

This theatrical tactic requires the punctilious preparation of the event, including the construction of a stage, the array of performers (i.e., artists, speakers), lighting, and sound. In addition, issues of audience recruitment and security precautions are central and require particular permissions for the use of public spaces, the support of local police forces, and substantial funding. This tactic is often used for grand events, which aim to be etched in a society's collective memory to change a particular discourse over a contested issue. It essentially hopes to achieve major support for a cause or power. For example, this spatial choreography can be observed in the "Yes to Peace, No to Violence" rally in support of the Oslo Accords, which took place in Kings of Israel Square on November 4, 1995. The Oslo Accords were agreements between the Israeli government and the Palestine Liberation Organization (PLO), representing the Palestinians as part of a peace process (officially called the Declaration of Principles) in 1993.[3] During this event, thousands of youngsters waved banners in the square, calling for peace in Hebrew and Arabic. After the assembly, Prime Minister Yitzhak Rabin was assassinated by a young Israeli religious extremist. At 11:14 p.m., Rabin's death was announced.

Place

Protests with theatrical designs cannot take place just anywhere. They require particular physical attributes that either already exist or are specially constructed for the event. In Israel, a prominent public space for protests is Rabin Square in

Tel Aviv. The square is an urban space, running approximately 260 meters from north to south and 160 meters from east to west; it is enclosed on three sides by six-story residential buildings with commercial arcades on the ground floor. On the northern edge of the square, the twelve-story City Hall building has a terrace and broad stairs that span Ben Gurion Street, connecting City Hall directly to the square. The site was originally named Kings of Israel Square but was renamed Rabin Square after Rabin's assassination in 1995. Historically, it was acquired by the Tel Aviv municipality in the late 1920s and was designated in the city's master plan to function as a square.[4] In the late 1940s, the city decided to convert the square into the civic heart of the city, building City Hall there next to a new open space that would function as a square.[5] The symbolic dimension of the square was further reinforced by the decision, approved by the City Council in 1974, to install a monument commemorating the Holocaust (designed as an inverted pyramid, an abstract sculpture in rusted metal), which made the square a national space.[6] In contrast to the empty plaza, the roads on the square's perimeter bustle with traffic, and the arcades are filled, day and night, with people who relax in cafés, visit shops and kiosks, and wait at bus stops—creating the buzz of normal urban life. Nonetheless, despite these everyday activities around the square, the spatial composition of both the square and City Hall suggests a hierarchical relationship between inhabitants and those in power.

These attributes of the square, with their contested evolution, have created a hybrid space, one that combines Sennett's two typologies—the "agora," an open space lined with commercial activity, and the "theater" with its rectangular geometry, which establishes an elevated hierarchy (balcony) and physical distance between the crowd and the speaker/performer.[7] This hybrid space is also physically unique in Tel Aviv: first, the consistent height of the buildings surrounding the plaza, a unique feature in Tel Aviv, is usually typified by its detached buildings; second, the square's size is large compared with other building complexes in Tel Aviv (and throughout Israel); and, third, the relationship between City Hall and the square is distinct for Tel Aviv, where institutional buildings are rarely situated in squares. These architectural features and the space's geographic centrality, along with the need for an arena for public debate over the Israelis' contested reality, have contributed to the square's evolution as an arena for political assemblies from the early 1930s to the present.[8]

However, starting in the 1970s, the square's increased recognition as a political arena partly resulted from the decision to install facilities in the plaza for national elections and to allow lectures and debates on controversial subjects to take place there.[9] This idea of debating in the square emerged during an increasingly contentious contest after Israel's occupation of the West Bank and Gaza in 1967, when disputes raged over the country's collective identity.[10] Key events included the political upheaval between the two major parties competing in 1977 and the rally in the square on September 25, 1982 (the "Protest of the 400,000"),[11] which called for a national investigation of the Sabra and Shatila massacres,[12] the withdrawal of Israeli forces from Lebanon, and the resignation of the government.

Since the 1980s, protests in the square have tended to have a similar rhythm. Generally, the crowd gathers on Saturday evening, after the Sabbath. Flags and banners are waved; those in the crowd move their arms and bodies to show their support for the speakers. The City Hall balcony has become a stage for speakers, celebrities, and high-ranking supporters. Speeches alternate with musical performances; the audience often responds loudly and enthusiastically; and every event concludes with the singing of the national anthem. Images from the protests are often transmitted live to millions of television viewers, and the demonstrations are normally synchronized with the end of the weekend evening news, then become the next morning's leading items. This ritual-designed order was in use during the most dramatic event in the square, fixed forever in the national (and international) consciousness, on November 4, 1995.

Context

The context of the November 4, 1995, rally was the 1993 Oslo Accords agreement (the Declaration of Principles) between the Israeli government, led by Prime Minister Yitzhak Rabin, and the PLO, led by Yasser Arafat. Descriptions of the public atmosphere in Israel in those days reveal a deep divide in Israeli society regarding whether to support the government-led peace process with the Palestinians, as many Palestinian terrorist attacks were taking place in central locations at that time. The opposition was very active, leading many demonstrations and distributing various posters not only criticizing the intentions and ideas of the Oslo Accords but also personally attacking Prime Minister Rabin and other political figures.[13] Eli Eshet, one of the organizers of the event, described the atmosphere among Israelis at that time:

> The public mood was fanatical, polar, and even extremely polar, for peace and against peace, pro-Rabin and anti-Rabin, followed by extreme and very, very unusual violent behavior. [There were] all sorts of parades with coffins and people wearing kufiyahs . . . and costumes of Arafat and swastikas.[14]

This climate led the Peace and Security Association[15] and the Efshar Association,[16] both headed by Colonel (Ret.) Shlomo Lahat, who also served as the mayor of Tel Aviv from 1974 to 1993, to publicly support the government in organizing a nonpartisan rally backing the government and its policy under the title of "Yes to Peace, No to Violence." In choosing the square as the location for the demonstration, organizers considered both practical reasons—its central location in Israel and its capacity to host mass demonstrations—and symbolic reasons—its associations with political gatherings and public debates.

> The square was chosen (a) because of its central location and (b) because of its symbolic meaning . . . if you expect hundreds of thousands, you have to arrange for a place where they can stand . . . there is no other place in the center. . . . When you do it in a closed space like this, a huge square like this, you see a sea of people. It leaves [a] great impression.[17]

Event

Crafting this theatrical event, its rhythm, and its detailed schedule was not the task of a mere few. The body of organization and planning included hundreds of people, who were responsible for the actual realization of the event on the ground. The organization included two key groups, one responsible for the event's design, including the stage, lighting, and media, and another responsible for security management during the event, including the police, municipality representatives, and the Shabak (Israel's security agency). The police played a major role in the execution of the event; they provided the permit for holding the rally, were responsible for the security during the event, and were thus included in the organization process from the start. In particular, due to the increased tension between rival groups in Israeli society, the escalating Palestinian Intifada in the 1990s, and the media's growing involvement in the assemblies, security was given additional attention and care.

> The fear was that someone would enter the assembly or approach the crowd with an explosive device. The other fear was that someone would use one of the roofs to snipe one of the key figures . . . there was a lot of work around issues of security and safety, and there was also the issue of the crowd; when hundreds of thousands of people arrive together to a place, they also can crush one another.[18]

The organization of the event mirrored the relationships and hierarchies among participants at the event. The organization's managerial team was located in a room on the balcony behind the central stage to ensure that the production ran smoothly. The police headquarters, technical teams, the media (journalists and photographers), artists, and leaders were also located on the balcony. Access to the compound was (more or less) restricted to those who confirmed their arrivals in advance.

Furthermore, on the day of assembly, the entrances to City Hall and to most of the restaurants and shops in the arcades surrounding the square were blocked by police with temporary checkpoints, which redefined the square's boundaries, turning it into a "sterile zone." Police officers and civilian ushers were responsible for maintaining order and inspecting the crowds to monitor who had entered the square from entrance points on peripheral streets around the square. Internal security agents were scattered around the area, including on the rooftops of the buildings surrounding the square. In addition, emergency teams—ambulances and firefighters—were also waiting in the area and ready for action. The increased media attention provided additional surveillance, documenting the event from above and on the ground.

> The whole thing is organized as a military operation. Look, first of all, we have to take into account that this kind of rally cannot start too early; it is the Sabbath. We do not want to cause a mass desecration of the Sabbath, though people are coming and travelling. But if you want people to come from all groups in society, you have to take into consideration this issue. The other factor is the varied media means, especially television, which follows specific broadcasting hours.[19]

Thus, in terms of distance, the event was planned and defined as a controlled central island within the city. There were two areas on the "island": the gathering area for participants, which was unrestricted, allowing freedom of movement and departure through any of the barriers; and the smaller performance area, which was designated for leaders and organizers and physically disconnected from the crowd. This spatial configuration—the key principle of this type of protest—created a setting with an illusion of freedom and safety, camouflaging the strictly controlled, surveyed, and searched boundaries of the crowd.

Socially, the rally brought together large crowds from all over the country. As an event planned from above, the organizers aimed to reduce social and ideological differences and, in turn, the distance between the diverse groups within Israeli society. The participants arrived in preorganized transport, buses, and cars. Local councils that sought to help the organizing body arranged some bus transport, while the organizing body sent some buses to prominent meeting points that were advertised in advance. The crowd included regular political activists affiliated with particular parties, members of kibbutzim, Palestinian supporters (Israeli citizens), and many others. Approximately 100,000 attendees were estimated to have participated in the event in the square and the streets adjacent to it.[20]

The event's meticulous organization required significant funding:

> It costs millions. Look, not only the buses . . . one would say . . . they are funded by the municipalities. But the buses in central meeting points cost money, a lot of money . . . and, if you set up a stage and employ a company to do this, as we did . . . they also ask for lots of money, and lighting and amplifying equipment and the public campaigns in the newspapers.[21]

The event followed the planned display, commencing at 7:00 p.m. with musical performances and lasting until approximately 9:30 p.m. The organizers aimed to create a festive atmosphere, using the square's lighting and distributing huge balloons and large signs supporting the parties affiliated with the coalition around the square. A large placard with the rally's motto—Yes to Peace, No to Violence—was hung on the western side of the square and on the southern side, where the stage was located. Stickers with the motto were also distributed throughout the crowd. The display ended with an Israeli singer's performance of the "Peace Song," accompanied by Prime Minister Rabin, Foreign Minister Peres, and others, and the release of hundreds of balloons. Following the song, as Prime Minister Rabin descended the service stairs below City Hall's terrace, he was shot by a young Jewish extremist.

Rabin's assassination exposed the deep fissures in Israeli society and triggered ongoing public debate about how to heal them. The square became the locus of memory of Rabin's assassination and a constant reminder of the tensions that led to it. Changing the name of the square was a memorial ritual, as was the monument placed at the exact site of the assassination. These acts reinforced the political formalization of the space and its assemblies, adding further symbolic meaning to the square, thus magnifying its theatrical dimension.[22]

Distance

The theater is a universal tactic that is used for spectacular events. It is based on a fixed spatial configuration, which separates the audience and the leadership. Due to its distinct physical structure, activists who use this tactic create event-spaces that preserve and sometimes further increase distance between participants and the leadership. The event's geographical location and its architectural and symbolic features are crucial; in most cases, protests that use this spatial choreography choose places that are associated with power.

Theatrical demonstrations attract many people who have previous experiences of protest activities but no links to specific associations. Recurrent participation in demonstrations may be regarded as a unique practice that is able to generate a distinct sense of commonality and specific bonds between people who repeatedly share the same experiences. The element that links these actors to one another is their sustained protest behavior.[23] People who engage in this type of event are often familiar with the space's geographic, cultural, and institutional meanings. As a huge endeavor, theater choreography suits large-scale events in which all key actors and participants are aware of their roles in the performance and show their support for an agreed-upon message. In theatrical demonstrations, the body is respectful and obedient. As such, theater is a type of action in which the body becomes part of the architectural features of the event-space. The mere presence of bodies sends a single message—they stand behind and support this event.

This spatial choreography is favored by institutionalized organizations and governments, as it is perceived as carefully coordinated with authorities and thus enhances the sense of predictability among participants. Therefore, the successful use of this tactic implies crafting an event with an a priori defined structure, lengthy preparation, and considerable funding.

THEATER | Tel Aviv, Rabin Square, November 4, 1995

ATTRIBUTES

- Hierarchical Relationships
- Planned Display
- Captured Audience

Figure 6.1. Spatially, theatrical protests tend to use spaces that are designed to be populated by the masses. Banners in Tel Aviv's Malchei Yisrael Square advocate an end to violence, hung up after the assassination of Prime Minister Yitzhak Rabin during a peace rally in 1995. Photo by Israeli Tsvika, National Photo Collection, Israel.

Figure 6.2. Rabin Square. Photo by author.

Key Features	**Rabin Square**
Location	Tel Aviv Centre, Israel
Buildings/activities	City Hall, Memorial Monuments, Leisure
Space	~40,500 sq. meters
Key value/concern	Symbolic
Spatial definition within the city	A void designed as municipal public square

Table 6.1. Key Features and Spatial Attributes.

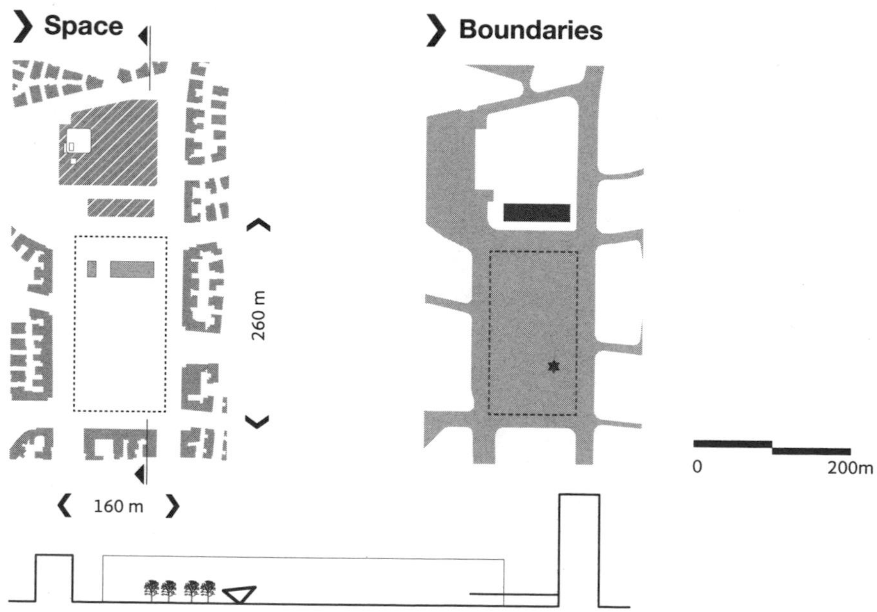

Figure 6.3. Rabin Square: Built form and space. Illustration by author.

Distance	Geography	Central locus of dissent, a focal point on a national scale
	Physical	Using design to define the distance between participants and leadership
	Meaning	The event as a means of reducing (communicative) ideological distance between rival groups in society

Table 6.2. Event and the Conceptualization of Distance.

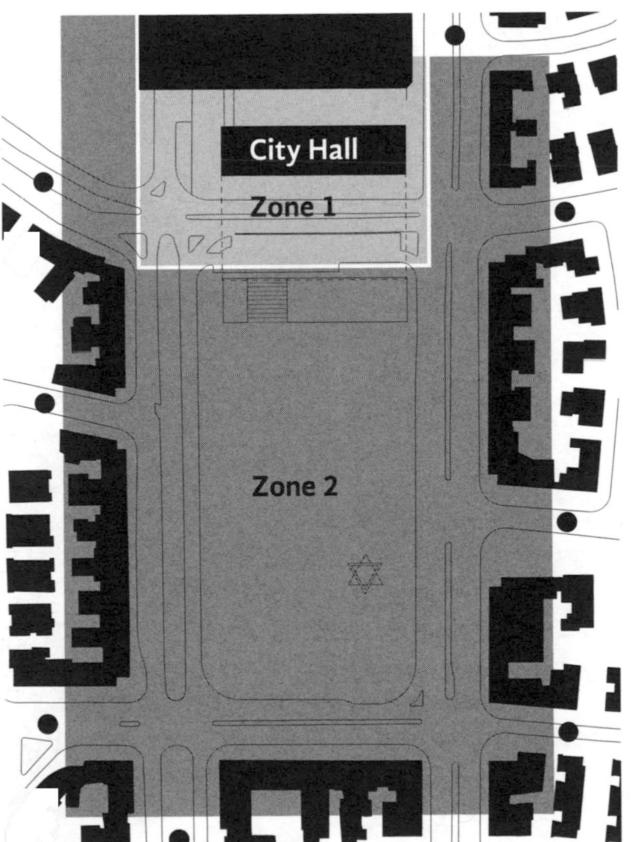

Zone 1 - Impermeable Checkpoint. Heavily guarded by police, barriers defining a sterile zone that includes the area of the balcony and the alley at the rear of the City Hall.

Zone 2 - Permeable Checkpoint. Metal barriers guarded by two to three policemen looking for suspicious individuals: checking IDs and contents of bags, asking about weapons; only pedestrians are allowed to pass. Surveillance Foot Patrol: teams with flashlights surveying the backyards of the residential buildings in the area. Surveillance in the crowd: police in civilian clothing among the crowd.

All Zones - Surveillance watchers: policemen on the first and second perimeters, roofs of residential and public buildings.

● Checkpoints

Figure 6.4. Rabin Square: Surveillance arrangements.

Figures 6.5 and 6.6. *Left*: Teenagers gather in Tel Aviv's Malchei Israel to light memorial candles after hearing of the assassination of Prime Minister Yitzhak Rabin during a peace rally there on November 4, 1995. Photo by Israeli Tsvika, Government Press Office, Israel. *Below*: Protests in the square have tended to have a similar rhythm. Generally, the crowd gathers on Saturday evening, after the Sabbath. Flags and banners are waved; those in the crowd move their arms and bodies to show their support for the speakers. The City Hall balcony has become a stage for speakers, celebrities, and high-ranking supporters. Speeches alternate with musical performances; the audience often responds loudly and enthusiastically; and every event concludes with the singing of the national anthem. Shown is a memorial service on the ninth anniversary of the assassination of Prime Minister Yitzhak Rabin, at "Rabin Square" in Tel Aviv, October 2004. Photo by Milner Moshe, National Photo Collection, Israel.

RITUAL | BUENOS AIRES, PLAZA DE MAYO, AUGUST 31, 2006

> On April 30, the Mothers were formed, the group of 14 mothers that . . . were forced to wait so much and suffered a series of humiliations in those places, so much that Azucena got up and said, "What are we doing here? Let's go to the Plaza!" If she hadn't said this, the Mothers wouldn't exist.
>
> Thursdays, always Thursdays . . . and we, no matter what's taking place, whatever it is, like what happened the other day . . . we, from 3:30 to 4 are in our place.
>
> Aida Sarti, September 4, 2006

Repetition is a key feature of protests that are designed as rituals. Repetition applies not only to time (i.e., doing the same thing over and over again) but also to how the act is performed physically in space and the ways in which the act's intention reveals itself through various symbols (e.g., placards and clothing). Although all protests may be understood as secular rituals, protests that use this spatial choreography, similar to that used in religious rituals, are based on a framework of mutual confirmation regarding the cause. The ritual provides a sense of *emotional support* and *refuge*, with participants following two key rules: (1) accepting their assigned roles with communicative intent and (2) committing themselves to the event's repetitious features, which are regarded as a means of effecting and sustaining transformation. This spatial choreography implies that endurance and persistence are the keys to making a difference. Endurance and persistence symbolize not only the fate of the participants in the cause but also the power of and cohesion among participants. This message serves to constantly remind the regime of the demonstrators' strength and will.

Ritual-based protests are built from the bottom up through encounters and interpersonal relations. These protests are often generated by a few individuals, and "their structure is such that they can be comprehended by the public and taken in at a quick glance."[24] As such, their role and message must be familiar to the public but adaptable enough to offer new insights. In this sense, powerful rituals are those that challenge agreed-upon constructs, specifically in terms of how bodies and spaces are used. The body is the center of these types of protests; it follows an agreed-upon choreography, seeking to take over a space and fill it with a set of movements that will leave a mark on spectators. These body movements, that is, the choreography itself, are filled with meaning both for the participants and for the viewers. Though repetitive, the choreography of the ritual is dynamic and may change over time.

Space plays a crucial role in this type of protest ritual, and it is part of the ritual's design. In choosing a place for action that is central or peripheral, institutional or informal, the ways in which the ritual responds to known symbols and updates them with new meanings are the key. Thus, although an action may only involve a few individuals, the ritual's power comes in the form of occupying space physically and ideologically. The message's precision, as manifested in the choreography of the action, is more important than its size.

The ritual is poetic; it is a spectacle with a small *s*, bringing a new rhythm to a place. However, it is a power display of the few, who are able to set up and organize an event that is not only temporary and unique but also cyclical. By appearing in the same place at the same time, using a particular uniform or acting in a defined sphere, preferably a central space or place with symbolic meaning, the ritual often attracts the attention of the media and the government. These principles assist in creating a "protest community" with its associated practices, language, and behavior, which may generate ties and solidarity among the people involved. Both may be expected to secure continuity, which is required for the development of collective actions over time.[25] An example of this tactic in a focal space is the case of the Mothers of the Plaza de Mayo, an association of Argentine mothers whose children "disappeared" under the military dictatorship between 1976 and 1983. The spectacle of elderly women in white scarves carrying placards depicting the faces of their missing children has become an icon of women's resistance movements in Latin America.[26] For over three decades, the Mothers of the Plaza de Mayo have fought for the right to reunite with their abducted children. Since April 30, 1977, they have gathered every Thursday afternoon in the Plaza de Mayo, meeting in front of the Casa Rosada presidential palace to walk around the plaza. On January 26, 2006, members of the Mothers of the Plaza de Mayo made their final annual March of Resistance around the Plaza de Mayo, chanting "no more!"

Context

The emergence of this plaza demonstration by the Mothers of the Plaza de Mayo should be seen in the context of the political climate in Argentina in the late 1970s. On March 24, 1976, the junta's commanders in chief, General Jorge Rafael Videla, Admiral Emilio Eduardo Massera, and Air Force Brigadier General Orlando Ramón Agosti, assumed power. They immediately issued the legal instrument of the so-called "Process of National Reorganization" and appointed General Videla president of the nation.[27] Only seven years later, a democratic government returned to power in December 1983. The military junta controlled the country using totalitarian methods, including the kidnapping, torture, and execution of thousands of people (estimates range from 9,000 to 30,000), who came to be known as the "disappeared."[28] This climate created extreme political distance between citizens and the state, and, in Argentina, those years are referred to as the "dirty war," which is associated with citizens' fear and anxiety. Trust was scarce, and political protests were almost impossible because of the military junta's repressive power. At the time, popular demonstrations in the plaza were strictly forbidden, and a gathering of more than two people was promptly dispersed by the ever-present security forces.[29]

The movement of the Mothers of the Plaza de Mayo started with a few mothers who were searching for their absent children, looking for clues in churches, military headquarters, hospitals, and police stations. In those days, churches were regarded as closely tied with the regime; thus, many families believed that the church would be able to influence the regime,[30] and mothers went to their priests and bishops, assuming that they would condemn the security forces' activities and support them in their search for relatives. In these locations, women identified other women in similar conditions, but, as one woman remembered, they did not immediately communicate or interact with one another because, "As Argentine women in a traditional society, they were wary and did not speak to the others around them. Although each mother was obsessed with the task of securing the return of her child, she believed this could be accomplished within a brief period of time."[31] However, some mothers were able to bridge this social distance and recruited others to action:

> In the Ministry of the Interior, I met another mother looking for her child. When I left the building, she was waiting for me outside, and she called me over. She asked me if they'd taken my child too. I told her what had happened. She said, "Come to the square on Thursday and join the Mothers. We meet every Thursday." I said yes, that I'd already heard something about the Mothers. She said, "Come, they won't ask you any questions. We're all women together." Within a few days of my son's disappearance, I was in Plaza de Mayo.[32]

On April 30, 1977, fourteen mothers, who met while searching for their children who were abducted by the junta, assembled in the Plaza de Mayo. Filled with anxiety, they arrived separately, with just bus fare and their identity cards in case they had to flee. At first, they had planned to act on Saturday but soon realized that, because stores and businesses were closed on the weekends, the plaza was empty on Saturdays. As a result, they decided to meet again the following Friday when there would be an audience for their demonstration.[33]

During the early years, the decision-making process took place at churches. Most of the mothers were very religious and used to pass notes on "tiny pieces of folded paper, like when you're in school, cheating in a test. Then, we hid them in the hems of our skirts in case we were searched later." They primarily met in small churches, as larger ones closed their doors to them when they discovered that they were the Mothers of the Plaza de Mayo.[34]

The mothers' profiles and their uniqueness as political actors are obvious from their organization's name, which indicates not only their protest's motivations and goals but also their societal role. Generally, they were older working-class women, who were housewives or employed in the fields of education and social work. Few women had an academic education or previous political experience.[35] In the early stages of the movement, they did not see themselves as part of a political movement, as one of them testifies: "What happens is that the movement of the Mothers didn't have anything political about it; we just left our houses, as God willed it, and we met there. And we were passive; we never carried a rock in hand, never had an aggressive action." Significantly, the mothers consciously distanced themselves from biological motherhood and moved toward political motherhood, manipulating the maternal role in a way that intensified the drama of their ritual in the plaza.[36]

Place

The Plaza de Mayo is an urban square that is located at the hub of political life in Argentina. As a physical space, it has three main features. First, the plaza is part of a wider *urban scheme* that includes significant national institutions, such as government offices, the financial district, and the city's commercial streets.[37] However, the plaza is dominated by institutional buildings (with no commercial entities), which adds to its formality. Second, the plaza is a rigid space—*rectangular* and *symmetrical*—with clear spatial definitions and physical boundaries. Third, the plaza is a *large* space (approximately 30,000 m^2), with greenery along the edges and the May Pyramid as a focal point in its center. The pyramid, a plastered masonry obelisk from 1811, marks the first anniversary of the Creoles' demand for independence from Spain. Replanned in 1884, the plaza became part of an east-west axis (May Avenue), with the Casa Rosada at one end and the Congress building at the other. The space's physical features and history have transformed it into a national symbol and a representation of the political powers. However, these exact physical features, particularly the scale of the place, which is designed for the masses, make the plaza a challenging space in terms of dissent and protest, especially for a small group of people.

The Plaza de Mayo was the immediate choice of the Mothers, mainly because of its proximity to the political powers. According to one participant, "Azucena got up and said, 'What are we doing here? Let's go to the Plaza!' If she hadn't said this, the Mothers wouldn't exist."[38] Thus, despite the incentive to abandon the plaza for a safer location, the Mothers sustained a symbolic presence in the form of a silent march around the May Pyramid. That form, so loaded with cultural and sexual associations, became the symbolic focus of what started as a literal response to the police's demand that the women "circulate." Thus, the ritual of the Mothers of the Plaza de Mayo involves challenging political and social distance by enhancing physical proximity in multiple ways: acting in proximity to key national symbols, acting in proximity to political powers, and creating intimacy in the form of a march in which they carry their message on their bodies.[39] The decision to continue marching in the plaza was associated with their aim to be visible: "We wanted people to see us, to know we were there, so we began to walk in the center of the square around the monument. Even if people supported us, they stayed outside the square. It was very dangerous for them to approach us. We were very alone in the beginning."[40]

Visibility and safety, both pragmatic considerations, played a key role in choosing the location. The Mothers realized the power of being visible, not just to make their political message effective but also to survive in a society that was annihilated by the military. They assumed that the junta, which legitimized its mission through its association with Christians and family values, could not suppress the Mothers in public.[41]

Event

The ritual of the Mothers essentially made visible the anonymous faces and the abstract numbers of the disappeared. Using their bodies, inscribing names, dates, and faces on their head scarves, the Mothers emphasized family ties and community, thus challenging the military regime's ahistorical erasure of their family member. The formation of the ritual took some time, as Aida Sarti explained:

> At first, we didn't march together when we were in the square. We sat on the benches with our knitting or stood in small groups, trying to disguise the letters we were signing to send to the churches, government officials, the military. We had to speak to each other quickly, in low voices so it didn't look as if we were having a meeting. Then, when the police saw what was happening and began pointing their rifles at us and telling us to move on, that we had to disperse, that we couldn't be more than two together, we began to walk in twos around the edge of the square. Two in front, two behind, because we had to keep moving but also had to be able to speak to each other, to talk about what we were going to do next.[42]

Two factors influenced the spatial and body-related form of the ritual. First, during the early years, the restrictions on the use of the space, the role of the police force, and their negotiations with the Mothers were crucial factors in the development of the Mothers' particular form of protest. The police objected to the Mothers standing together in the square, which first pushed the latter to walk around the pyramid.[43] According to a participant, "The police came and kicked us off because there was martial law and we couldn't stay there, and the police asked themselves what we were doing, 'What are these women doing here?'. . . So we would walk, two by two; for a time, we walked two by two." Second, manipulating existing constructs and representations of femininity in the early stages of their activism, women consciously modeled themselves on the Virgin Mary, the ultimate mother who transcends the public/private dilemma by exposing her private concerns in public. The Mothers exploited deeply rooted stereotypes of femininity, representations that often limited the visibility and experiences of women, by marching as if in a ritual procession, with serious faces, eyes turned upward in supplication, and heads covered in a peaceful, rapt, and pleading protest.[44] This exercise allowed them to act within the traditional roles of women in Argentinian society.

Indeed, from the early days, the body of the mother was the focal point of the ritual, a carrier of a sacred memory, with the obelisk serving as a reference point—an object and physical anchor that contributes to the form of the ritual and serves as a carrier of meaning (as in the case of annual marches). The power of the ritual is its simplicity and unique features: (1) motion: the occupation of the square, marching clockwise in circles around the central pyramid to demonstrate their resistance;[45] (2) clothing: white kerchiefs that are worn on their heads, listing the names of their children;[46] (3) temporal and spatial repetition: the same dynamic every Thursday between 3:30 and 4:00 p.m. One Mother explained the group's consistent gatherings: "Thursdays, always Thursdays. Because first we had said Saturday. . . . Then, it changed forever to Thursdays. And we, no matter what's taking place, whatever it is, like what happened the other day with Blumberg, we, from 3:30 to 4:00 are in our place."[47] The Mothers did not aspire to achieve some kind of fixed content during their weekly half-hour protest, meaning that, at 4:00 p.m., the ritual is over until the following week. Similarly, the demonstrations have no clear beginning; women just arrive and start marching at 3:30 p.m. In later years, they began using pictures of their disappeared children.

The Mothers' activism has an emotional dimension, which runs deep into the core of the interpersonal relations among the Mothers.[48] These interpersonal relations contributed to the ritual becoming not only a political spectacle but also a means of collectively coping with grief in public.[49] Using the ideas of Dominick LaCapra, the ritual was a means of *working through* their losses. In his work, LaCapra distinguishes, in nonbinary terms, between *acting out* and *working through* an interrelated response to loss or historic trauma.[50] Referring to Freud's "Mourning and Melancholia," LaCapra argues that mourning can be considered a form of *working through* and that melancholia can be regarded as a form of *acting out*. On the one hand, Freud viewed melancholia as characteristic of an arrested process in which the depressed patient, locked in compulsive repetition, is possessed by the past and still identifies with the lost object; on the other hand, mourning offers the possibility of engaging trauma in a way that allows an individual to begin anew. Historical losses necessitate mourning—and possibly critical and transformative sociopolitical practices as well. However, when absence is the cause of mourning, as in the case of the Mothers, mourning may become impossible, continually returning individuals to endless melancholy.

The ritual, its form, and its members have undergone various changes through the years. From 1978 to 1979, the junta worked hard to repress the Mothers' protests, thereby increasing their suffering. Police were sent to the demonstrations, arresting and harassing the women; as a result, many women stopped coming to the square. By the end of 1978, the army sealed off the square with barriers, and the women could barely access the square in 1979. Around 1980, the junta's pressure on the Mothers was starting to mount, especially because of the economic crisis.[51]

The Mothers did not realize that they were embarking on a journey that would transform them into political activists.[52] However, in 1979, they were registered as the Asociación Civil Madres de Plaza de Mayo, creating an organization that helped enlarge the movement with supporters from rural areas. From a movement of very few, they became a network of hundreds, including Mothers living in interior provinces and support groups around the world.[53] The formal organization also reveals the Mothers' second strategy in addition to the weekly protest for which they are known; this strategy included communicating with government officials, cooperating with other human rights organizations in Argentina and abroad, and connecting with international organizations, such as the United Nations. In 1980, they began to publish their own bulletin.[54] In early 1980, other institutional political agents joined the Mothers' cause, and they managed to create a national network.[55]

The movement finally led to the end of the military regime, with some 30,000 people joining their weekly protest.[56] With the reestablishment of democracy, the Mothers continued their weekly protest, but their membership declined. In 1986, the movement split into two branches, one taking a more radical political stand and the other staying closer to the original goals of the movement.[57] When they became a registered organization, the Mothers declared that their main goal was to receive an answer to the question of where their children were and what happened to them. However, they also stressed their commitment to working toward building a just Argentina in which this history would not repeat itself.[58]

After years of being occupied by the Mothers, the Plaza de Mayo came to be identified with their long struggle. Some of the Mothers are buried around the central pyramid, further strengthening this identification. In December 1981, four years after they first came to the square, they began to hold a yearly ritual in the square—a twenty-four-hour march to celebrate Human Rights Day.[59] The Human Rights Day March of December 1983, the last march against the military regime, included 30,000 silhouettes of the disappeared.

Distance

The foundation of the ritual is the body and interpersonal relationships. The ritual is based on an agreed-upon choreography of the body, which is set by organizers in advance. This choreography is used as a means of creating unity and clarifying their message. During the ritual, physical proximity among actors not only helps create a solid entity in space but also reflects the familiarity and trust among participants.

The repetition of this ritual as a event-space provides actors with the opportunity to engage in the spatial choreography and its associated meaning. Importantly, the body and the space are interlinked in the ritual, and the material space serves as a transformative tool rather than static decoration. Spaces and bodies are emerging and changing, and the ritual as a spatial choreography is thus a flexible event-space that evolves over time without spatial or temporal limitations.

This tactic has no particular scale, and it can be used by the many and the few. The organizers define the way of challenging distance, which is influenced by the choice of place and the configuration of the spectacle. In this sense, different from mass protests, this spatial choreography allows protesters more freedom in defining the components of the performance. Thus, although this spatial choreography has no particular scale and can take place anywhere, it is powerful when it successfully modifies agreed-upon meanings that are associated with the space or the body.

RITUAL | Buenos Aires, Plaza De Mayo, August 31, 2006

ATTRIBUTES

- Assigned Role
- Bounded Space
- Repetitiveness

Figure 6.7. The white kerchiefs the Mothers wear were adopted from the cloth diapers of their missing children. Photo by author.

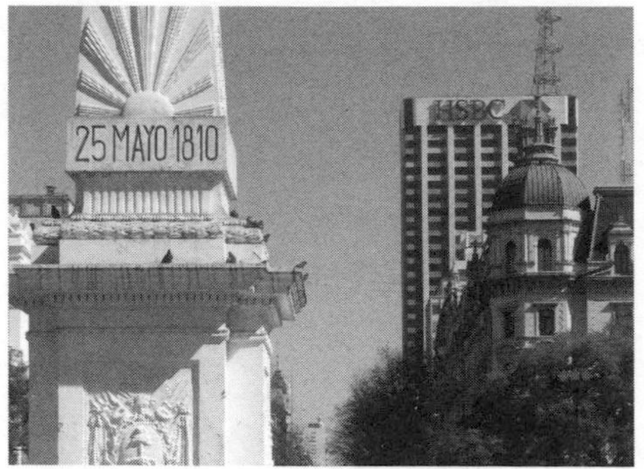

Figure 6.8. Pirámide de Mayo, detail. Photo by author.

Figure 6.9. Plaza de Mayo, 2007. Photo by author.

Key Features	Plaza de Majo
Location	Buenos Aires, Argentina
Buildings/activities	Government/national structures, symbolic monuments, recreation
Space	~31,200 sq. meters
Key value/concern	Symbolic
Spatial definition within the city	Symbolic, the hub of political life in Argentina

Table 6.3. Key Features and Spatial Attributes.

❯ Space

130 m

240 m

❯ Boundaries

0 200m

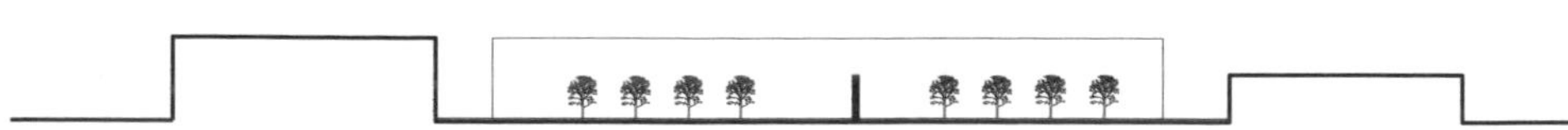

Figure 6.10. Plaza de Mayo: Built form and space. Illustration by author.

Figure 6.11. The Mothers in the Plaza de Mayo, Buenos Aires, July 2006. Photo by author.

Distance	Geography	Central locus of national power
	Physical	Using spatial attributes as part of ritual's design
	Meaning	Performing pain in public space, violating the distance dictated by those in power

Table 6.4. Event and the Conceptualization of Distance.

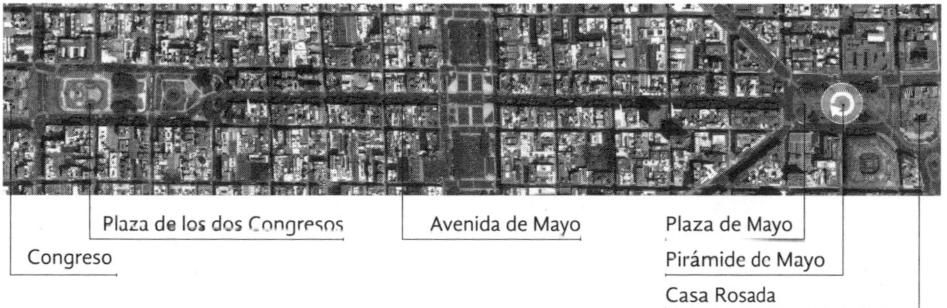

Figure 6.12. Plaza de Mayo: Urban context and space of gathering. Illustration by author.

Figure 6.13. Body is following agreed choreographic movements in space. The Mothers marching in the Plaza, 2007. Photos by author.

BARENESS | TEL AVIV, KING GEORGE, JANUARY 26, 2008

> We are invisible, but not entirely invisible, they know that we're there, that's the point. . . . Then, there are those who walk by and give us thumps up, it happens, not often, but it happens. There are those who throw at us some kind of a curse, you know . . . in the beginning the decision was to be silent, and not to react to the violence, and we tried very hard not to react to the violence unless someone actually attacked us; sometimes it did happen.
>
> Alia Strauss, December 24, 2009

Bareness is about exposing a human being's vulnerability. With no captive audience or public support, using minimal means to project a message, this tactic attempts to reach its audience by merely placing one's body in space. It is a performance of the few; thus, in using this choreography, participants are exposed to the possibility of being attacked or harmed—either physically or emotionally—by the crowd. This departure point—"swimming against the tide" alone or with a few others—enhances the vulnerability of protesters, and this approach is difficult to adopt. However, the vulnerability of humans and their loneliness are exactly what is memorable. This spatial choreography seeks to capture one of people's greatest fears: fragility.

Bareness, like the ritual, is often generated by a closed group of activists presenting a message to the masses. However, bareness involves approaching the crowd, the common people, rather than the ruler, and actors thus often choose to act in everyday places. There are two key reasons for acting in these spaces: (1) The conception of power: actors using this tactic aim to change public opinion from below. They do not aim to accumulate any power in government or to socialize with public figures and media personalities. They do not attempt to participate in the formal decision-making process or to press their message in a conventional manner. (2) The conception of space: daily places provide relative flexibility in defining the array of the act. Protesters using this tactic rarely modify or challenge the spatial rules of a place; spaces are regarded as geographical locations and represent opportunities, acting as channels through which their message can be projected. As such, this type of protest does not generally create an event with a capital *E*, but it can be considered an episode in time-space. "Bareness episodes" might expand spatially (taking place in multiple venues) or temporally (extending their program), but they will retain their modest features and scope.

As a tactic of the few with limited ability to grow, the performative components of such actions are often known in advance by the participants. The action's performative features (e.g., standing, gathering, and singing), dress code, and schedule (i.e., the timing and duration) tend to be minimalistic and distinct. This contributes to activists' visibility in space, which helps expose them to ideologically distant crowds.

Bareness involves being distant and distinct from the crowd. Isolation helps bring activists ideologically and socially close to one another, though this unification is not necessarily free of conflicts and activists are not immediately unified. This tactic is often used in decentralized groups of activists and thus enhances flexibility among actors, geographic spread, and multiplicity. WIB used this tactic, triggered by the outbreak of the First Intifada (1987). The group was formed by a small group of Jerusalemite women. Started as a weekly vigil of women dressed in black, the organization soon became a national network of some thirty vigils across Israel. At the group's peak, the Jerusalem vigil, known to be the largest, was estimated to include some 350–400 activists,[60] with a steep decline after the Gulf War (1991) and an even steeper decline after the Oslo Accords (1993). Today, only four vigils are active,[61] in Jerusalem, Haifa, Tel Aviv, and Gan Shmuel, with 8–15 women participating in each.

Context

In the same spot every Friday, WIB stand in silence with signs from 1:00 to 2:00 p.m. for their weekly vigil. Wearing black to symbolize their mourning for the tragedies suffered by both Israelis and Palestinians, they carry signs with the slogan "Stop the Occupation" in three languages (Hebrew, English, and Arabic).[62] WIB's aim is to convince Israelis that "what happens to the Palestinians is their problem and our problem, and it's hurting us."[63] However, the pain is ideological rather than personal. Fighting against Israeli occupation, these activists do not have direct contact with Palestinian women.

WIB's social positioning in the streets challenged Israeli society's conceptions of women and their bodies. Thus, some passersby made hostile, sexist, and violent comments that predominantly related to the women's bodies, which were regarded as removed from their natural place.[64] This verbal violence and periodic physical assaults characterized the dynamic between vigil participants and the crowd in the early years, and these reactions also influenced the group's spatial choreography. This dynamic reflects patriarchal society in general and Israeli patriarchy in particular, which associates gender with nationalism, religion, and tradition, thus hindering the free participation of women in politics.[65] Today, threats have dissipated, though these women still suffer verbal attacks,[66] and two police officers regularly attend the Jerusalem vigil.

Special significance should be given to the protesters' identities as Israeli citizens. As an Israeli movement, WIB chooses to protest in venues within Israel rather than in the West Bank or the Gaza Strip.[67] The clear majority of WIB activists are Israeli Jewish women between the ages of fifty and eighty,[68] and to become a WIB member, one must fit two eligibility criteria related to gender and nationality/civilian identity. The activists' female identities are regarded as critical and powerful: "In many ways, we prefer to be in a separate movement . . . because, in many movements, when it's men and women, the men just naturally feel that they have the right to be the leaders. It's so natural to them; it's so natural in our society for the men to be the leaders."[69]

The contact among activists involved in the first vigils in 1988 was conducted via general media exposure and through word of mouth among friends. Growth was spontaneous and flexible, and when decision making was required, participants used paper notes that were distributed during the shifts. For communication among participants, WIB has used faxes and, more recently, a Facebook group. The decision to create the Facebook page took place in a meeting held on March 13, 2010, in Jaffa. The thirty participants who arrived were not in full agreement regarding this tool, as most of them did not use Facebook; thus, the 190 members of the Facebook group do not represent all the activists involved in the movement. In addition, though their strategy was successfully "exported" worldwide, WIB does not have an independent website; rather, they have a page on the (Israeli) "Coalition of Women for Peace" website, and a description of their early activities appears on the international website of WIB.

The formation of WIB in the late 1980s should be understood in the context of a wider phenomenon of "autonomous women's peace movement[s]."[70] Various writers analyze the role of the feminist agenda in the formation of WIB, mentioning factors such as inspiration due to the success of women's movements abroad, such as the Mothers of the Plaza de Mayo; the weakness of more traditional forms of protest;[71] and the marginalization of women in mixed-gender political organizations and political life in general.[72]

Place

For WIB, place matters, and their vigils take place at traffic junctions. These sites are not loci of power, that is, "well-established places of public demonstration, or sites of particular contention." Rather, they are "regular" places, which ordinarily do not provoke controversy.[73]

> . . . they got us maximum exposure (i.e., standing in junctions). . . . In Tel Aviv, the first place where Women in Black stood for many years was the Tnuva junction, where . . . several streets come in, and there's a lot of traffic there, and so we stood there . . . then one of the younger women,

> who joined later, was very adamant that we should be in a place where people really could meet pedestrians; there are no pedestrians who go by that junction . . . The women, who, from the beginning have been standing there, didn't want to leave, and so we formed two groups . . . the younger women started standing at the end of Ben Zion Boulevard on Fridays . . . there is really massive pedestrian [movement] on all sides. At some point, after about a year those of us who kept standing at the Tnuva junction realized that we had gone down to approximately 6–7 women, so we said, ok, it's time to join, and we did.[74]

The decision to carry out acts of dissent in small groups at junctions is pragmatic and based on three considerations: (1) proximity, a crucial factor for women with families who want to attend the vigil; (2) familiarity (small, familiar places near their homes); and (3) visibility, where the relatively small scale of these locations enhances their impact. Their mere silent presence in the mundane space, wearing black, helps them to stand out from the crowd. In WIB, the body plays a significant role in personalizing the struggle. The body is marked and not taken for granted; the body is the message—knowledge is performed and communicated through the protesting body. In their black clothing, WIB activists project images that confound existing cultural codes and thus become more difficult to tolerate because they challenge the daily appearance of secular women.

The essence of this approach is replicated in different ways nationwide, and the map of the vigil locations shows the many sites of these coordinated acts, which are all located within Israel's boundaries before the 1967 war. These two spheres—the physical and geographical—are the group's focus and mirror its aim to attract a crowd.

Over the history of the movement, bareness can be considered one of its underlying principles, and WIB neither accumulated any power in government nor socialized with public figures or media personalities. The women never attempted to participate in the formal decision-making process or to pressure officials in a conventional manner.[75]

Event

Each WIB vigil is absolutely autonomous, and its participants are able to determine the time, place, and composition of the shift and are responsible for placards and signage. In annual meetings, WIB members hold general discussions about the situation on the ground and members' new initiatives. This diffuse structure is based on the personal relationships within each vigil group, which enhance members' commitment to smaller groups. For example, almost from the very beginning, the Jerusalem vigil stood in a round plaza commonly known as "Paris Square" (officially: "France Square"). The square is located at the intersection of five roads facing the Franciscan College of Terra Sancta on one side and the Kings Hotel on the other; the square is only a few minutes' walking distance from the prime minister's official residence. Many cars pass by the square, and pedestrians pass through it and along its perimeter.[76] Different from the Jerusalem vigil, the Tel Aviv vigil switched locations in the mid-1990s. The original location was a traffic island on a busy street on the eastern border of the city. The vigil moved from a four-lane road with heavy automobile traffic to a junction located at the end of a small boulevard in the city center. This new location has more pedestrian movement, especially on Fridays. Both locations, in Jerusalem and Tel Aviv, reflect WIB's choices, specifically, places that are not formally defined and do not have their own symbolic meaning.

The vigils' symbolism is a straightforward gesture that includes three major features: a black outfit, which "symbolizes the tragedy of both peoples, the Israeli and Palestinian";[77] hand-shaped signs, stating "Stop the Occupation" in one of three languages: Hebrew, Arabic, and English, and the female identity. Some of their signs also portray the female symbol (♀) combined with the peace symbol (☮),[78] and the women stand in silence facing the crowd (cars or pedestrians).[79]

In essence, vigils eliminate class discrimination among participants. All the women play the same role during the event. In the early years, verbal assaults and physical violence characterized the dynamic between vigil participants and the crowd, which led to a police presence at some of the vigils. According to an internal document from the Jerusalem vigil, the police responded to 75 percent of its requests for protection.[80] In the early years, when larger vigils were threatened with violence, the Jerusalem vigil—the largest in Israel—appointed one of its participants to act as an usher during its demonstrations. At that time, participants were specifically asked to avoid confrontations and to react nonviolently. Although some vigils (e.g., Haifa) were harassed by police, their reactions to police during the vigils seems to have been based on a policy of cooperation as long as they were allowed to proceed with their vigils at the set locations.[81] Today, threats have become scarce, though the group still suffers some verbal assaults.[82]

> . . . right away, at the beginning, there was one woman who took it upon herself to be in contact with the police, and there were times when the police came, mainly in the early years, and maybe had a car somewhere watching. Because we have a right to hold a vigil—if you have less than fifty people and you don't have any sound equipment—then it's perfectly legal to hold a vigil, and it's not legal to attack other people. So [the police] would come and protect, but I have in my bag, I have the number, anything happens . . . if someone decides to attack us, I can call that number.[83]

Distance

Being ideologically distant from the mainstream, WIB uses this spatial choreography to change the discourse from below. With no grand motives, WIB hopes to create a event-space that will be distinct and perhaps evoke discursive change, increasing public awareness of a cause that might be perceived as abstract. Bareness is based on interpersonal relations and personal networks, which are crucial for recruiting individuals to high-risk activism.[84] Either way, actors using bareness seek proximity and interactions with people in space. This proximity to other people can best be achieved in everyday, informal places rather than symbolic spaces associated with the power of the regime. However, bareness is about forming a "closed crowd," a group of activists that emphasizes permanence over growth. For this purpose, it defines boundaries and rules, and "it establishes itself by accepting its limitation. It creates a space for itself which it will fill."[85] Thus, it always keeps its distance from the crowd and the regime. It sacrifices its chance of growth but gains control over its actions and the ability to maintain a clear, direct, and uncompromised message in time and space. This purity is both the tactic's strength and its weakness. Thus, although bareness is spatially positioned in the mundane and the concrete, it remains distant from the people and the power, and thus it often remains an abstract call.

BARENESS | Tel Aviv, King George, January 26, 2008

ATTRIBUTES

- Physical Vulnerability
- Spatial Informality
- Reserved Communication

Figure 6.14. Vigils stand in traffic junctions. These sites are "regular" places, which ordinarily do not provoke controversy. Women in Black, Tel Aviv, January 2008. Photo by author.

Figure 6.15. *Left:* Women in Black (Nachshon Vigil). Photo by Yair Gil. *Right:* Women in Black Pin. Daphna Kaminer's Archival Collection.

Key Features	**King George/Ben Zion crossroads**
Location	Crossroads all over Israel
Buildings/activities	Vehicle and pedestrian movement
Space	~700 sq. meters (including roads)
Key value/concern	Informal, mundane
Spatial definition within the city	Hectic crossroad of vehicles and pedestrians

Table 6.5. Key Features and Spatial Attributes.

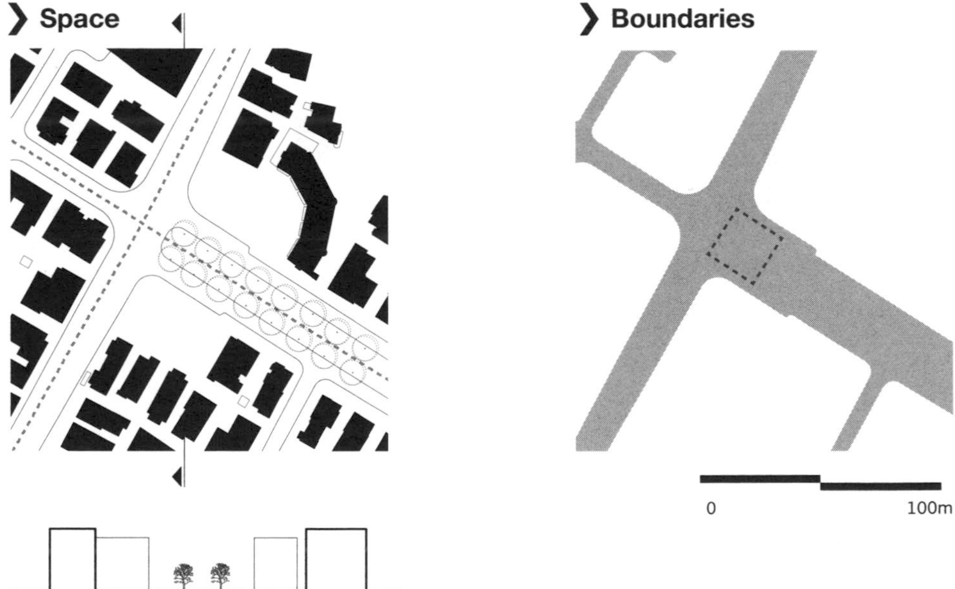

Figure 6.16. King George/Ben Zion crossroads: Built form and space. Illustration by author.

Distance	Geography	Key spots in the city center
	Physical	Informal distance between protesters and crowd
	Meaning	Bringing the reality of Palestinians (who are mentally perceived as distant) to everyday Israeli contexts

Table 6.6. Event and the Conceptualization of Distance.

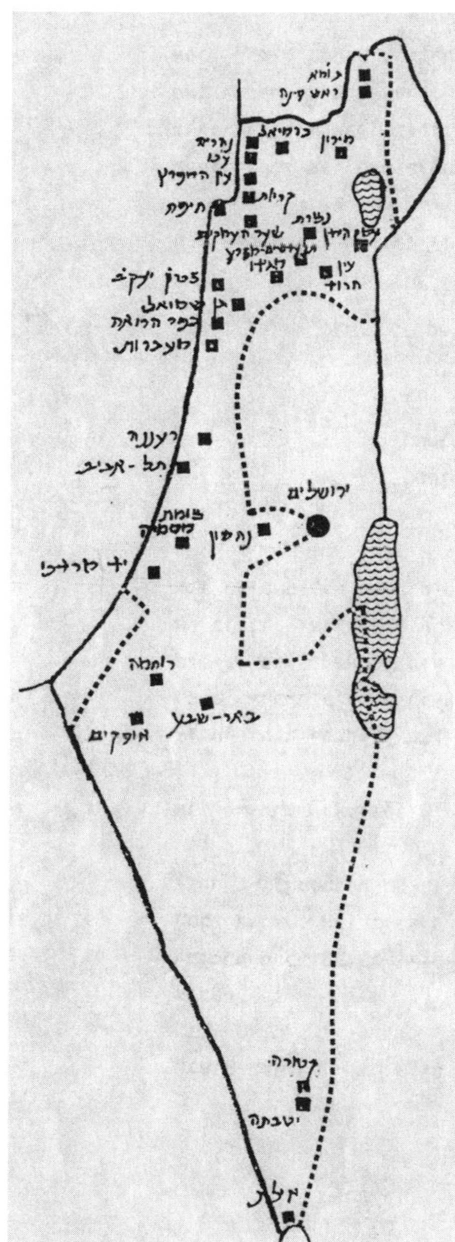

Figure 6.17. Map of vigils, June 18, 1990. Photo from the Dafna and Reuven Kaminer Collection.

1. Gome Junction (North)
2. Rosh Pina (Village)
3. Meiron (Village)
4. Nahariya (City)
5. Acre (City)
6. Ein Hamifratz (Kibbutz)
7. Kiryat Bialik (City)
8. Haifa (City)
9. Shaar Hammakim (Kibbutz)
10. Nazareth (City)
11. Emek Hayarden (Kibbutz)
12. Tel Adashim—Mizra (Village + Kibbutz)
13. Ein Harod (Kibbutz)
14. Megiddo (Area of small villages)
15. Zichron Yaakov (City)
16. Gan shmuel (Kibbutz)
17. Cfar Haroee (Village)
18. Maabarot (Kibbutz)
19. Raanana (City)
20. Tel Aviv (City)
21. Nachshon (Kibbutz)
22. Jerusalem (City)
23. Yad Mordechai (Kibbutz)
24. Ruchama (Kibbutz)
25. Beer Sheva (City)
26. Ofakim (City)
27. Ktora (Kibbutz)
28. Yotvata (Kibbutz)
29. Eilat (City)
30. Masmiha (Near Gedera City)
31. Karmiel (City)

Figure 6.18. The decision to carry out acts of dissent in small groups at junctions is pragmatic and based on three considerations: (1) proximity; (2) familiarity; (3) visibility. *Top:* Women in Black, Haifa. Photos by Yair Gil. *Bottom:* Women in Black, Tel Aviv. Photos by author.

ميني ماركت الكمال
ميني ماركت الكمال
מיני מרקט אלכמל
ساندويشات * مواد غذائيه * مواد تنظيف وكل مستلزمات البيت
بس ولادي وبناتي
لجميع الاجيال
050-46898

7 Processions

Previous page: Putting one foot in front of the other produces magnified rhythms of sound, creating a dynamic performance that enhances social bonding. Shown is a protest against the war in Gaza, Baqa al Gharbiya, Israel, August 1, 2009. Photo by author.

TARGET | ISTANBUL, TAKSIM SQUARE, MAY 1, 1977

> As a central location in Istanbul, compared with other spaces, Taksim's distance can be said to have equal weight vis-à-vis the periphery. Until the 1st of May of 1976 and 1977, in general, the meetings centrally held in Istanbul, beginning with the meetings of political parties, used to take place in Taksim. . . . The reason that we chose Taksim is because of its central location, the transportation being easier compared with other places, and also because it could be viewed by its surroundings; we thought that its impact would be higher.
>
> Mehmet Karaca, 2005

Protests that consider targeting as a spatial choreography aim to "conquer the city" by reclaiming city streets through processions that end at defined, known, and symbolic locations. The procession's start and end points are equally meaningful. As with military powers, space is seen through a geographical lens. The city is regarded as a battlefield that is a composite of multiple parts. However, this multiplicity is not without order; even if they are not hierarchically organized, the procession paths include significant landmarks and desired targets. Accordingly, the procession's spatial strategy includes special attention to the different parts of the city and their connectivity and proximity to the gathering place (often a symbolic location or a locus of power). So the protest's physical manifestation is the outcome of a plan or schedule that is designed to attain a defined objective.

The concept of distance is primarily associated with the physical and geographical meanings, that is, remoteness or the degree of remoteness, in any relationship to which spatial terms are transferred or figuratively applied. In terms of an event's spatial design, the target tactic requires high familiarity with the city's spatial array. Choosing the paths to take toward a congregational central point is a crucial component in choreographing the event and reducing the distance between the city's geographical center and its periphery. This spatial approach requires careful coordination, scheduling, and planning of the physical distance between locations, which is based on a particular hierarchical reading of the city that focuses on scale and linearity.

This spatial choreography for events seeks to be etched in the collective memory or to achieve a consensus regarding a particular societal discourse. To create an impact, this choreography requires many participants and disciplinary tools that allow the organizers to control and manage the event. It shares many characteristics with the theatrical choreography, though in much more complex and dynamic ways.

Thus, the visual-aesthetic dimension is central in developing a sense of rhyme and pattern for the overall event.

The target choreography implies careful preparation, including audience recruitment, security precautions, permits to use public spaces, the support of local police forces, and substantial funding. Thus, in executing these protests, political leadership is essential, and hierarchy among actors is maintained throughout the event. This approach was used in the May Day demonstration that was organized by the Confederation of Progressive Trade Unions of Turkey (DISK in Turkish) in 1977. Thousands assembled to celebrate that day, and many were killed in the chaos that ensued. The assailants, who took the lives of thirty-four[1] people and who were responsible for hundreds of casualties, were not (and have not been) identified. However, this tragedy did not deter equally large crowds from showing up again on May 1, 1978. However, in 1979, the government thwarted a massive May Day demonstration by imposing a citywide curfew and stationing a regiment of soldiers in the square. May Day celebrations in the square were banned until 2009.

Place

Taksim means "allocation," and the name derives from the water distribution chamber located there. The dams, aqueducts, and fountains that bring water to Istanbul are centuries old; as the city grew, new systems were added. The construction of the Taksim water system began during the reign of Mahmut I (1730–1754), and it was completed during the reign of Mahmut II in 1839.[2] From the Taksim distribution center, water was sent to different districts of the city. Artillery barracks and a courtyard, originally built between 1803 and 1806, occupied a large portion of the site. The barracks were rebuilt and renovated several times because of damage from uprisings and fires, but they were ultimately demolished.[3] During World War I, the barracks were abandoned; after 1921, the courtyard became a stadium, and the interior of the barracks was used for casinos and workshops. In 1940, the building was demolished to create an open space for a park. Apart from the barracks and the water reservoir, cemeteries also occupied the open space. However, the Beyoglu district expanded, and new, upscale residences were built around Taksim, close to the lively Western lifestyle of Beyoglu.

Weakened after many years of ongoing warfare, the Ottoman Empire was occupied by foreign powers after World War I. Then, led by Mustafa Kemal Atatürk, the Turkish War of Independence began in the cities of Asia Minor. The powers of the Entente, or Allies, occupied Istanbul on March 16, 1920, and they remained there for two years (until 1922). The last meeting of the Ottoman Parliament was on March 18, 1920, and the Grand National Assembly of Turkey opened in Ankara on April 23, 1920, under the leadership of Mustafa Kemal Atatürk and several of his friends from Istanbul, who had escaped the occupation. With the declaration of a new constitution on January 20, 1921, Ankara became the new capital of Turkey. On October 29, 1923, the new regime was declared a republic, and a new ideology of progress, modernization, secularization, and nation building held sway. Until 1946, single-party rule dictated how Turkey was spatially organized.[4] New railroads connected outlying localities, uniting them in a "national space," and cities were organized according to the social, political, and cultural institutions that spread the new ideals across the nation. Modernity was also reflected in changes in the city's physical forms and in the architecture.[5] Expressing the aspirations of the young republic, plans were made and implemented in Ankara, the new capital, which included monumental new buildings and styles. The state's power derived from decision making that was based on the norms of modern knowledge and the centralized distribution of resources. During the 1930s, municipal laws were passed for the appropriation of land and for its financing. Plans for large cities were mandatory, and professional architects and engineers undertook the construction of new buildings.[6] Inevitably, the application of these new laws was another matter, given the government's limited resources; in addition, how much (or how little) the new ideology was internalized by large segments of the population is debatable.[7]

Taksim Square, built in 1926, was the first square with the first monument to be planned and designed in the new republic. The Italian architect Giulio Mongeri designed the base of the monument and the landscaping around it, and the Italian sculptor Pietro Canonica created the statue of Atatürk surrounded by his friends during the War of Independence.[8] The Grand Rue de Pera (known previously as Cadde-I Kebir), leading from Beyoglu to Taksim, became İstiklalCaddesi (Liberty Street), while the street by the water reservoir and the barracks (known previously as Barracks Street), leading to Pangaltı, became CumhuriyetCaddesi (Avenue of the Republic). Renaming perhaps cannot completely erase memory, but it does create a new language through which younger generations dictate and relearn the meaning of the space.

Taksim Square, along with its monument, did not reduce the vast space in front of the barracks; instead, this loose spatial definition and its political symbolism—as an embodiment of the universal ideals of civic rights, secularism, and progress—make the square a potent site for popular action.

City growth and development continued to affect the spatial form of the square. In 1930, when an international competition was held for land-use planning in Istanbul, the winner of the competition, Herman Elgötz, proposed major replanning of Taksim Square, but his plans were not implemented. In 1936, Henri Prost, one of the planners in the competition, was offered the task. He accepted, and his plans for Beyoglu were implemented in 1939.[9] Between 1939 and 1949, the planning and rebuilding of Istanbul continued along the modernist lines designed by professionals. Prost offered to expand Taksim Square, with the Monument of the Republic and the narrow circular space surrounding it as its defining features, by razing the barracks and building spectacular public buildings (e.g., exhibition halls) and broad boulevards.[10] Interestingly, Prost designated the historic area of the city for public ceremonies rather than Taksim. In his plans, Taksim would abide by narrower definitions, functions, and uses of modernity, namely, the political representational forms that aimed to involve and reach the masses.[11]

The year 1950 marked the beginning of the post–World War II era. The multiparty regime, the liberalization of the economy, the aid from the Marshall Plan, new highways to replace railroads, and the growing population brought about the formulation of rural areas with large cities. The new party, which replaced the previous regime, pursued populist cultural and economic policies. Between 1950 and 1960, Istanbul's population nearly doubled, approaching two million. The political ideology of space did not seek to symbolize the new, modern nation; it instead regarded space as an economic resource for liberal interests. Land speculation increased due to major migration to the city, and Istanbul was once more becoming the leading city for commerce and industry. Large boulevards were constructed across the historic area, connecting it to other parts of the city with no consideration for its historical significance. Several neighborhoods were erased in the process. Along the new boulevards, dense construction took place without regard to style or quality.[12] In the early 1940s, a new park had been constructed in Taksim (based on Prost's plans), which replaced the old barracks. It was named for Mustafa İsmet İnönü, Atatürk's second in command in the earlier regime, who became president after Atatürk's death. When the new regime came to power, a plinth for a monument to İnönü already existed. However, the new regime changed the name of the park and rejected the monument, and Taksim's image changed once again. As in the 1920s, the discourse of political power in the 1950s erased Taksim's representational form once again.[13] It was again an open space, a *meydan* for the rising tide of newcomers to Istanbul, whose aspirations differed from those of the power elite.

Regarding Taksim Square, three points should be emphasized: (1) With its huge concrete plateau surrounded by offices, banks, international hotels, and prestige projects (e.g., the opera house and art gallery), the square does not position individuals in a meaningful social hierarchy. Rather than an abstract space, it is a lively, inclusive space, a place bustling with traffic and people, both locals and tourists. Its vastness and diverse facilities allow for different activities—sitting near the monument or in a café, shopping, eating, and commuting.[14] (2) This place maintains a reciprocal *daily* relationship between the space and the crowd's trajectories, which gives it meaning and defines its role in the city. (3) The square and its surroundings are dynamic places that are constantly evolving and developing and are influenced by national and local political dynamics. However, due to the square's significance to the Turkish people, modifications and changes to it are contested and constantly challenged.[15]

Context

Ottoman rulers were familiar with political upheavals and demonstrations, especially in times of economic hardship or modernization of the army and the state. Masses often gathered around familiar spaces such as army barracks and mosques. The most hospitable of such spaces was the Beyazit Meydani (Beyazit Square) in the historical peninsula, with its proximity to the market, the Beyazit Mosque, and institutions of learning. This proximity was effective for both reactionary demonstrations against social change and revolutionary changes against a conservative regime. An example of the former was the funeral of Marşal Fevzi Çakmak, an opponent of the single-party regime, at the Beyazit Mosque and its aftermath, and an example of the latter was the 1958 student and intellectual demonstration against the rule of the Democrat Party.[16]

After the military coup of 1960, a new constitution was adopted in 1961, which laid the foundation for the separation of powers, on the one hand, and for the civic organizations that clamored for economic and democratic rights (e.g., labor unions and other professional organizations), on the other hand. The import-substitution models of economic growth encouraged the development of cities around growing industries. The new constitution weakened the power of governments, which, more often than not, were coalitions of various small parties. The unstable political governance and deepening economic crisis of the 1970s were concomitant with the clash between the municipal powers, whose electorate leaned toward the left, and the right-wing center that pursued patron-client relations in favor of populist support systems. City centers, streets, and public institutions (such as universities) became battlefields for different groups that organized along different political lines. As the city with the largest population and the most social organizations, Istanbul was inevitably the stage for the largest demonstrations.

The Turkish word for "demonstration" is *gösteri*, which can also be translated as "stage performance." Hence, political protests by crowds in city spaces are referred to as "protest demonstrations" (*protestogösterileri* in Turkish), and these events were frequent, large, and well organized during the 1970s. New roads and transport facilities made Taksim accessible as a focal stage; people would converge there, and the protest demonstrations would end with public speeches. If we accept that protest is a method of involving people in political partnerships, then we must also accept that protest has a specific *form*, which is negotiated both by particular groups and by a regime. Thus, understanding the spatial dynamics of protests is not simply a question of control, legality, or collective behavior. It is about reclaiming national, local, or communal spaces and their symbolic attributes.

From the perspective of the politics of place, May 1 celebrations have extended beyond Taksim's geographical boundaries. Starting from the two boundaries of the city, with Taksim as the meeting point, the demonstration procession reclaimed the city as part of its universalist discourse on labor. From a historical perspective, mass demonstrations that celebrated May 1 as a labor day were allowed from 1910 to 1912 under Ottoman rule and from 1921 to 1923 and 1976 to 1978 under the Republic.[17] In other years, although some spontaneous demonstrations occurred, the government repressed these events and punished those who participated in them. In 1976, DISK organized the May 1 demonstration in the social and political climate described above. No major incidents occurred, and, in the following year, the event was rescheduled, this time with widespread publicity.

Event

DISK's general plan was to reclaim city streets in the form of a procession ending at a defined, known, and symbolic location.[18] The idea was to approach Taksim from two points in the city, gathering in Besiktas and moving via Barbaros Boulevard and Saraçhane Square and across the Golden Horn, eventually meeting in a large central location: Taksim Square. The accessibility of the starting points via public transport increased the event's visibility and impact.[19] The meeting was also a focal event at the national level, with participants coming not only from Istanbul and the Marmara region, where industry is dense, but also from all over Turkey. The crowd (400,000 people, according to some estimates) was heterogeneous and included, apart from DISK members, unions from the Confederation of Turkish Trade Unions (TÜRK-İŞ), members of independent unions, teachers' associations, technical personnel, architecture and engineering associations, authors, artists, lawyers, doctors, youth groups, and women's associations.

Planned as a dynamic performance, the demonstration was citywide, creating a unique overlap of urban settings and cultural codes of collective behavior in a state-citizenship context. The entire city played a role, as is often the case with demonstrations or parades, with Taksim Square serving as a key reference point.

> Where and how the 1st of May was going to be celebrated was decided on and the central organizing committee, mentioned above [i.e., DISK], was established. Following this, what demands would be brought forward in that particular year, the contents of the banners and the pankarts (those things that they carry with the slogans written on them, couldn't find the word in English), slogans were decided upon. Of course, if there were demands coming from below and if these did not contradict the decisions of the center, they were also considered. These preparations of 1976 and 1978, the preparations of the publications, the posters, their distribution across the country, etc., took approximately two months.[20]

At 9:00 a.m., the crowds began to gather at the two starting points, with their own flags and *pankarts* (placards). Celebrations began, which included music and dancing. At 1:00 p.m., in organized processions, the crowds marched along the prescribed routes. They sang national and international marching songs in unison. All along the route, young actors gave street performances. Economic and democratic rights were demanded; political slogans were shouted; and there was a festive atmosphere.

A stage with microphones, flags, and posters had been set up in Taksim Square at the entrance to the park, thus creating a focal point in that vast space. At 3:00 p.m., the president of DISK, Kemal Türkler, was to deliver his speech on the significance of the day and on the workers' demands for economic and democratic rights. However, the procession took longer than expected to reach the square. Meanwhile, in the square, the sound system was blasting marching music and folk songs. Sitki Coskun, DISK's organizer and office manager, stage-managed the event. In between the musical pieces, he read poems by Nâzim Hikmet (a left-wing poet who died in exile) amid the excited cheers of the participants. The president's speech was scheduled for 3:00 p.m. However, because the marchers' arrival was delayed, he began speaking at approximately 5:00 p.m.; even then, the Tarlabası branch of the procession had not yet reached Taksim.

To understand what happened next, it is necessary to understand the "order" of the procession and the ways in which it gave a new meaning to the place and to the participants. By "order," two interrelated systems are evoked, that of the assembly and that of the space. The order of the assembly and its ritual components (marching, gathering, and singing), dress code, and schedule (i.e., the timing and duration of the event) represented how the participants saw themselves—on the one hand, as supporters of the universal discourse of the left, and, on the other hand, as a community of different fragments of society and the working classes. It was an orderly celebration on a national scale. The order of the procession was both a mechanism for constructing meaning and a device for negotiations between the state and citizens.

The discursive order of the assembly considered the order of the city—its topography, boundaries, traffic movement, and buildings (including governmental buildings, religious buildings, and residential homes). Naturally, the routes were temporarily adapted to the order of the assembly, with barriers, blocked routes, and adjusted traffic rules to regulate the crowd's movement. Order was also maintained externally (by the police) and internally (by DISK), as a precaution to avert any potential violence. Thus, in addition to the police force, there were around 20,000 workers from factories and DISK members deployed to maintain security. They were identifiable by their red aprons. They did not carry guns; they only carried the poles supporting their banners. Their responsibilities were to maintain order, to prevent the possible infiltration of unknown outsiders, and to prevent any assaults by outsiders. Order, both for the assembly (maintained by DISK and the state) and for the space (the city and the square), was incredibly important, not only serving as a device of control but also creating new meanings for those who had gathered. This overlapping order (of the assembly and of the space) and the sheer scale of the event endowed the procession with enormous significance, appropriating and altering the square's meaning for good.

However, the extent of the subsequent violence marked the enduring meaning of the event. Mehmet Karaca described the violence as follows:

> Although I can't say the precise time, President Kemal Turkler's speech ended at around 6 o'clock. It ended with an invitation to a one-minute silence in respect for the memory of those who had lost their lives in the struggle for the cause of workers' rights. In that moving moment of respect, in that huge, totally packed space in the Taksim Square, total silence reigned. The sound of a gunshot, coming from somewhere around the entrance to Taksim from the Tarlabasi direction broke that silence. Then everything started, with that first shot.[21]

The first gunshot was followed by others and by the arrival of armored police vehicles, approaching from Siraselviler and Istiklal Boulevards and advancing toward the crowds in the square, firing sound bombs with high-pitched sirens. The bombs and the continuous sirens from the armored vehicles created a mass panic, resulting in several people being trampled by the crowd and others being crushed under police vehicles.

The celebratory event ended in tragedy and resulted in restrictions on mass protests thereafter. As a result, the monumental nature of this particular point in time-space increased in the collective memory of Turkish citizens: a monument that is neither an object nor an assemblage of diverse objects but a social space, defined by what happened there and, in turn, by what did not and may not happen there (prescribed/proscribed, scene/obscene).[22] No matter how temporary the appropriation was or how permanently its traces were eradicated, the very existence of the demonstration on May 1, 1977, with the memories and associations that it evokes, has permanently changed the face of Taksim Square.

The assailants were not (and have not been) identified. However, this tragedy did not deter equally large crowds from showing up again on May 1, 1978. However, in 1979, the government thwarted a massive May Day demonstration by imposing a citywide curfew and stationing a regiment of soldiers in the square. May Day celebrations in the square were banned until 2009. This political show of force "was intended to threaten and challenge not only the working class but all progressive forces. Conversely, it has helped to convince the general public of the existence of such a danger."[23]

After the turmoil of the 1970s, 1980 started with a major fracture in Turkish history. In February 1980, liberal economic policies replaced import substitution models of economic growth, and policies supporting an export-oriented market economy were implemented in the face of an economic depression and political upheaval. On September 12, 1980, a military coup took place, abolishing political parties and social organizations and banning public gatherings in spaces that even remotely implied political aims. In 1981, a new constitution was written under the watchful gaze of the military, restricting political democracy and easing the transition toward a liberal economy. This constitution has been modified several times, although residues of it remain.[24]

Distance

The target spatial choreography perceives cities as complex, fragmented entities. This choreography involves the creation of an inclusive map of action that captures the city's diverse geographies. The target is a hybrid tactic that combines a procession with a spectacle. It is based on a geographical configuration, which connects and bridges different ends and groups in the city. The event's geographical location and its architectural and symbolic features are crucial, and, in most cases, protests that use this tactic choose places that are associated with power. As a major endower, the target suits large-scale events in which all the key actors and participants are aware of their roles in the performance, showing support for an agreed-upon message. Successfully using this tactic requires an a priori defined plan, lengthy preparation, and significant funding. Similar to theater choreography, target choreography also has a captive crowd; however, in this case, the body has multiple roles and tasks, and participation is physically demanding.

Figure 7.1. Daily life in Taksim Square; at the back is a monument to the republic. Photo by author.

 **TARGET** | Istanbul, Taksim Square, May 1, 1977

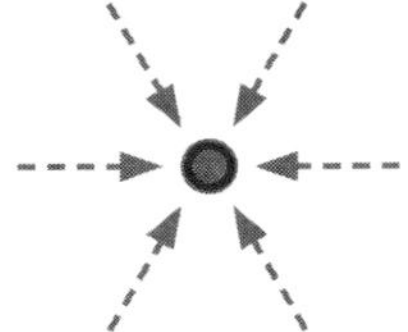

ATTRIBUTES

- Assigned Roles
- Symbolic Reclaiming
- Coordinated Performance

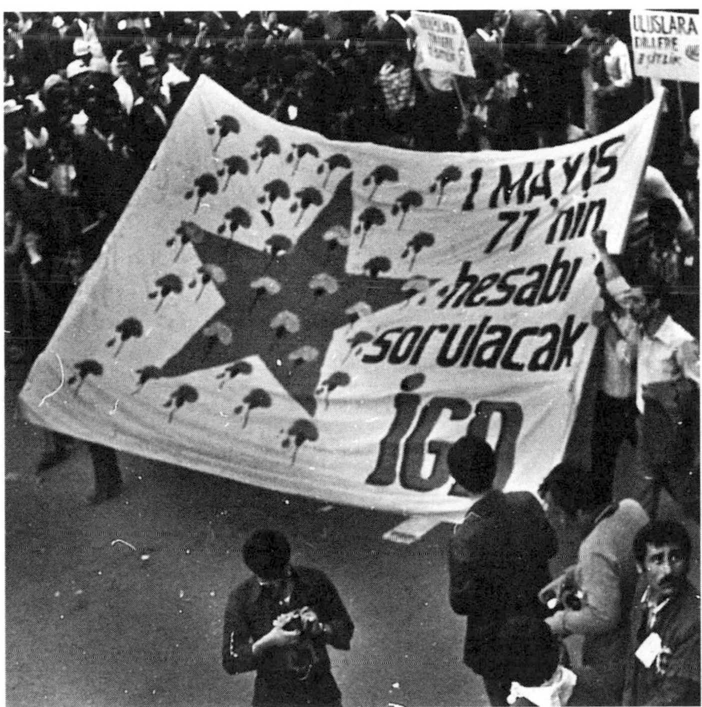

Figure 7.2. At 1:00 p.m., in organized processions, the crowds marched along the prescribed routes. A detail from the procession, Istanbul, 1977. Photo from Cengiz Kahraman Collection, Istanbul.

Figures 7.3 and 7.4. *Left:* A monument to the republic, Taksim Square, 2006. *Right:* Taksim Square from above, 2006. Photos by author.

Key Features	**Taksim Square**
Location	Situated in the European part of Istanbul, Turkey
Buildings/activities	Government/ national structures, symbolic monuments, recreation
Space	~20,500 sq. meters
Key value/concern	A major tourist and leisure district famed for its restaurants, shops, and hotels
Spatial definition within the city	The heart of modern Istanbul

Table 7.1. Taksim Square: Built form and space. Illustration by author.

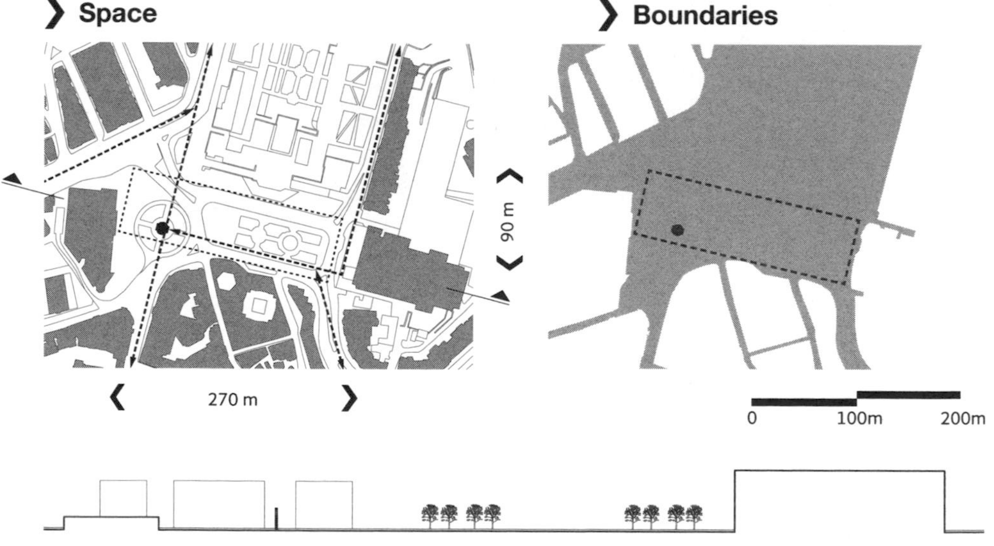

Figure 7.5. Taksim Square: Built form and space. Illustration by author.

Distance	Geography	The paths of processions towards the central gathering point as a means of reducing the distance between the center and the periphery
	Physical	Using the different parts of the city and their connectivity to the gathering place
	Meaning	"Conquering" the city by reclaiming a defined and known symbolic location

Table 7.2. Event and the Conceptualization of Distance.

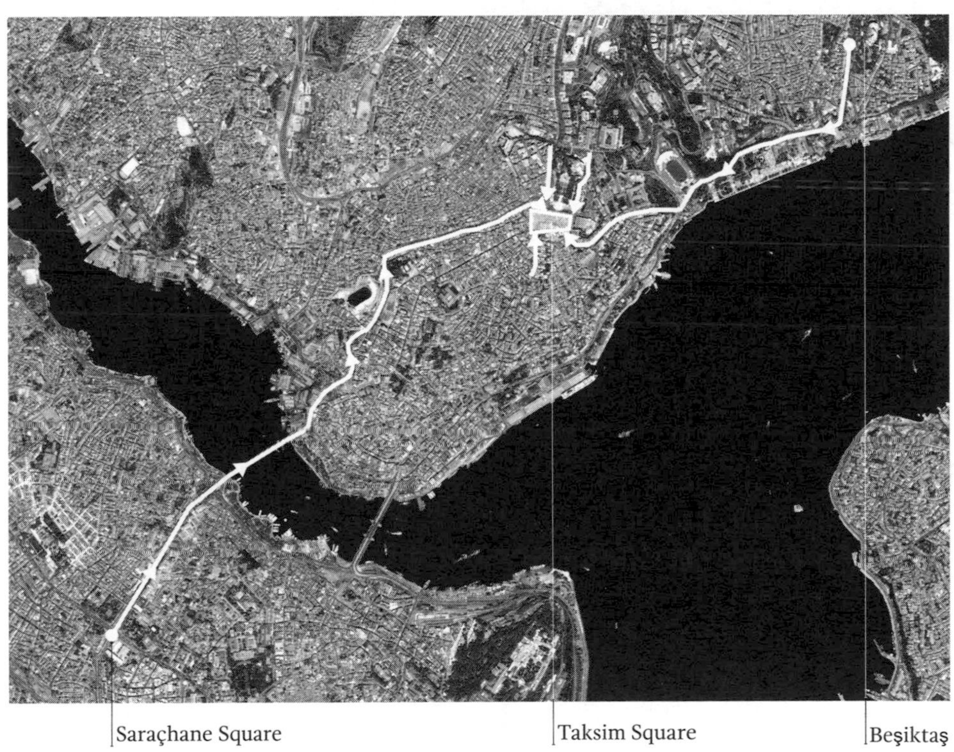

Figure 7.6. Aerial view of the procession route. On the morning of the meeting, the workers and other participants, under their own banners, flags, and placards, met at two key points. Those who met in Besiktas were to march by way of Dolmabahçe, through Gumussuyu Street, ending in Taksim Square; the others were to arrive via the Unkapani Bridge, from the direction of Tepebasi and Tarlabas. Illustration by author.

Figure 7.7. *Left*: Images from the procession, 1977. Photos from Cengiz Kahraman Collection, Istanbul.

Figure 7.8. *Bottom*: Panic after the shooting and the bloody end of the meeting, 1977. Photo from Cengiz Kahraman Collection, Istanbul.

CONJOINING | LEIPZIG, AUGUSTUSPLATZ, OCTOBER 9, 1989

Karl-Marx-Platz was the large, open square that was more easily and more quickly reachable compared to Marktplatz, and, furthermore, the police were standing in such a way each time that they were blocking the way to Marktplatz. It wasn't possible to reach Marktplatz because it was the central square. Thus, it was necessary to make a detour away from the city center and travel outwards toward the Ring. It was the movement away from the police because they blocked the street and for a long time; it was not possible to break through the blockade.

Rainer Müller, January 24, 2007

Conjoining is a coordinated tactic, which takes time to evolve. Its spatial manifestation is a spectacle of people marching through the city in the form of a ring. Conjoining is a tactic that requires density. Just a few people cannot create an impact. During this type of protest, each participant primarily sees the multiple heads of other participants; participants are presenting themselves to one another. The spatial form of the ring, with its different points of entrance and exit, implies closure and boundlessness, proximity and endlessness. This spatial configuration reconfirms the power of the participants, thus sending a decisive message to the rulers.

The conjoining choreography is based on deep familiarity with and sensitivity to the city's infrastructure. The city and the people are not considered separate; they are instead regarded as one entity. However, rather than smooth or unified, the ring is built from multiple adjacent points that are regarded as one ring. Along the ring, there are points of punctuation marked by landmarks or institutions and entry points where people can join in or withdraw from the event. These points affect the rhythm of the movement, which is crucial to the creation of the event's image. Gaps in the ring might result in disintegration and possible subsequent dispersal. Thus, when successful, no distance or gaps exist between people, and this ring might be considered a closed entity, "doubly closed, to the world outside and in itself."[25] The design of such an event requires careful appreciation and analysis of a city's infrastructure as a means of creating a planned sequence. Thus, though minimalist in its intervention in space, this spatial choreography's effect is monumental.

The conjoining tactic is the outcome of a social process and thus evolves. It brings different groups—aggregates—from different settings to develop a synchronized performance on a city scale. The Monday demonstrations were a series of peaceful political protests against the socialist government of the German

Democratic Republic (GDR), and they used the conjoining tactic. After regular prayers for peace in the Nikolai Church in Leipzig, the demonstrations began on September 4, 1989, and they eventually filled the nearby downtown Karl Marx Square (today known again as Augustusplatz). Informed by (West German) television and friends about the events, people in other East German cities began repeating the Leipzig demonstration, meeting at city squares on Monday evenings. By October 9, 1989, just after the fortieth anniversary celebrations of the GDR, what had begun as a few hundred gatherers at the Nikolai Church swelled to more than 70,000, all united in peaceful opposition to the regime. That day, East Germany also saw demonstrations in Dresden, Halle, and Lindow Magdeburg. The next week, 120,000 showed up in Leipzig, with military units again held on standby in the vicinity. A week later, the number more than doubled to 320,000, proving that most of the population opposed the regime. This pressure led to the fall of the Berlin Wall on November 9, 1989, marking the imminent fall of the socialist GDR regime.

Context

In the late 1980s, a dissident movement had evolved in the GDR, the socialist state that was established in the Soviet zone of occupied Germany following World War II. The GDR was a repressive regime supported by the Ministry of State Security (Stasi),[26] which consisted of a network of approximately 85,000 full-time employees and over 100,000 informants, who collected vast amounts of information to intimidate citizens and to eliminate any active opposition. Under GDR rule, information was limited, and the overall policy glorified the conditions in the GDR. The movement began because of people's increasing disillusion with the regime, and the disjunction between the slogans that celebrated the GDR as a model of socialism and their own daily experiences.[27] The city of Leipzig was a focal point in the movement, which contributed significantly to the final demise of the GDR and German reunification in 1990.

The evolution in Leipzig may be explained by a combination of several factors, including the city's role as a center for theology students, which encouraged their involvement and enabled them to serve as mediators between the church and the activists.[28] In particular, the dissident movement depended heavily on the Lutheran Church, which at that time enjoyed an intermediate status in the GDR. During the early years, the atheist socialist regime was hostile to the church of its establishment; nevertheless, in later years, the regime reached a detente with the church, which was formalized in a 1979 agreement entitled "Church of Socialism," which normalized the relations between the state and the largest religious organization based on "primacy of state interests."[29] This status enabled opposition groups to gather in churches. In a sense, the movement evolved around the church, though not directly from it, and persistent tension exists between the different agendas of the young activists who eventually led the way and the church's voice. This tension is directly addressed in the testimony of Christian Führer, a pastor who focuses on the political and institutional context of the events, and Rainer Müller, an activist who perceives the political upheaval from personal and environmental perspectives.

Christian Führer, the pastor, describes the movement as follows:

> In 1980, a protest movement developed among the Protestant churches in the East and West against the placement of middle-range ballistic missiles, and it was this that spurred the movement Friedensdekade (Decade of Peace). There were ten days in autumn, which were especially dedicated to reflection, personal involvement, and prayers for peace. . . . And in 1981, together with the city-youth pastor, I arranged a midnight devotional prayer. We thought that only a few would come, but there were about 130 who came—unusual youth—most of whom had never been in the church. . . . That was in autumn of 1981, and it was the decisive opening of the church. The Friedensdekade and the opening of the church for the unconventional and protest groups in the country as a result of this devotional midnight prayer, and the next important step, beginning in 1982, was the desire of the base groups to have a peace prayer every Monday in the Nikolaikirche. Not just on special occasions, not just for the Friedensdekade, but rather every Monday beginning on September 20, 1982.[30]

The activist Rainer Müller offers a different perspective:

> I grew up in an area thirty to forty kilometers south of Leipzig, in an area of brown coal surface mining and chemical industry where a large amount of environmental destruction and polluting was going on. Where every summer a village was bulldozed away and disappeared in the brown coal surface mining. So, villages were being destroyed and many people took their lives; every year in our village someone died because of hopelessness. . . . The relationship was always tense. It was always a conflict between those people who were active in the church groups and wanted to bring about change in the GDR, and those parish members who wanted to keep the status quo. . . . These people always worked against us; in all of the GDR, the church leaders worked against the active human rights groups, peace groups, and environmental groups. Simultaneously, they were active in the church and cooperated with people against the state. . . . The church itself was caught between its own claim to be the descendant of Jesus and

> the Sermon on the Mount and its support of the people who were fighting for a united society and the church's subordination in this authoritarian state. And within the church, these people, the church leadership, stood against us. Outwardly, they sometimes backed us.[31]

Though approaching the events differently, the two interviewees agree on three key points regarding the dynamic of the movement. First, under GDR rule, protests were risky. Fear of and distance from the regime were apparent in daily life. In fact, only one large-scale protest against the regime took place (June 16, 1953). Construction workers in Berlin spontaneously went on strike to protest changes in their work schedule and benefits. Their strike spread to the provinces, with people also demanding free elections, unrestricted rights to form political parties, and the release of all political prisoners. The intensity and scale of this protest surprised the regime, and these events were suppressed with the help of the Soviet military.[32] Second, gathering in churches contributed to the movement's growth. Churches provided physical and social/communal spaces, later serving as departure points for mass demonstrations in the fall of 1989. Third, although the relationships between activists and church leaders could be tense, the political action through the repetitive ritual of Monday prayers seemingly decreased the tension. Rituals were also a means of enhancing trust and decreasing social distance. The ongoing meetings have reduced the sense of risk among individuals and encouraged other individuals to publicly express their opposition to the regime.[33]

Protests usually take place outdoors. However, in this case, indoor spaces played a crucial role in the evolution of the protest and its dynamics. As an indoor space, Nicolai Church provided a place for the evolution of the peace prayers since 1982, a ritual that took place every Monday from 5 to 6 p.m. This ritual had an enormous effect on social distance, and it enhanced the sense of familiarity and embeddedness. Activist Rainer Müller describes the scene:

> The churches opened the doors for the protest and for people who wanted to express themselves in a closed society and avowed the images from Leipzig, open church, the Nikolaikirche here [*sic*]. . . . At 5:00 p.m. the prayer for peace began, then ending around 5:30–5:45, and everyone was kindly ushered out, and by 6:00 the doors of the church were closed, regardless of how many police officers were standing outside and arresting people. The church was closed then, and it had nothing to do with what was going on outside. No one among the church leaders carried this responsibility. They just stood at the windows and watched or, at best, reported it to the church leadership.[34]

The arrests associated with the peace prayers further established these prayers as a protest ritual in the minds of the people.[35]

Place

When discussing the location of these events, one must address the structure of the city and its contested evolution. Leipzig, located approximately 160 kilometers (99 miles) southwest of Berlin, is one of Germany's most densely populated cities. Historically, Leipzig served as a trade city and was once a major European center of learning and culture in fields such as music and publishing. Leipzig's centrality increased during the GDR regime, and the city became a major urban and industrial center, which also resulted in severe environmental problems. However, compared with other cities in the GDR, Leipzig inhabitants were more exposed to the conditions in the West because of the city's trade fair, which attracted Western businesspeople. In addition, because the Stasi apparatus was centered in Berlin, Leipzig residents had more breathing room compared with those living in the capital.[36]

Spatially, the city of Leipzig has developed, like many medieval cities, around the historical city. In terms of spatial morphology, the historical city is surrounded by a ring road, which receives traffic from the main roads between the outer districts. The ring road itself is 2.9 kilometers long, which indicates the compactness of the historical core. Along the city's inner-city ring road is the city's largest square, Augustusplatz,[37] which is also one of the largest squares in Europe, serving also as the central hub for Leipzig's tram network. The square is defined by the Opernhaus on its northern edge, the Neues Gewandhaus (with the Mendebrunnen) on the southern side, and the main buildings of the University of Leipzig, including the City-Hochhaus Leipzig, on the western side, which borders the city center.[38] In the city core, the institutional and governmental buildings are located in a relatively small area, resulting in congestion. Furthermore, within the perimeter of the ring are two churches involved in the movement, and two others lie outside the borders of the city center, one adjacent to the ring and another farther north.

These features—(1) the scale and length of the ring (only 2.9 kilometers), a walkable distance, and (2) the geographical spread of the churches in proximity to the ring—create a unique spatial condition. The religious buildings, indoor spaces that are considered sanctuaries, are juxtaposed with the ring and the city core, outdoor urban spaces that are regarded as spaces that are controlled by the regime. This unique overlap has allowed various communities, which have developed separately in different locations in the city, to create a coordinated event in which people march through the city in the form of a ring.

Event

The spatial choreography of Leipzig protests is a unique dynamic between indoor and outdoor spaces. This dynamic does not usually occur in political protests, and as a tactic, it plays a significant role in challenging social, spatial, and political distances. It contributes to social embeddedness, personal networks, and familiarity with city spaces, which ultimately influenced the events of September 25, 1989, when over six thousand participants joined in the first of thirteen demonstrations. This dynamic is clearly portrayed in the testimony of Rainer Müller:

> There was the good idea to take the one church, the Nikolaikirche, as a starting point and to go to the Thomaskirche as a religious meeting place, where people might want to go just by chance per se. Then, we could use this opportunity to attract attention from Western journalists from the Norddeutschen Rundfunk, who happened to be reporting about the Leipzig fair from the market square or from windows. And exactly in that moment, during a simulcast at that location, and entirely official, a train of demonstrators, as regards content, moved along from one church, over the market square, to the other church. With one exception, the peace march, such a thing had never happened; the first public demonstrations took place, which were being filmed simultaneously and reported live in West German television, or on the same evening with moving pictures. We planned all of this and made arrangements with the individual journalists.[39]

As Rainer Müller indicates, the first demonstrations in 1988 had nothing to do with the ring; instead, participants walked city streets within the city, moving from one church to the next or from one church toward the market.

> It was on September 25, '89 . . . there was a dynamic that cannot be ascribed to any individual will or to any preparation from within the church. On one side, there were the police officers, where the crowd didn't flow, but the people came out of the church, they had to, and there a few thousand of them and it was only a short way past the Nikolaikirche, over the Ritterstrasse to the then Karl-Marx-Platz. We also used the wide Grimmasche Straße, a street we had used in the past as well, from the Nikolaikirche to the Thomaskirche in '88. Thus, everyone who had been participating for a longer time knew in what direction to go because it is a wide street and one can either go to the market, as a central place, or to the Thomaskirche. But then it didn't move any further in the one direction because there were too many people.

Why Karl-Marx-Platz?

> Karl-Marx-Platz was the large, open square that was more easily and more quickly reachable compared to Marktplatz, and, furthermore, the police were standing in such a way each time that they were blocking the way

to Marktplatz. It wasn't possible to reach Marktplatz because it was the central square. Thus, it was necessary to make a detour away from the city center and travel outwards toward the Ring. It was the movement away from the police because they blocked the street and for a long time, it was not possible to break through the blockade.

Along the ring were several important landmarks, including the train station, which symbolized the opportunity to travel to the West, and the Stasi headquarters:

> The next goal was the Staatssicherheit. That was a building everyone knew, the Runde Ecke [the Leipzig Stasi headquarters]. It led automatically from the church's exit, which was normally the side entrance and not the front entrance, to the north, out of the Nikolaikirche yard, from the Nikolaikirche yard over the open exit of the square at the wide Grimmashen Steinweg, to the Grimmasche Straße, and from this wide pedestrian boulevard, offering much room, the masses streamed toward the open square of the Karl-Marx-Platz. And from there, the people went vertically downwards, topographically, see, where one can walk conveniently. It is more convenient to walk downwards and upwards. The way continued towards the train station, and, at the train station, the way automatically led to the next church, which everyone knew would be open, or, as was the case previously in the autumn of '89, there would be a peace prayer.[40]

The repetition and familiarity with these landmarks and protest routes also helped expand the scale of the movement:

> The people of Leipzig knew first of all the direction toward the Nikolai, toward the Augustus, toward Karl-Marx-Platz, then to the train station, and then the people knew automatically that the next stop was the next church that was visible. Even though it was often already dark, everyone knew where the next church was. From the Reformed Church in the Ringstraße, one passed the Stasi and then ended up at the Thomaskirche.[41]

On October 2, 1989, 80,000 people participated in the demonstration. On October 9, the government prepared tear gas containers, and the hospitals were prepared for a bloodbath. The GDR prepared for civil war. At 5:45 p.m., before the end of the peace prayers, the army and police withdrew. The numbers increased from one event to the next: 100,000 people participated on October 16, and 325,000 people participated on November 6. The regime gradually responded to the ongoing mass mobilization with reforms: opposition groups were legalized, and free elections were scheduled for 1990. The borders to the West were opened in early November.[42]

Distance

Conjoining is a spatial choreography that is based on multiplicity, on the dynamics between various groups and locations in the city. The group's evolution is processual, which contributes to a sense of community and social embeddedness. Based on indoor-outdoor dynamics, togetherness is a fundamental psychological mechanism to overcome fear,[43] and personal networks play a key role in individuals' involvement in this type of protest. The spatial manifestation of conjoining is a grand event in which people march through the city in the form of a ring. Though not smooth or unified, the ring is created from multiple adjacent points that together are regarded as a ring.

The conjoining choreography is based on deep familiarity with and sensitivity to the city's infrastructure. The city and the people are not considered separate; they are instead regarded as constituting one another. Political leadership and organization plays a secondary role in this type of choreography, which is based on small groups who make their decisions in a decentralized way.

 **CONJOINING** | Leipzig, Augustusplatz, October 9, 1989

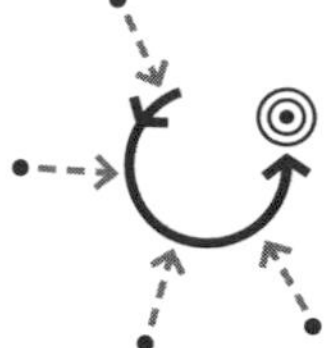

ATTRIBUTES

- Planned Sequence
- Spatial Reclaiming
- Concretizing Alliance

Figure 7.9. Participants present themselves to one another at a Monday demonstration at Nikolai Church in Leipzig on September 4, 1989. Photo by Armin Wiech, Archiv Bürgerbewegung, Leipzig.

Figure 7.10. Monday demonstration in front of Nikolai Church in Leipzig on September 4, 1989, following the peace prayer inside the church. Photo by Armin Wiech, Archiv Bürgerbewegung, Leipzig.

Figure 7.11. Nikolai Church, 2007. Photo by author.

Figure 7.12. Augustusplatz: Built form and space. Illustrations by author.

Key Features	Augustusplatz
Location	City center of Leipzig
Buildings/activities	Cultural educational buildings, monuments
Space	~34,000 sq. meters
Key value/concern	Historic and social landmark
Spatial definition within the city	Part of the city's inner-city ring-road and a central hub for its tram network

Table 7.3. Key Features and Spatial Attributes.

Distance	Geography	Creating a closed circle of people on a city scale
	Physical	Each participant primarily sees the many heads of other protesters
	Meaning	Challenging authorities by repossessing the city

Table 7.4. Event and the Conceptualization of Distance.

Figure 7.13. Augustusplatz: Urban context and space of gathering. Illustration by author.

Figures 7.14. *Left*: Augustusplatz, Leipzig, 2007. Photos by author. *Bottom*: Leipzig, October 30, 1989. Photo by Armin Kühne, Stadtgeschichtliches Museum Leipzig. "And the people walked so, with the footprints of their shoes, children's shoes, women's shoes, men's shoes, but no boots and no marching intact. And the army of police officers and patrol cars had to pull back, and the people could exit the churches and walk around the Ring unchallenged." Pastor Christian Führer, January 17, 2007.

> This route is significant, as it passes directly past and through the key ceremonial and the most recognisable spaces and buildings in the UK. First, we passed Big Ben, a symbol of British politics, the sound of the bell tolling—you hear it on all of the news/political programmes—as well as the bell tower with its clock faces on all sides, are both highly representative. After the parliament buildings, the route travelled through Whitehall, where all the government departments are located as well as crucially, Downing Street, where the official residence of the Prime Minister is located—the heart of government in the UK. As we passed these places, I remember the march being more crushed and also louder with whistles and boos and chants, all directed at these places and the people who occupied them—especially at Downing Street.
>
> Ailsa Gunson, January 22, 2007

Synchronicity is about shrinking global geographic and ideological distance and producing an *orchestrated transnational spectacle* that is based on a network of national movements. Being so socially diverse and geographically expansive, this tactic connects individuals around a particular issue, creating ad hoc connections among people from more than one country, who mobilize around a common concern.[44] In achieving this goal, synchronicity uses the "network" concept and escapes hierarchical leadership.[45] The task of this transnational network is to nurture *connectivity and solidarity* among different protest groups in different locations around the world as a means of constructing an orchestrated spectacle on a global scale. The event's choreography is based on some key agreed-upon design elements, such as (1) the action repertoire, (2) the unification of slogans, and (3) the identical timing of protests. Although these elements are contextualized, their essence and simultaneous timing suffice to create a *unified rhythm*. Thus, synchronicity should be considered a global-local dynamic, with transnational goals on the one hand, but with the particularities of place on the other. The "place" of the protest should be understood as an expression of a symbolic appropriation of "the world" rather than as an event that takes place in multiple localities. The place is abstract, serving as the event's image that can be regarded as an image of "global alliance," which is responsive to an identical political climate.

Socially, synchronicity is about sociodemographic diversity, about decreasing social distance and increasing the normalization of protests and protesters.[46] Spatially, as a transnational effort, its use of urban space is direct, and the event's repertoire is basic, often a procession that ends at a known central point. The procession routes are significant in terms of length, geography, and symbolism (e.g., passing by buildings that represent power). The spatial performance often involves simply marching in the streets and conveys a peaceful message to which most demonstrators and viewers adhere. This type of orchestrated event is highly photogenic to members of the media, enabling demonstrators to reach a wider constituency and capture the public's imagination.

However, synchronicity is a recent phenomenon that has been criticized for the very principles that make it an impressive spectacle. This type of action is often seen to be about objecting to something rather than standing for something. Furthermore, the activists' loose networks, which depend very little on a central leader or common ideology, result in the diffusion of ideas among movement actors.[47] This diffusion, which builds up momentum, attracts participants, enables communication across the diverse groups present, and provides the symbolic glue that holds together similar groups from different countries, has been called a "travelling circus."[48] This pejorative name suggests that these types of actions are significant in the eyes of the press and politicians but that they are often immature and superficial.

Synchronicity requires thorough preparation to maximize coordination and minimize unexpected events by considering public order policies on local, national, and even international levels. This coordination process relies significantly on ICTs.[49] This tactic was used, for example, during an antiwar protest on February 15, 2003, which was a coordinated day of worldwide protests against the invasion of Iraq. This coordinated action was to be the largest transnational antiwar protest in human history, with 10 to 15 million people demonstrating around the world. All demonstrations took place on Saturday, February 15 (in their respective time zones). The demonstrations varied in size, from small ones that brought together only a few neighborhoods to very large ones on the national level.[50] Even though the transnational character of the protests influenced the uniformity of the slogans used during the demonstrations and the written materials distributed beforehand, there is no detailed account of materials used across the globe.[51]

Context

After the September 11, 2001, attacks on the World Trade Centers in New York, the United States began its "war on terror" with the support of a wide international coalition. During the early months of 2003, an international campaign was mounted in support of a military attack on Iraq, claiming the country had weapons of mass destruction and connections to al-Qaeda, which prepared the public for a US invasion of Iraq on March 20, 2003.[52] Parallel to the national campaign, different organizations and individuals across the globe started protesting against the invasion. The plan to hold an international day of demonstrations was first presented publicly at the European Social Forum meeting in Florence (November 2002) in the presence of some six hundred organizations. In the beginning, the large coalition against the upcoming war in Iraq was predominantly European, but it very quickly expanded across continents. The European efforts combined with an already existing trend of transnational antiwar efforts,[53] then led by a US-based international coalition, Act Now to Stop the War and End Racism (ANSWER), which had already protested against the war. On October 2002, another coalition, United for Peace and Justice (UFPJ), formed in the United States and joined the European Forum's meeting in Copenhagen in December 2002. During that meeting, the attendee parties agreed to the ideas and infrastructure for a worldwide action on February 15, 2003. Sidney Tarrow defines this type of protest as "socially mobilized groups with constituents in at least two states, engaged in sustained contentious interaction with powerholders in at least one state other than their own, or against an international institution, or a multinational economic actor."[54]

Synchronicity is a mode of collective action that combines action forms that have been associated with less institutionalized organizational forms—such as protesting—with those that have been associated with more institutionalized forms—such as lobbying.[55] As described by one of the demonstrators, "There was a definite sense that London—and so myself, my friends—was now, due to our government's alignment with the USA, more of a target for terrorism. We were now more at risk. I felt a need, with many others it seems, to separate myself from the actions of the government (who I had actually voted for previously), and somehow say 'I don't agree,' 'I am not part of this,' and 'they do not speak for me.'"[56]

The coordination among national umbrella organizations played a key role in planning the event,[57] which took place not only in Europe and the United States but also in the Middle East, Asia, Australia, and even Antarctica. Joris Verhulst notes two organizational factors that contributed to the success of the event: "the dynamics of the social fora and the use of world-wide electronic communication technologies."[58] The first provided an arena in which to initiate and promote transnational coordination, and the second functioned as a complementary channel, which enhanced mobilization and helped participants agree on similar terms of demonstration and, in turn, create a truly transnational character for the demonstration. As a result, "the transnational character of the protests was clear *before* the protests took place."[59] Prior to the demonstration, the media and posters displayed around the various cities publicized the event. Information about the event was also disseminated through social circles, as one of the demonstrators testifies: "I do remember realizing a week or so beforehand that this protest would be large and in some way historic and not like other marches."[60] This testimony reflects one of this tactic's key features: attracting first-timers to participate to achieve diversity and thus enhance the normalization of the overall event.[61] As she further testifies, "I don't normally protest (this was my first demonstration) so I must have also realized, again probably through the media, that this protest would be more representative of general society and not just made up of more hard-core 'professional protesters.'"[62]

The aim of the event was simple and clear. As noted by one of the leading organizations, Stop the War Coalition (StWC), the idea was "to stop the war currently declared by the United States and its allies against 'terrorism.' We condemn the attacks on New York. . . . But any war will simply add to the numbers of innocent dead."[63] However, different perspectives could be found in the diverse crowd. The variety was also evident in the different (though corresponding) agendas of the coalitions involved and the different slogans used by participants.[64] Thus, locality, culture, and context played a role in the composition of the demonstrations.[65] In the case of London, for example, a mixture of "formal" slogans were directed at the government's actions or specifically at UK Prime Minister Blair or US President Bush, and "informal" homemade slogans offered humorous takes on the situation.[66] As stated, "There were many banners and posters, some homemade, some supplied by political organizations. . . . There were some even supplied by the tabloid papers. There was a lot of humorous content or 'cheek' on the banners—'Make Tea Not War,' showing a grinning Tony Blair wearing an upside-down teacup rather than a helmet and carrying a rifle, and my absolute favorite: a tiny square of paper stuck onto the top of a wooden pole that you had to get close to read. Other posters referred to the need to distance ourselves from the government's actions—'Not in My Name' being very prominent—and most, I would say, were directed squarely at Tony Blair and George Bush personally."[67] This dynamic supports the idea that transnational demonstrations or "global non-state networks" are grounded in the "micro-spaces of daily life rather than on some putative global stage."[68]

Event

The largest rally, with 1,050,000 participants, took place in London.[69] The London demonstration was organized by the Stop the War Coalition, the Campaign for Nuclear Disarmament (CND), and the Muslim Association of Britain. The demonstration took the form of a march that started at two meeting points, both of which led to a final gathering area in Hyde Park.[70] According to one protester, "The march started to the east of central London and then followed the river, along the north bank, westwards directly to Parliament at the Palace of Westminster. From there, the march route turned back on itself and then moved up through Whitehall and into Trafalgar Square. From there, the route turned west, through Piccadilly Square and along Piccadilly and finally out to Hyde Park, where people would gather and there would be various speakers and events. The route didn't cover a large part of the city—on a normal day, you could walk from the river to Hyde Park in less than thirty minutes."[71] The route of the march was carefully planned; it passed directly through key ceremonial and very recognizable spaces and buildings in the United Kingdom, including Big Ben, a symbol of British politics; the parliament buildings; Whitehall; and Downing Street, where the official residence of the Prime Minister is located—the heart of government in the UK. The sounds of the procession were critical and added a festive element to the event. At some points, groups of people were playing drums; at others, people were wearing costumes and performing, and noise was also amplified with the help of whistles and shouting. Sometimes, the cheering happened in waves, from one point in the procession to another, thus connecting participants who were physically distant from one another.

Spatially, the procession was designed to create a situation in which demonstrators would march in different areas of the city but still be able to see one another. The procession's length was relatively short, but its multiple physical layers created an architectural effect that enhanced excitement among demonstrators, as conveyed below:

> Above us, the bridge was crowded with people, leaning over the edges, all waving, cheering, and whistling at the main march below. All these people were on their way to start points back east. Some sections of the route along the river were so busy that new joiners were being directed across the bridges, onto the south side of the river, where they would walk back towards the east until they reached Blackfriars, and then they would cross north and finally begin their march—about an hour's walk behind us, and, by that point, we ourselves were not even halfway through. Seeing all the people on the bridge also gave a sense of the range of people participating in the march—normally, you would only see the same fifty to one hundred or so people around you all the way through the march, but we could see hundreds of people above us.[72]

Targeting large audiences and aiming to temporarily unite diverse groups, the event's festive nature is also supported by a strong sense of safety among participants, which is provided by the police force. In London, the police force settled along the route, lining either side of the march and observing the participants. In sensitive locations, such as Downing Street and Whitehall, the police presence was increased. In addition, police and media helicopters flew above the marchers' heads. When the demonstrators gathered in Hyde Park, the demonstration changed from being a march to being a rally, and the participants listened to speeches and music performances.

In sum, synchronicity, especially in transnational protests, is about protesters distancing themselves from the state's political leaders and creating a transnational coalition. The effect on participants is strong, tending to make them feel that social and geographical distance is reduced on a global scale: "It suddenly became clear that we were involved in a significant event and that so many people, from all sorts of places, with all sorts of backgrounds, all felt the same way and felt strongly enough to give up the best part of a day to say something."[73] However, this distance from local state leaders also contributes to the feeling that the protest has no "address." Although the massive event did not stop the war or change policies regarding Iraq, it was a crucial event for the social capital of the antiwar coalition, and its effects may be a goal in themselves, as they laid the foundation for future engagements and protests.[74]

Distance

Synchronicity is a tactic of the many—in terms of people, places, and organizations. Although it could be a tactic of the few, its effects derive from its ability to redefine space, time, and, most particularly, the dynamics between the local and the global. Synchronicity requires detailed preparation, often being used in transnational protests that are composed of wide-ranging and diverse groups, organizations, and individuals. These types of groups use protest actions as part of their repertoire to target international actors, including intergovernmental organizations (IGOs), multinational corporations, and, more generally, the forces of global capitalism, rather than states directly. In this sense, actors distance themselves from the state, focusing on larger universal concerns.

With regard to social distance, synchronicity involves defining a choreography that will, at least temporarily, "shrink" the geographical distance and ideological differences between countries and groups. In doing so, it strengthens cooperation among actors by creating unified transnational opposition to an issue. Mobilization is achieved through social media, which enables participants to transmit messages and pictures during the action, enhancing the visual impact and increasing its reach to potential allies in the world outside the movement and across national boundaries. Governments or elites tend to tolerate and even support such protest events and thus contribute to their normalization.[75]

SYNCHRONICITY | Worldwide, February 15, 2003

ATTRIBUTES

- Orchestrated Spectacle
- Geographical Shrinkage
- Simultaneous Rhythm

Figure 7.15. The demonstrations varied in size, from small ones that brought together only a few neighborhoods to very large ones on the national level. London, February 2003. Photo by Ailsa Gunson.

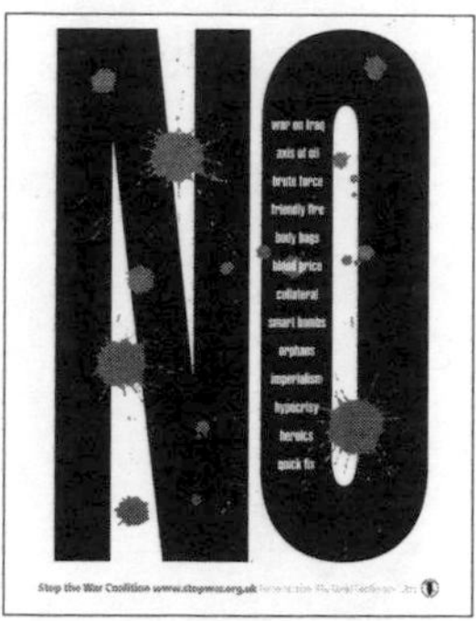

Figure 7.16a and b. Posters of the Stop the War Coalition, 2003, by David Gentleman.

Key Features	Processions and Gatherings
Location	Key ceremonial and recognisable spaces and buildings
Buildings/activities	Governmental and symbolic
Space	1,400,000 sq. meters (Hyde Park)
Key value/concern	Visual impact
Spatial definition within the city	Major routes

Table 7.5. Key Features and Spatial Attributes.

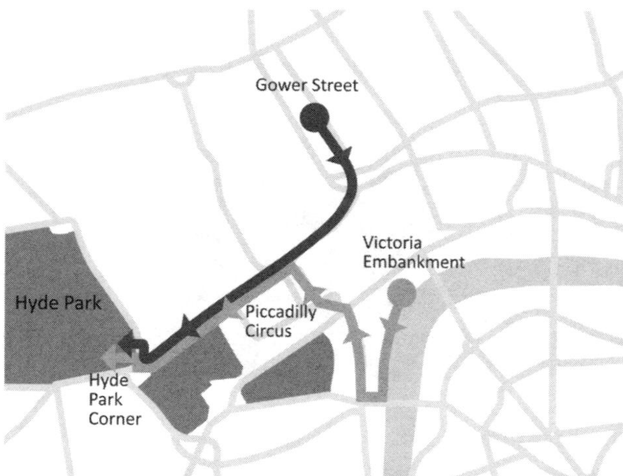

Figure 7.17. The largest rally, with 1,050,000 participants, took place in London. The London demonstration was organized by the Stop the War Coalition, the Campaign for Nuclear Disarmament, and the Muslim Association of Britain. The demonstration took the form of a march that started at two meeting points, both of which led to a final gathering area in Hyde Park. March began at 12:30. Route A (5.6 km): Marchers coming from the north to assemble outside the British Museum in Gower Street. Route B (5.6 km): Marchers not coming from the north, including those from London, to assemble at Victoria Embankment. Illustration by author.

Distance	Geography	Enhancing connectivity and solidarity among the various protests in different countries
	Physical	An agreed-upon action repertoire in central spaces worldwide
	Meaning	A “global society” that is sensitive to an identical political climate

Table 7.6. Event and the Conceptualization of Distance.

Figure 7.18. Synchronicity requires thorough preparation to maximize coordination and minimize unexpected events by considering public order policies on local, national, and even international levels. London, February 15, 2003. Photo by Ailsa Gunson.

KEY VENUES: London 750,000 (police estimate) to 2,000,000 people (Stop the War Coalition estimate); **Glasgow** 50,000 (*Guardian* estimate) to 100,000 people (*World Socialist* estimate); **Dublin** 80,000 (police estimate), 90,000 (BBC estimate), 100,000 (*Guardian* estimate), or 150,000 people (Socialist Worker estimate); **Belfast** 10,000 (*Guardian* estimate) to 20,000 people (Socialist Worker estimate); **Rome** 650,000 people (police estimate); **Paris** 100,000 (*USA Today* estimate) to 200,000 people (World Socialist website estimate); **Toulouse** around 10,000 people; **Berlin** 300,000 (police estimate) to 500,000 people (organizers' estimate); **Madrid** 660,000 (government source's estimate) to 2,000,000 people (GLW estimate); **Barcelona** 350,000 (Delegación de Gobierno), 1,300,000 (Barcelona city hall and police), or 1,500,000 people (GLW estimate); **Valencia** 500,000 people (GLW estimate); **Seville** 200,000 (government sources estimate) to 250,000 people (GLW estimate); **Las Palmas de Gran Canaria** 100,000 people (GLW estimate); **Cadiz** 100,000 people (GLW estimate); **Oviedo** 100,000 people; **Malta** 1,000 people (SW estimate); **Oslo** 60,000 people (police and socialist worker estimates); **Bergen** around 15,000 people; **Stavanger** 10,000 people; **Copenhagen** 20,000 to 30,000 people (WSWS estimate); **Stockholm** 35,000 people; **Gothenburg** 25,000 people; **Brussels** 100,000 people (WSWS and GLW estimate); **Luxembourg** 14,000 people; **Amsterdam** 70,000 (*USA Today* estimate) to 75,000 people (WSWS estimate); **Vienna** 30,000 people (SW estimate); **Bern** 40,000 people; **Ljubljana** 3,000 people; **Mostar** 100 people; **Zagreb** 10,000 people (WSWS estimate) [Croatia also saw protests in **Osijek**, **Vukovar**, **Knin**, **Zadar**, **Sibenik**, **Split**, and **Dubrovnik**]; **Prague** 1,000 people; **Budapest** 60,000 people (SW estimate); **Warsaw** 10,000 people (SW estimate); **Lisbon** 80,000 people; **Belgrade** 200 people (WSWS estimate); **Moscow** 400 people (WSWS estimate); **Kiev** 2,000 people (*USA Today* estimate); **Istanbul** thousands (SW estimate) [Turkey also saw demonstrations in **Adana**, **Ankara**, **İzmir**, **Zonguldak**, **İzmit**, **Antalya**, and **Mugla**]; **Athens** 150,000 people (WSWS estimate); **Dhekelia** 500 (*USA Today* estimate) to more than 800 people (SW estimate); **Montreal** 100,000 people (SW and WSWS each estimated 150,000); **Toronto** 80,000 people; **Vancouver** 40,000 people; **Victoria** 8,000 people; **Halifax** 4,000 people; **Ottawa** 6,000 people; **Chicoutimi** 1,500 people; **New York** 300,000 to 400,000 people (WSWS estimate); **San Francisco** 60,000 to 200,000 people [Feb. 16] (accounts vary as to the total number present); **Los Angeles** 50,000 (WSWS estimate) to 60,000 people (GLW estimate) [CNN said "thousands"]; **Colorado Springs** 4,000 people; **Seattle** 50,000 people (GLW estimate); **Chicago** 10,000 people (GLW estimate); **Puerto Rico** a small number of people (*USA Today* estimate) [US also saw demonstrations in towns such as **Gainesville, Georgia**; **Macomb, Illinois**; and **Juneau, Alaska**]; **Mexico City** 10,000 people (*USA Today* estimate); **Montevideo** 70,000 people; **Sao Paolo** 1,500 people (police estimate); **Buenos Aires** 50,000 people; **Damascus** 10,000 (GLW estimate) to 200,000 people (CBS and *USA Today* estimate); **Beirut** 10,000 people (CBS estimate); **Tel Aviv** approximately 2,000 (*USA Today* estimate) to 3,000 people (GLW and WSWS estimate); **Shibuya** 5,000 people (SW estimate); **Tokyo** [14.2], 25,000 people [Japan also saw demonstrations in **Osaka** and other cities]; **Kuala Lumpur** 3,000 people (SW estimate); **Taipei** 2,000 people (WSWS estimate); **Calcutta** 10,000 people (BBC estimate); **Dhaka** 2,000 people; **Seoul** 2,000 people (WSWS estimate) [protests also took place in the South Korean cites of **Pusan, Taegu, Taejon, Kwangju, and Wonju**]; **Hong Kong** 1,000 people (WSWS estimate); **Johannesburg** 8,000 or 10,000 (AllAfrica.com estimate) to 20,000 people (SW estimate); **Cape Town** 5,000 (*USA Today* estimate) to 20,000 people (WSWS estimate) [protests of thousands of people also took place at **Durban** and **Bloemfontein**; **Sfax** 3,000 people (SW estimate); **Melbourne** 150,000 (BBC estimate) to over 200,000 (organisers' estimate); Sydney 200,000 people (BBC estimate) [an estimated 600,000 demonstrated in cities around Australia]; **Auckland** and **Wellington** 10,000 people.

Figure 7.19. List of key venues where demonstrations took place with estimated numbers of participants. Sources: Multiple websites.

ELASTICITY | CARACAS, AUTOPISTA FRANCISCO FAJARDO, APRIL 11, 2002

> Parque del Este to PDVSA [Petroleum of Venezuela] was the motivation of the march, so to speak. Why? Because it was a disavowal of the dismissal of the people, and that was the location of the main offices of PDVSA, principally the one in Chuao, and therefore the march left from here and went to Chuao. The reason to go to Chuao was because PDVSA was there; that's why the podium was there. Now, when the march left PDVSA for the center, that was a combination of spontaneity, the people wanted, or many people wanted, to go to Miraflores, at the same time it was induced, that is, many of the speakers that were on the platform, some of them, were connected with the idea of the conspiracy, they began to say, "TO MIRAFLORES!! TO MIRAFLORES!!" The march took off for Miraflores.
>
> Teodoro Petkoff, June 14, 2007

Elasticity is a sociospatial condition that deeply influences how space is perceived and lived. Elasticity suggests a counterposition to modern space, which should be regarded as emerging or becoming. It welcomes the notion of the unexpected, presenting a future about which we can never be certain. In protests that are regarded as elastic, space is also elastic (even when strictly regulated and based on a modern conceptualization of zoning). It is fluid, becoming. The idea of becoming involves a process-based ontology of movement, in which the world is considered a dynamic and open-ended set of relational transformations.[76] Thus, protests that use this tactic challenge the concept of space as a preexisting, three-dimensional container within which things and events occur. Space is a process, and, similar to protest, it is better conceived as a verb than as a noun. Because becoming, rather than space, is central to protests, such demonstrations can take place anywhere. Becoming does not occur through or around a space's physicality; instead, it is part of what makes the physical space.

Elasticity refers not only to conceptions of space but also to the dynamic among people. It allows the dynamic of an open crowd, which abandons itself to its natural urge for growth. "An open crowd has no clear feeling or idea of the size it may attain; it does not depend on a known building which it has to fill; its size is not determined; it wants to grow indefinitely and what it needs for this is more and more people."[77] This conception of an open space and crowd also affects perceptions of scale by negating the hierarchical conceptualization of scale, which is embedded in an ontology that focuses on the notions of event-space and an event-reaction.[78]

Elasticity, as an open-ended sociospatial condition, implies that the spatial choreography of this type of event is unknown to the organizers and to the government in advance. What is known in advance is a general idea and an estimation of the rhythm or the intensities among particular objects and entities. The event's loose configuration threatens those in power. An event with no leadership, which is not channeled through agreed-upon city spaces, is unpredictable and thus less controllable. However, the ruling power's lack of control over the event does not necessarily imply a promise of change. It instead implies that an elastic protest, as with the concept of becoming, is "a form of thinking, open to and attuned to its own capacity for variation, cultivating in the process an affective orientation, not so much of optimism, but of hope."[79]

Building moment by moment, this type of protest rejects linearity. The distance between participants is not fixed or defined; it is instead lived. A protest can be regarded as a river full of swirls; at one level, it goes faster here and slower there. For example, this tactic can be seen in a protest that took place on April 9, 2002, when the Confederación de Trabajadores de Venezuela (CTV)—the country's largest trade union federation, which is traditionally affiliated with the opposition's Democratic Action (Acción Democrática) Party—called for a two-day strike. Two days later, amid rapidly escalating tensions, people marched to the Petroleum of Venezuela (PDVSA) headquarters in defense of its recently dismissed management board. Unexpectedly, the organizers decided to reroute the march to Miraflores, the presidential palace, where a pro-Chávez demonstration was taking place. Supporters and opponents of President Hugo Chávez clashed at the Miraflores Palace. According to BBC News, a sector of the armed forces asked for Chávez's resignation, holding him responsible for a massacre during the demonstrations. Chávez was taken to a military base, while Fedecámaras president Pedro Carmona was appointed as the transitional president of Venezuela, following mass protests and a general strike by Chávez's opponents. Carmona's first decree reversed the major social and economic policies that composed Chávez's "Bolivarian Revolution" and dissolved both the National Assembly and the Venezuelan judiciary. It also changed the nation's name back to República de Venezuela from República Bolivariana de Venezuela. Carmona's regime was then toppled, and Chávez resumed his presidency on the night of Saturday, April 13, 2002.

Place

To understand the dynamics of protest in Caracas, locating the events in the context of the city's sociospatial configuration is necessary. As has been previously argued, elasticity is a sociospatial condition that deeply influences how spaces are perceived and lived; it stands against the rational ideas of the modernists' movement in architecture and planning. At its core, the modernists' legacy is based on the positivist idea that sociospatial progress and development can be achieved through planning regulations and design control. This premise influences the development of numerous cities worldwide, including Caracas, which is characterized by an ongoing political struggle to control the fluid elasticity of city spaces.

The geographical location of Caracas plays a crucial role in its sociospatial evolution. It was founded on the main axis of the valley known as San Francisco. Caracas is walled in by the mountains, which impede its access to the sea. In the early decades of the twentieth century, until the 1930s, the city's development did not follow a defined urban policy. This condition can partly be associated with the role of the ruling power between 1909 and 1935, the dictator Juan Vicente Gómez, who regarded Caracas as hostile to his power and preferred to reside in the city of Maracay. In 1936, a debate over the future of Caracas resulted in the preparation of the 1939 Monumental Plan, which proposed the creation of spatial organization through a monumental arterial road that would revitalize the city's dense central quarter. This arterial road, named Bolívar Avenue, stretched the length of the city, passing through the new town center, with the capitol as the main building at the bottom of Calvario Hill.[80] The plan was a sea change in the city's development, which aimed to control its rapid growth. This goal continued being pursued after World War II, at which time the Comisión Nacional de Urbanismo (CNU; National Urban Planning Commission) was created, which recognized, for the first time, the metropolitan area of Caracas.[81] CNU's city planning work was continued by the Direction of City Planning at the Ministry of Public Works, which designed the General Development Plan for the Caracas Metropolitan Area in 1958.

The 1930s and 1940s were significant in terms of the city's development, and major interventions occurred, including the Sistema de la Nacionalidad, a large roadway system, and monuments, military facilities, and housing projects. As in many other parts of the world, the interventions heeded the ideologies of the modern movement, which favored automobiles as the main method of mobilization. These interventions thus included the design of new avenues and major demolition in the historical quarter, neglecting the development of an organized public transportation system.[82] Most of these interventions, particularly in the eastbound expansion of the upper middle class, inspired by American-style suburbs, including residential complexes, commercial buildings, and public spaces, were marked by the dominant role of the state (with the aid of the private sector), which was affluent due to oil revenues. Through these large-scale interventions, the city was developed in a linear shape, partly due to the long east-west axis that contains the main arterial roads and highest density of urban buildings.

However, during the 1960s and 1970s, Venezuelan authorities adopted anti-urban ideals. Urban growth should be controlled, and the growth of the cities—especially Caracas and other cities in the central-northern coastal region, including Valencia and Maracay—should be limited because megacities are hard to manage.

Although no explicit policy ever advocated these ideas, the tendency was to reduce investment in housing related to social interests or in the settlement of low-income migrant families arriving in Caracas. As a result, an informal city, with self-constructed neighborhoods and no city planning, climbed the mountains surrounding the valley. Although this informal city developed rapidly, the main morphological scheme—characterized by the long axis of the main valley—has become more defined rather than changing much.[83] A sociospatial assemblage was created, with specific power relations existing between the heterogeneous parts of the city.[84]

According to Petkoff,

> Chavismo was in the west; anti-Chavismo was in the east—or, rather, in part of the east because one part of the east is one of the largest [poor] barrios in Latin America, known as Petare. But, in general, the east of Caracas and the southwest are the neighborhoods of the middle class, as well as the rich. Therefore, initially, the city was divided, the Chavista city . . . where Chavismo moved in and created a kind of unwritten rule, whereby everyone moves in their ambit only. So, when the march went to Miraflores, in a certain sense, it was moving into another space. Afterwards, with time, this obviously became subjective; the objective fact became subjective; that is, the residents of Caracas became conscious of the fact that the city is divided in two parts, theirs and ours, and everyone has their own "them" and "us"; the idea is that the city is divided in two.[85]

At the beginning of the twenty-first century, Caracas is a socially and spatially disintegrating city. Its mass transportation networks, specialized mobilization, urban air terminals, ports and airports, protected natural areas, mass entertainment facilities, on the one hand, and its violence and dynamic, undefined, emerging, and increasingly informal cultural spaces, on the other, have transformed the city into a hybrid scene that is prone to conflicts, hodgepodges, changes, and violent confrontations.[86] According to Teodoro Petkoff Malec,[87] this condition should be understood as the "impoverishment that Venezuelan society went through in the twenty years prior to Chávez and that has continued through the Chávez years." According to Petkoff, some sectors have fared better than others: "The situation has improved a bit for the sector known as E, the poorest of the poor, those who were previously called marginal, who certainly are eating a bit better and who have more income than they had before." However, overall, the polarization in the city has increased, and the social disintegration has contributed to increased urban violence and criminality. As he further argues,

> The situation of neglect that is felt by the residents of the city, the deterioration of the public health system, which has made it so the children of the poor begin first grade and three-quarters of them leave school, there is no

> process of educational formation sufficient to counter the terrible influence of television . . . another criminological factor that is very important in Venezuela. The example of the elites—the social and political elites—is one of corruption, so, of course, the poorest Venezuelan as well as the low-level public servant will tell you, "If the minister steals, why shouldn't I steal?" . . . the example of corruption scandals, the frequency with which high-level functionaries, bankers, etc., are denounced, the known fact that businesses take part in private as well as public and official corruption, all these things that permeate society are generating the terrible urban violence that we live through, and political violence is a reflection of urban violence.[88]

Thus, in the early twenty-first century, the context of protests in Caracas involves the societal and spatial assemblage of powers and movements within the city. In that sense, Caracas should be viewed as both a particular city in the world, with its own physicality and narrative, and as a city with a global orientation and a temporal spatiality, which focuses on the interactive co-constitution of agents through relations of exteriority and unequal capacities.[89] This tension between the structured, hierarchical, and narrativized city and the open-ended sociospatial conditions in Caracas is embedded in the profoundly unequal relations of power, resources, and knowledge.

Context

This elastic and fragile social-political context, with its spatial manifestations, has nurtured the protest culture in Caracas. In fact, since the mid-1980s, Venezuela has been perceived, both at home and abroad, as a constantly mobilizing society. Furthermore, protests are seen as legitimate actions and as a right. With the Chávez government, there has been even greater recognition of the right to protest, which has been institutionalized.[90] The statistics show that "from October 1989 to September 2003, there were 12,889 protests in the country, an average of 2.52 per day, including weekends and holidays." In addition, between 1999 and 2003, coinciding with the years of the Chávez government, when a new political elite was attempting to implement an alternative project for the country, "the daily average of protests [rose] to 3.50."[91] In that respect, the protests in Venezuela are an expression of the multiple economic, social, cultural, and racial fractures that have defined Venezuelan society since colonial times.[92] In contemporary times, these fractures have centered on a class-based political polarization of society, in which the popular classes—consisting of some parts of the unorganized working class and the unemployed and informal sectors—and the organized working, middle, and upper classes—consisting of the salaried working and professional sectors and capitalist groups—are pitted against one another. The Chávez regime recognized and capitalized on this development, politically outstripping the other parties who were unable or unwilling to adapt to these new sociopolitical realities.[93]

The early twenty-first century was characterized by a confrontational atmosphere, an agonistic dynamic, which later manifested itself in street protests.[94] These types of protests indicate that a society is undergoing a period of turbulence or sociopolitical transformation.[95] The novelty was that, in late 2001, sectors of the upper and middle classes, who could be distinguished "by the Venezuelan phenotype and by the way they dress, and many women, mostly middle class,"[96] also took to the streets. This new ingredient has increased the visibility of protests because these new sectors have economic resources, and, above all, they are backed by the private mass media, which share and promote the aims of such mobilization.[97]

Heavily stimulated through the media, especially through television, mobilization took real form after January 2002, with a "large part of the Venezuelan population, who [did] not identify with Chávez, who [felt] attacked by his discourse and who oppose[d] him."[98] According to Barry Cannon, the opposition's strategy was to deny the existence of class polarization in Venezuelan society by attributing its existence solely to the discourse of the president. The hegemonic struggle became discursively centered on "democracy," and, in this way, the differing opposition fragments found a centralizing ideological discourse that could successfully obscure the fundamental class divisions in Venezuelan society.[99]

The demand of the students and the opposition was phrased in abstract terms: "Their demand was abstract—liberty, in general terms—and this is the great novelty of this era . . . what affected them was the abuse, the violation of the right to decide which option they would like to see, that is, values that are abstract but very strong."[100]

Event

The prelude to April 2002 was a series of highly publicized work stoppages and marches, which reexposed the social polarization in Venezuela. Most opposition marches were held in the wealthier sectors in eastern Caracas, while marches supporting Chávez were held in the poorer western sectors. During the opposition's stoppages, informal workers continued to work.[101] Geographically, the march on April 11 had planned to proceed from Parque del Este to one of the PDVSA offices in Chuao. However, it became an enormous demonstration, not only in terms of the number of participants but also in terms of the spatial scale of the occupation.

> The period from January to April 2002 is the period in which the opposition won the streets, took the streets, literally snatched the streets away from Chavismo—even though Chávez also mobilized many people—but the streets were most definitely dominated by the opposition. Within this context of

> polarization, confrontation, and citizen mobilization in both camps, there occurred the dismissal of the upper management of PDVSA, which Chávez carried out . . . an aggressive act that provoked enormous irritation and led to the declaration of a two-day strike, culminating in a march.[102]

The events began at PDVSA. Choosing this location was symbolic, as PDVSA was perceived to have violated the opposition. The dynamic of the event was not planned, and an exchange of volleys between those on top of the bridge and those underneath it followed. This shift in the dynamic of the protest, particularly the way it spilled onto the Autopista Francisco Fajardo, was a shift from a target-oriented gathering of a collective mass to an unknown spatial movement of that collective mass. This shift was a powerful statement about distanciation from the spatial order and the disembedding of the middle-class sectors through the "re-occupation of the city." Furthermore, it challenged the sociospatial agreed-upon distances that were manifested in the city's spatial configuration.

On its end, the government tried to maintain social and spatial distance by stopping the opposition from marching into the center of the city, creating a repressive apparatus that blocked particular routes and locations. Thus, the power of these events involved taking back this right to march in all parts of the city, not merely demonstrating in one particular area. This action represented the demand of the protesters (particularly the students) to have their right to go to the city center and to march anywhere recognized. This act had a symbolic value, which went beyond dismantling political and social polarization, because it not only challenged the ruler's ideas but also destroyed spatial polarization. Indeed, students played a key role in the events, which is not new. According to Petkoff,

> The Venezuelan student movement has always been politically oriented . . . the political parties had a lot of influence in the universities, especially the leftist ones; the left was a minority in the country but a majority in the universities, so the student movements had a very high rate of membership in political parties. Many of the students, not knowing any other president than Chávez, have lived eight years under Chávez and emerged. Certainly, you have to take into account that, basically, they are middle-class kids, so when the student movement emerges, they come from the social sector that has been confronting Chávez, which is the middle class.[103]

The appropriation of the city's spaces played a major role in the protest. Protesters had the explicit intention of breaking spatial polarization and taking back their civil right to demonstrate all over the city. The government's actions, limiting such demonstrations in the name of order and control, were political, deepening the polarization in the city by denying democratic rights.[104] However, as some scholars have argued, the commitment to democracy was circumstantial—not ideological. Different sectors of the opposition were willing to actively conspire to achieve the downfall of a democratically elected government and to support a clearly authoritarian project in the name of "democracy," which indicates that "an authentic preoccupation with the strengthening of democracy" did not motivate them; instead, "they [found] in the Chávez project a threat or obstacle to their propositions."[105]

The opposition's protest strategies have been radical, including intensive media campaigns, a coup, an indefinite general production stoppage, sustained campaigns of popular mobilization, and repeated appeals for military intervention. All these tactics show the abandonment of dialogue in favor of outright insurrection. Thus, to a certain extent, the opposition's strategies can be seen as equally polarizing and ideologically driven as any of the activities of the Chávez government.[106] On April 13, 2002, two days after the coup that occurred during an opposition march in the city's wealthier east side, the poor from the peripheral barrios returned Chávez to power. This sequence of events contributed to two parallel narratives, which represent the two visions of Venezuela.

This contestation can be regarded as an antagonistic condition, a reality in contemporary polarized cities, which is embedded in perpetual conflicts, even within an ordered setting. This contestation contributes to the elasticity of space and power, enhancing the conditions of instability. This state of affairs can be viewed pessimistically, as one of Venezuelan society undergoing a process of deepening polarization. However, pragmatists might argue that Venezuelan society must open a dialogue toward achieving consensus,[107] and structuralists might suggest that the task involves developing an agonistic democracy, that is, "[creating] institutions which allow for conflict—when it emerges—to take an agonistic form, a form of adversarial confrontation instead of antagonism between enemies."[108]

Distance

The elastic protest is an act that challenges agreed-upon social, political, and spatial distance in radical and unexpected ways. These protests challenge the accepted hegemony. Because it does not maintain any sort of distance, elasticity might ultimately result in aggressive actions, such as coups or violence. This particular form of action opens up spatiality and the political sphere to new possibilities, but it also presents societal and personal risks. Elastic protests are not based on negotiations; they are instead based on confrontations and antagonism (that do not start at the time of the event), which are part of people's evolving perceptions about spaces and places.

Thus, elasticity is a condition rather than a planned event. As a tactic, it is the opposite of the theater, with its organized spatial choreography and its aim to create a temporally unified collective. Elasticity is about constructing people, though in a way that is unknown to the organizers. The knowns are limited, and the organizers (though they might be able to affect the dynamic in some way) are limited in their ability to control the event as a whole. The event's loose configuration threatens the contemporary project of the nation-state, with its aims to coordinate, administer, and distribute resources to address uncertainties. Elastic protests are about exposing uncertainties and enhancing risks. They are about opening up spatial configurations and imagining the spaces of the (unknown) future.

Figure 7.20. Removing the physical distance between people is a multifaceted mental task that requires people to suppress their fears, take risks, and expose themselves to others and to the unknown. Venezuelans protest against President Hugo Chávez in Caracas, April 11, 2002. At least 300,000 opponents of Chávez marched through Caracas, pressing ahead with an indefinite general strike as his embattled government tried to start up a dialogue to ward off the threat of economic chaos. Photo from REUTERS/Stringer.

ELASTICITY | Caracas, Autopista Francisco Fajardo, April 11, 2002

ATTRIBUTES

- Becoming
- Space as Continuum
- Temporal Rules

Figure 7.21. Venezuelans fill the highways while protesting against President Hugo Chávez, in Caracas, April 11, 2002. Photo from REUTERS/Kimberley White.

Key Features	Autopista Francisco Fajardo
Location	Starting point: Parque del Este
Buildings/activities	From PDVSA Building to Palacio de Miraflores (~ 11.5 km)
Space	NA
Key value/concern	Symbolic national structures and monuments
Spatial definition within the city	The most important motorway in Caracas, the only west arterial road that connects to the east of the city.

Table 7.7. Key Features and Spatial Attributes.

Figure 7.22. Avenida Bolívar (looking east to west), a place for political gatherings and demonstrations for both members of the opposition and supporters. Photo by Fabiola López-Durán.

❯ Space

km 1 km 2

❯ Boundaries

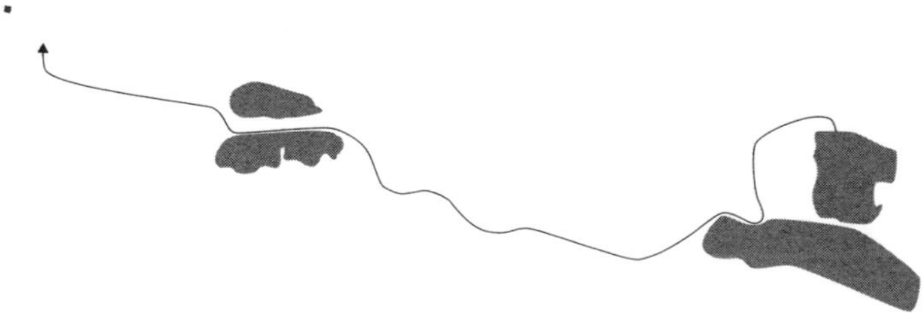

Figure 7.23. Autopista Francisco Fajardo, Caracas: Built form and space. Illustration by author.

Figure 7.24. Avenida under Puente Llaguno, the place of confrontation between the police and Chávez supporters. Photo by Fabiola López-Durán.

Distance	Geography	Starting at a location that is associated with violation, then spreading throughout the polarized city
	Physical	Elastic, spontaneous configuration
	Meaning	"Conquering" the city by reclaiming the right to protest and challenging the regime's conceptualization of the city

Table 7.8. Event and the Conceptualization of Distance.

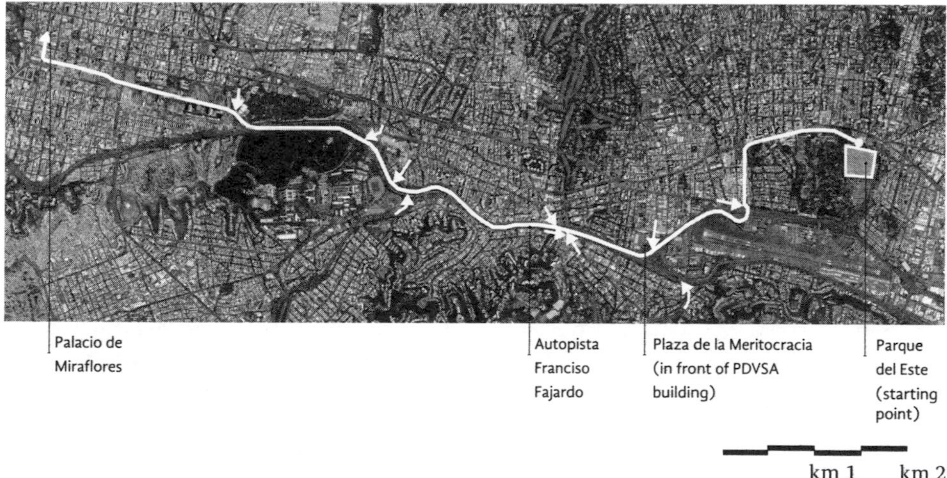

Figure 7.25. Autopista Francisco Fajardo, Caracas: Urban context and route of march. Illustration by author.

Figure 7.26. National guardsmen shoot at protesters in Caracas, April 11, 2002. A Venezuelan general said that President Hugo Chávez's government had "abandoned its functions," and the South American country was under the control of the armed forces. Photo from REUTERS/Stringer.

8
Place-Making

Previous page: In this type of action, the body is secondary to the object, but the two are closely related. The object's creation and survival rely on the body. Resurrection City, Washington, DC, 1968. Photo by Tunney Lee.

REICONIZATION | BEIJING, TIANANMEN SQUARE, JUNE 4, 1989

> Someone erected a statue of the "goddess of democracy" without authorization in dignified Tiananmen Square, and this evoked various comments among the people. . . . All citizens have the duty to cherish and protect Tiananmen Square. This is equal to cherishing and protecting our motherland and to cherishing and protecting our own rights. The square is sacred. No one has the power to add any permanent memorial or to remove anything from the square. Such things must not be allowed to happen in China.[1]
>
> Wu Ye, June 1, 1989

Protests that aim to achieve radical collective shifts in society will search for a means of differentiating their actions from other events. To do so, protests can create memorable new icons—at least in their interpretation during particular events—for public display. The choice of an icon and its meaning is linked to the distance between the state and its citizens. In cases of extreme distance between citizens and the state, the protesters' choice of an icon will tend to provoke antagonistic or revolutionary meaning; in cases of moderate distance, the protesters' choice of an icon might attempt to provoke a discourse without trying to destroy significant state representations. Thus, the reiconizing tactic might be considered a tactic that aims to change a place's ideology through its semiotics. Objects, such as buildings or squares, denote certain functions and connote certain ideologies in relation to these functions. All objects have primary functions, which are denoted (utilitarian functions), and a complex set of secondary functions, which are connoted (symbolic functions).[2] The protesters who use this tactic play with the primary and secondary functions and evoke new meanings. Thus, using the ideas of Gayatri Spivak, who distinguishes between representations that speak *of* and representations that speak *for*,[3] the spatial choreography of reiconization can be conceived as a tactic that publicly displays representations that speak *for* to challenge the representations that speak *of*.

The reiconizing approach requires careful attention to the *choice* of the image/object. This type of choreography is not only about choosing names or using particular signs but also about creating a symbol that conveys meanings, feelings, perceptions, and beliefs that have not been thus attributed in the particular context that is associated with the action. At the same time, this "new" icon must be legible to the public at large. It must simplify meaning but not dilute it. Protesters play a key role in creating and spreading the icon; thus, the number of actors that support the icon is vital to its dissemination and influence on the public at large.

However, the power of this type of action is about not only creating the icon but also displaying it. The relationships between the icon and the place are critical to the meaning of the event as a whole. Spaces, especially monumental places, often include many symbols that carry particular contextual meanings; thus, the act of presenting something new is a powerful act of appropriation—not only of the place but also of its agreed-upon meanings—which can also be perceived as a violent act. Thus, in its radical form, this tactic will take place at a key focal point in the city, one that includes symbolic icons of the ruling powers, and it might dismantle these icons or replace them with new ones.

The icon's power is its ability to be replicated and, through replication, to spread and evolve in other contexts. When successful, meaning when it is adopted by the public, the icon is impossible to repress. If it leaves a mark on a space, it might irrevocably change the place's symbolic meaning, even if it is only displayed in that space temporarily. As a tactic, dramatic reiconization was used in the Tiananmen Square protests, which were led by labor activists, students, and intellectuals in the People's Republic of China (PRC) between April 15 and June 4, 1989. The participants were generally critical of the ruling Communist Party of China (CPC), and they demanded democracy and broader civic freedoms. The demonstrations were focused in Tiananmen Square in Beijing, but large-scale protests also occurred in cities throughout China. The PRC government's subsequent military crackdown on the protesters in Beijing left numerous civilians dead or injured. Protests in other cities throughout China, including Shanghai, remained peaceful.

Place

Tiananmen Square lies between Tiananmen Gate, the "Gate of Heavenly Peace," and the entrance to the Imperial City to the north and Qianmen Gate to the south.[4] Chang'an Avenue, which is used for national parades, passes in front of Tiananmen Gate. The Great Hall of the People lies along the west side of the square, and the National Museum of China, dedicated to the revolt in 1919, is located along the east side. The Monument to the People's Heroes and the Mausoleum of Mao Zedong are situated at the center of the square. The central location of the former, a 37.4-meter-high granite obelisk, which was completed in 1958, blocks the Imperial Way (facing north toward the gate and denying entrance from the south) and establishes the square as a locus of power.[5] However, the monument, dedicated to fallen heroes, is impersonal and conceptual—an abstract object, which symbolizes the founding of a new China.[6] Abstraction characterizes the design of the square, which is flat and bare, with trees lining its eastern and western edges. The space is heavily monitored by uniformed and plainclothes police officers, and closed-circuit television (CCTV) is installed in the lampposts in the square. The site's vastness gives visitors a sense of being small and ephemeral. Its walls and monuments and the coordinated distance from the historical Forbidden City—as well as the distance to and between the monuments—enhance the sense of order and the power to control this order. The physicality of the space represents both the Chinese people's passion for clarity in human relationships and status and "the will to power."[7] The square is about the *negation of death*; it is about *durability*. As argued by Lefebvre, "Monumentality transcends death. . . . A monument transmutes the fear of the passage of time, and anxiety about death, into splendour."[8] Thus, in Tiananmen Square, no arbitrariness, signs of life, or the chaos of daily life can be found.

The evolution of Tiananmen Square can be traced back to the reign of the Ming dynasty in the early fifteenth century. With the end of imperial rule in 1911, the center of power moved next door to the Forbidden City. The space was a pleasure park, and, shortly after 1911, it became a park that functioned as an enclave for the rulers. At the time, the Tiananmen Gate was perceived as an intersection of the north–south and east–west axial roads in Beijing.[9] It was not an independent place; it was instead an intersection that emerged from the juxtaposition of other urban elements. However, only after 1949, when the Tiananmen Gate area was chosen as the venue for staging the opening ceremony of the new state, was Tiananmen Square perceived as a "sacred place." Mao Zedong's choice was carefully planned, interweaving the narrative of the socialist regime with the May Fourth Movement in 1919, which was regarded as a turning point in China's "new democratic revolution."[10] As the capital of the newly established Republic of China (1912–1949), Beijing needed a spatial layout that was more adaptable, and the formerly private palace square beyond Tiananmen Gate was opened to the public.[11] Thereafter, a number of reconstruction projects were carried out to enhance the space's role as a national emblem of the socialist regime.[12] The square's development as an open area of approximately fifty acres required the destruction of numerous structures that surrounded the historical square.[13] The square was designed to host approximately 400,000 people, and, after Mao's death, it was further expanded to accommodate some 600,000 protesters.[14] Chang'an Avenue, which intersected the north-south axis of the city, developed into the busiest road in Beijing.

The design history of the place illustrates how, when revolt becomes revolution and a new political order replaces the old, the new regime's task is not to obliterate the space of the old regime; it should instead create a new spatial order that not only builds on the old but also invests it with new meaning(s).[15] Thus, Tiananmen Square went from being one of the most closed and segregated centers in urban history, which the Chinese people were forbidden to access, to become the antithesis of the forbidden, a space that was reconstructed to represent the people.[16] The square was considered a strict and static monumental complex, which externalized

Mao's vision of China's revolution, history, and people on a spatial plane, which went unchallenged.[17] However, since 1976, the situation has changed. The events of 1976 and 1989 can be regarded as an ongoing interplay between the efforts of the state to dominate spaces and the endeavors of oppositional movements to appropriate them.

Context

During the 1980s, the PRC was facing mounting economic and social problems, which, in turn, promoted the radicalization of liberal elites who were already critical of the government and contributed to the alienation of other students and urban residents. These dynamics were further accelerated due to domestic restrictions, which limited opportunities to go abroad to escape local realities.[18] As a result, students were more involved in domestic political activity,[19] and from 1988 to early 1989, dissident activities (i.e., conferences, posters, small-scale demonstrations, and petitions) started to increase among intellectual elites and radical students in the PRC, who called for political reform and democracy. These actions paved the way for the student movement that was active between April and June 1989.[20]

On April 15, 1989, the sudden death of Hu Yaobang, a former general secretary of the CPC, triggered the subsequent events of 1989. Hu was considered an outspoken and reform-minded leader, who lost his power in 1987, partly because of his support of the student movement in 1986. Two major events in the next few days contributed to the mobilization of additional participants. The first was the demonstration held at the Xinhua Gate, where the CPC Central Committee and State Council are located. After three days of demonstrations, participants were dispersed by the police, and rumors of violent police misconduct contributed to the mobilization of more students.[21] The second event was Hu's official funeral, which served as a point of contact between the government and the demonstrators. An organization for the students of Beijing was then formed, and it decided to call for a citywide boycott of classes.[22] Following these events, a critical student movement evolved, with the square being used as the center of their activities. The protesters' seven demands can be summarized as calls for democratization, free speech, and free education.[23] However, although it started in Beijing, the movement soon became a national one, gaining the support of millions throughout China.[24] Not only students but also other societal groups that wished to demonstrate for reform participated in the protests, which occurred concomitantly in other Chinese cities. Within a month of its launch, the movement included millions of supporters in some eighty cities throughout China.[25]

Guthrie describes the character of the dissident movement that became visible from April to June 1989 as a two-tiered structure: the first tier included student leaders and emphasized the role of organization in mobilizing students; the second tier included "ordinary people," who were mobilized through the use of symbols and public rhetoric. The connections between the two tiers and between different groups that took part in the movement were not strictly defined; nevertheless, the organized character of the student tier enabled the participation of different groups that were mobilized to use different tactics.

The movement, which did not emerge out of any existing organization, was spontaneously organized and relatively noncentralized. It started with the student organization of Beijing University, which quickly inspired more university organizations and a general organization for students in Beijing. These organizations did not have prior histories or legitimized leaders, and, overall, they were not necessarily coordinated in their mutual activities. As previously noted, the movement had *unidirectional effectiveness*, that is, the ability to mobilize people to action but difficulty in then controlling the actions of the mobilized participants.[26]

The first demonstration took place in Tiananmen Square on April 17, and approximately 600 young teachers and students participated.[27] Over the next few days, the students continued to hold demonstrations and participate in various activities, while the movement was becoming more organized and demands were being drafted. On April 27, some 150,000 students marched through police lines into Tiananmen Square; they received support from some 350,000 Beijing residents. In May, other groups, such as journalists and workers' organizations, became involved in the demonstrations.[28] At the peak of the movement, approximately 100,000–200,000 students occupied the square every night, a number that dropped to approximately 10,000 by the end of May. Martial law was declared on May 20, but by then the number of people in the square was estimated at over one million. From June 3 to 4, the government violently ended the demonstrations.[29] The protest continued for a month and a half, after which it was brutally squashed by the regime.

Event

Iconization, or the creation and public display of national icons, is the practice of those in power. The ruler decides on the configuration, meaning, and location of such icons. Thus, reiconization is a challenging task, not only because it requires an idea of what constitutes an icon and where it can be placed but also because it is a risky action that steps on the ruler's toes. Reiconization involves violating distance by dismantling abstract symbols, representations, and regulations and placing them in the context of the here and now. It is about counteracting the negation of death by contaminating the durable with bottom-up ideas. When this icon-making act is not coordinated, it can be a real threat to power.

The attempts of the students, who used the square's existing monuments as their field of action, included diverse but related place-making actions. First, a few hours after Hu's death, flowers were laid in his memory at the foot of the Monument to the

People's Heroes. On April 19, a portrait of Hu, made by students from the Central Academy of Fine Arts, was hung on the monument's plinth in opposition to Mao's portrait in Tiananmen. Under this new image, students gave memorial speeches, and, at approximately 6:00 p.m., a veteran of the 1976 demonstration called for the crowds to look to the future rather than to the dead.[30] Second, on May 20, a banner that read "Long Live the People" was hung in the square. On May 23, Mao's portrait in the square was splashed with paint. Third, on May 25, a replica of the Statue of Liberty was carried through the streets of Shanghai and placed in front of its city hall. Lastly, the action that was perceived to violate all political distance was the placement of the *Goddess of Democracy*, a seven-meter-high statue, in front of Mao's portrait on May 30. Although inspired by statues such as the Statue of Liberty (a young woman holding a torch), the goddess was not a replica; she projected an image of a young Chinese woman. The goddess functioned as the students' monumental symbol, which was placed in the square and added to the five monuments that would stand there permanently.[31] These acts were all part of the icon-making process—a means of externalizing and spreading protesters' intentions.

Apart from the "icon-making" actions in the square, other actions enhanced the protest's visibility, including students' participation in Hu's official funeral on April 22, an act that subverted its original meaning as an official ceremony; the televised dialogue between one of the student leaders, Wu'er Kaixi, with Premier Li Peng, which took place while Kaixi was hospitalized because of his participation in the student hunger strike; and the hunger strike of some three thousand students in the square.[32] The strike became an effective mobilization tool that drew millions of supporters, including hundreds of thousands of students throughout the country, within a few days; it also led to a leadership crisis within the government following the failure of its negotiations with the students and, ultimately, to the declaration of martial law on May 20.[33] In the final days of the protest, the events that attracted attention to the square were (1) the placement of the *Goddess of Democracy*; (2) the hunger strike by four intellectuals; and (3) the establishment of the Democracy University.[34]

All these actions transformed the space from a monumental and abstract space into a living space, where people remained during the day and overnight, negotiating, debating, and commemorating.[35] The space became human and negotiable. After its placement, the *Goddess of Democracy* served as an icon that represented the movement's needs and desires. However, although event participation was extensive, social distance remained. The student movement was tainted with elitism and self-interest, especially considering that university students in China represent the top 1–2 percent of the college-aged population and that most of them are urbanites.[36]

At least from the government's perspective, the protests were considered a total violation of political distance. Culturally, civil disobedience conflicts with the traditional patriarchy of Chinese society, where obedience is both revered by and expected from the young. Politically, government leaders viewed the civil disobedience in Tiananmen Square as a direct threat to the Communist Revolution.[37] Although some attempted to bridge the distance and develop dialogue between the parties, these negotiations failed because both student and government leaders denied their respective followers adequate representation. As shown here, broken negotiations matter because a significant portion of public violence actually occurs in the course of organized social processes that are not intrinsically violent. However, political regimes differ dramatically in the latitude that they allow for nonviolent collective claim making.[38]

The government reacted accordingly. The *Goddess of Democracy* was destroyed when a tank drove into it at full speed during the military crackdown in the square. On May 26, a military operation led to the evacuation of Tiananmen Square. Army regiments began entering Beijing, first disguised as civilians, and violent clashes between civilians and soldiers filled the streets. The final assault started on the evening of June 3; by the morning of June 4, the movement had been repressed and the protesters evacuated. Estimates of the number of killed and wounded vary, and due to the censorship of this information by the Chinese government, numbers are not definitive.[39] In addition, many were arrested.[40]

In sum, the distinctiveness of Tiananmen Square stems from the relationships between physicality and events, which manifest the agreed-upon and contested paradigms of nationhood. The protesters' occupation and control of the square and its defense by those in power symbolized the control of the Chinese state. Thus, the square should be seen not only as the container of the struggle but also as the physical object of the struggle.[41] However, although the *Goddess of Democracy* was destroyed, her ghostly image continued to haunt the regime. The icon could not be erased from the minds of the Chinese people.

Distance

Reiconization involves changing the political discourse and, in extreme cases, government rule. The icon, then, is a metaphor for this call to action, and it must be explicit. This tactic is made possible through not only institutionalized organizations but also by bottom-up movements, as it is about changing conceptions. It does not necessarily translate into concrete demands, but it puts those in power in danger because it challenges the premises of political ideas or decisions. Icons characterize many of the loci of power worldwide; thus, adding additional icons in a space might be perceived as a real threat to those in power and a concrete risk to activists.

This spatial choreography always symbolizes the need for change, substitution, and transformation. The notion of distance plays a crucial role in both the meaning of the icon (i.e., the extent to which the icon challenges the ruler's ideas), as developed by the protesters, and how it is perceived by those in power. Extreme political distance between the ruler and ruled results in the icon's total negation by the ruling power; however, in cases of moderate political distance, icons can be regarded as part of the negotiations over the future of the place. Importantly, icons are abstract; they are simplifications of meaning. The actual practice of place-making, bringing these icons to the site and performing rituals (e.g., speeches, gatherings, and shows), makes them concrete, thus boosting their significance and loading them with meaning. In addition, the icon's power is its ability to spread across time and space; once it receives attention after being placed in a concrete location, the icon has no boundaries. In this type of protest, the body is the carrier of the icon. However, the link between the new icon and place is stronger than the one between individuals or between people and place. As such, reiconization primarily focuses on challenging political and physical distance; challenges to social distance, if at all, are secondary. Thus, at its core, reiconization is about mobilizing dissent around an object that represents the protesters' claims and, in so doing, challenging or violating political distance.

❯ **REICONIZATION** | Beijing, Tiananmen Square, June 4, 1989

ATTRIBUTES

- Central Locus
- Symbolic Appropriation
- Image Supremacy

Figure 8.1. *Goddess of Democracy*, May 30, 1989, in Tiananmen Square. The statue was unveiled in front of the Great Hall of the People and the Monument to the People's Heroes to promote the pro-democracy protest against the Chinese government. Photo by Catherine Henriette/AFP.

Figure 8.2. Reiconization involves changing the political discourse and, in extreme cases, government rule. As such, the icon is a metaphor for this call to action, and it must be explicit. This tactic is made possible not only through institutionalized organizations but also by bottom-up movements, as it is about changing conceptions. In Tiananmen Square, a soldier guards the flag. Photo by author.

Key Features	**Tiananmen Square**
Location	Centre of Beijing, China
Buildings/activities	Government/national structures, symbolic monuments
Space	~440,000 sq. meters
Key value/concern	Symbolic, historical, cultural
Spatial definition within the city	A gigantic national public square surrounded by cultural and governmental monuments

Table 8.1. Key Features and Spatial Attributes.

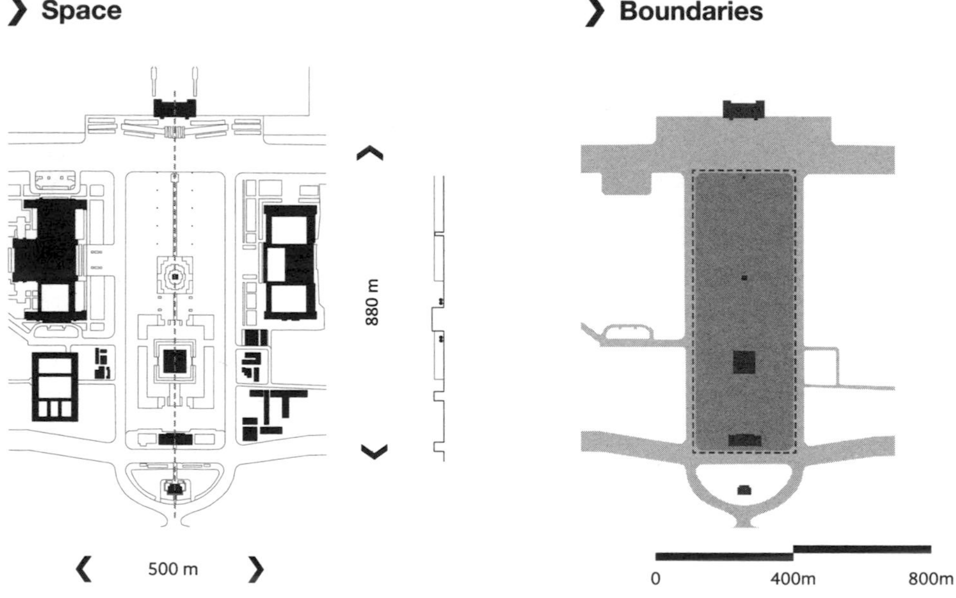

Figure 8.3. Tiananmen Square: Built form and space. Illustration by author.

Distance	Geography	Central iconic location with social and cultural heritage on a national scale; actions take place beyond physical boundaries
	Physical	Placing a symbolic object in the square that is associated with a competing political agenda
	Meaning	A revolutionary act against political distance and the structure dictated by the ruling power

Table 8.2. Event and the Conceptualization of Distance.

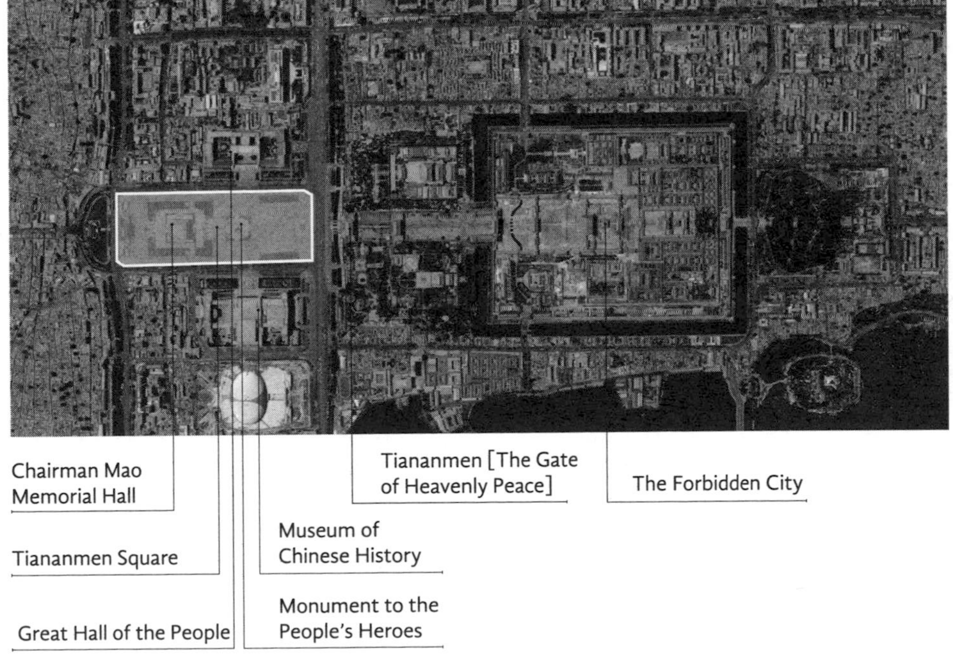

Figure 8.4. Tiananmen Square: Urban context and space of gathering, Illustration by author.

Figure 8.5. *Top*: Hundreds of thousands of Chinese gather around a ten-meter replica of the Statue of Liberty, called the *Goddess of Democracy*, in Tiananmen Square, demanding democracy despite martial law in Beijing, June 2, 1989. Families of those killed in the crushing of the 1989 Tiananmen Square protests on June 2, 2010, demanded that China end its silence and open a dialogue on the bloodshed. Photo by Catherine Henriette/AFP.

Figure 8.6. *Bottom*: Hong Kong, China, June 4, 2014. Thousands of people attend the Tiananmen Square 25th anniversary candlelight vigil. Photo from Lewis Tse Pui Lung/iStock by Getty Images.

CITY DESIGN | WASHINGTON, DC, NATIONAL MALL, MAY 13–JUNE 24, 1968

> The problem, first of all, was finding a site. So you have to plan without a site, like an ideal plan that would fit everywhere, in order to look for a site. And so first thing we had to say is how many people . . . and then we decided that it must have services, toilets obviously, and other kinds of services, day care, and so we had an essential program.
>
> Interview with Tunney Lee, May 4, 2004

A protest that is based on a city-design approach aims to challenge the ruler in his playground. It involves conceptualizing a new territory (a task often restricted to bureaucrats and planners) with a new spatial configuration that is defined and implemented by protesters. As such, city design is based on two primary interrelated sets of rules: morphological rules, which define the place's character and physical identity, and social rules, which define the dynamics and the activities that occur within them. The challenge concerns developing a sustainable new area that will both support personal needs (e.g., shelter and health care) and cultivate a collective cause (i.e., ideology). Protests that use this tactic should be considered an ongoing political, spatial, and aesthetic struggle. Thus, this tactic is not about having an instantaneous impact or about creating a spectacle; it is instead about cultivating everyday practices within an a priori sociospatial framework, and the physical setting is regarded as a manifestation of activists' ideas.

Spatially, city-design protests are about *flattening* space, viewing it as a tabula rasa on which new counter *design* rules can be applied. These rules include the definition of the project's scale, schedule, physical design, facility program, layout of objects, infrastructure development, materials needed, construction plan, security, and management. This tactic does not require a particular context and can be used everywhere. However, the chosen location may carry symbolic meaning as a means of attracting the attention of the ruler and the public. If these projects take place in a "center" with political significance, the setting will challenge the ruling power's space, and time will indicate the intent of a dialogue. If these acts were to occur on the outskirts, where the space is less controlled and flexible, the project would, in effect, suggest a claim over territory and perhaps a claim for autonomy. Therefore, the location should be a place that not only is equipped with adequate infrastructure to support the action (e.g., access to water and electricity) but can also accommodate the message that is projected by this space.

As an act that aims to develop a holistic system, a center of life, its success depends on the protesters' abilities to establish and manage a complex project. Similar to the responsibilities of the ruler, the use of this tactic and its successful implementation require (1) centralized leadership who conceptualize the project and (2) devoted participants who will agree to the new spatial and social rules. In these types of projects, participants are obviously recruited in advance and are willing to commit themselves to a long-term stay. Their participation implies a strong commitment to the cause.

Importantly, distance and distancing are key in the process of initiating city-design protests. Distance is not only about the protest's specific geographic location but also about the ways in which this location serves as a staging ground for other activities and thus influences distant locations and viewers. The leadership aims to reduce its physical and ideological distance from other potential actors or venues by demonstrating its high-level organization and implementation skills, thus expanding its influence. This tactic requires long-term preparation, funding, and experts. It was used in the case of Resurrection City in 1968, which was initiated by the Southern Christian Leadership Conference (SCLC) to call attention to the nation's neediest people. In 1967, one in seven Americans lived in poverty. The SCLC embarked on its so-called Poor People's Campaign by staging a march in Washington, DC, to draw attention to the nation's poorest people. In the midst of organizing the march, on April 4, 1968, Martin Luther King Jr. was assassinated. The SCLC pressed forward with the Poor People's Campaign just weeks later, and people settled on the National Mall in an encampment that they called Resurrection City. Jesse Jackson led protesters in direct actions around the city; however, the protest failed after participants became bogged down by heavy rains and unclear agendas. In the middle of the protest, word came that presidential candidate Robert Kennedy had been assassinated in California. Soon afterward, Resurrection City was closed.

Context

The Poor People's Campaign was conceived and planned by the SCLC, which was led by Martin Luther King Jr. in late 1967 and early 1968. The campaign sought to address the economic problems in black ghettos, given the growing tensions throughout the country, which included the rise of alternative forces calling for the use of violent methods and riots. King saw the Poor People's Campaign as the last chance to save the country from deteriorating into a state of chaos, hatred, and violence.[42] Touring the country to inspire the nation to address poverty and racism, King motivated people to join the campaign for fair jobs and incomes and the right to a decent life, beginning on April 22, 1968, in Washington, DC.[43] According to the campaign's strategic outline, several thousand people would convene in Washington to live together in a temporary town that would act as a center of protest. From this center, people would be mobilized in a mass demonstration, which would lead to other steps, such as boycotts of selected industries. Importantly, the campaign was intended to mobilize not only blacks but also members of all races to unite under the common goal of resisting economic inequality rather than focusing on racial injustice alone.[44] King's assassination on April 4, 1968, did not halt or drastically change the campaign schedule. After the assassination, Rev. Ralph David Abernathy was nominated to be the president of the SCLC, and he led the campaign through multiple sets of actions that included "a wagon train of poor people through the South; a shanty town in Washington; movements of poor people to Washington from all parts of the United States; a huge march on Washington; and continued escalating demonstrations in the Nation's Capital."[45] To do so, he developed a complex organizational mechanism. One of the main purposes of the wagon train, in addition to getting people to Washington, was to make the Poor People's Campaign visible to the rest of the country.[46] Resurrection City should not be considered merely a protest; it should instead be regarded as an ambitious project that attempted to challenge the distance between the government and the poor. Resurrection City's spatial manifestation reflects the social and political power structures of the actors that initiated it.

Place

The Washington Mall is the "front stage" of the US government. The Mall is a national park of more than one thousand acres that contains many of the country's significant natural and cultural resources.[47] The open spaces and parklands,[48] which were commissioned by President George Washington, were intended to create an ideal stage "for national expressions of remembrance, observance, celebration, and expression of First Amendment rights."[49] The monumental aspect of the capital aimed to represent the nature of government and the relationship between the rulers and the ruled. The site hosts numerous activities and special events each year, and it is seen to represent national values in its blending of "formal history and tradition and informal contemporary life."[50] Owned and maintained by the federal government, the park offers a large stretch of "nature" in the midst of the city's bustling urban environment.[51] Protests in the park are often large-scale activities, and the enclosed, detached nature of the Mall minimizes the protests' interference with the daily dynamics of the city.

Resurrection City was chosen as a site for pragmatic (size and access) and symbolic (visibility) reasons. During a meeting on March 10, 1968, Ken Jadin presented a survey on the issue. Among the options raised, the following were mentioned:

> 1. The mall would be the easiest to handle; 2. The S.W. area bordered by main and 4th, eye and buildings including Arena stage and some

apartments, would probably hold 2,500 to 3,000 people (better capacity estimate later). This would be relatively easy to handle; 3. The S.E. (& some S.W.) area cleared for freeway.[52]

Other options included a church and other parkland possibilities. Of the sites that the team of planners considered and suggested, the Washington Mall, which was perceived as one of the easiest sites to manage, required a permit.[53] The final location of the encampment was an area adjacent to the Lincoln Memorial. This area resulted from a landfill that, following the adoption of the Senate Parks Commission Plan of 1901 (McMillan Plan), became part of the legacy of the City Beautiful movement under the direction of Daniel H. Burnham.[54] The place, a wide lawn surrounded by trees, offered a flexible platform for the construction of Resurrection City and provided the organizers with suitable physical infrastructures and the symbolic advantage of being close to Washington monuments, especially the Lincoln Memorial.[55] As noted in the memos of the SCLC,

> Washington is the center of government power, the national capital, and a symbol of the American economic system. The federal government, based in Washington, has the power and resources to do many things to end poverty. Visibility was a key issue in choosing the location, as further elaborated by the SCLC: "If the American people will wake up to these evils, they can make their government respond. We have learned that the government does not respond to these situations until it is confronted with dramatic, powerful, massive actions."[56]

Indeed, as indicated in the quotation above, the site is a meaningful representation of power. However, two points should be clarified: Resurrection City aimed to use the site as a central residential base from which protesters could go out into the city for various events at federal agencies. It was not just a self-contained encampment; instead, it was a staging ground for additional actions. However, spatially, it was an extremely isolated space, with little connection to the daily life of the city. As such, it was less disruptive to the city's routine and economy, and it could be regarded as a constrained island of dissent.

Spatially, the development of Resurrection City included two parallel phases involving professional city planners: planning a structure for the encampment and obtaining a permit for an appropriate site on which to erect it.[57] The plan for the temporary city, which was prepared prior to the selection of the actual site, mainly focused on the expected character of the demonstrators and challenges such as security, health, and social interactions. Structurally, the city was carefully designed using planning terminology (e.g., neighborhoods and blocks) and a hierarchical sociospatial logic, as summarized in an SCLC fact sheet: "1 community = 4 neighborhoods =

1000 people, 1 neighborhood = 4 blocks = 250 people, 1 block = approximately 60 people."[58] The idea was that each community would have an information/supply center. For administrative purposes, Center I (located in Community I) would be the main center.[59] Importantly, this suggested structure was regarded as generic and adaptable to various site possibilities.

The key idea was that most construction would take place on-site with the protesters. As noted by Tunney Lee, one of the planners who participated in the project,

> We came up with the idea of 4 by 8 sheets of plywood, with minimal cutting. . . . We bought the materials and we had volunteer carpenters organize the work crews . . . the raw material was put on the site and work crews would come and build these . . . it really can't go wrong, part of this thing was how simple it could be done. . . . I think first we built one to make sure we could do it, work out with the carpenter, and then we had volunteers, many volunteers showed up.[60]

According to the plan, the temporary city was to include larger structures for services and smaller ones for living, with a main street that would serve as a central community area to both functionally and symbolically unite the diverse elements therein. Although the plan eventually had to be adapted, the main street retained its public character as the place where services were provided.[61] With all the preparations completed only a few days before the protest was to start, the site was approved, and the building process began. Poor people and volunteers, who formed work groups to work more quickly and efficiently, constructed most of the structures during the first week or two of the city's life.

Event

In terms of space, the activists successfully reclaimed the country's most iconic national space by constructing an alternative city. More specifically, they initiated a megascale event in a focal location; this required long-term planning and negotiating with authorities prior to the event regarding permitted actions based on an estimation of participation and growth. In that sense, the Resurrection City encampment could be considered an attempt to challenge agreed-upon distance and to control this change by creating an "accepted island" of dissent with clear boundaries.

Resurrection City's spatial design and components also influenced the dynamic among participants.

> As new groups arrived, they came very fast, so there weren't enough volunteers, so the groups would build it themselves. One of the carpenters would help them, but, you know, pretty soon people started to do their own things

> with it . . . each group would see what the other group was doing; some groups were smaller; some groups were bigger, so they just adapted . . . they stayed pretty much with the plan, but it was very loosely organized.[62]

In addition, during the weeks of construction, the committee attempted to have a representative at Resurrection City at all times. Once the city was more or less standing, it functioned less like a centralized community and more like an umbrella group that had similar goals but that did not act together at all times. Throughout the entire period from May 12 to June 24, demonstrators took an active part in community life through a variety of roles, first building shelters and later working as rangers and marshals, helping with food and child services, and performing other roles. The leaders of local groups had important roles in internal matters and in mobilizing people to demonstrate. Finally, Resurrection City had a mayor. As a whole, the city was organized like a real city, including a security force, which was considered important not only to protect residents from outside threats but also to maintain order inside the compound.[63] Although Resurrection City was located on the Mall, its boundaries were controlled and constrained, and the police force was not visibly present at the compound and did not take a lead role in regulating its activities. The site was also watched twenty-four hours a day by the so-called Security System, through which members of the community provided safety and security for those within the community. "They will watch for outsiders who are not authorized to be on the site and will prevent vandalism, theft, and any trouble that may develop."[64]

The residents of Resurrection City came mostly from the rural south and large cities in the Northeast and Midwest. Most of them were black, but there were also white, Native American, and Hispanic residents, among others. The residents tended to organize themselves into groups according to their original affiliation (e.g., the New York group or the Chicago group). Although there were supporters and volunteers from DC's black community, most of the white DC community saw Resurrection City as strange and even threatening.[65] The aim of the campaign in general and of Resurrection City in particular was to shift the focus from the local level to the national level and to include social organizations, religious institutions, and actors in the federal government. As King stated, "We hope, with growing confidence, that our campaign in Washington will receive at first a sympathetic understanding across our nation, followed by dramatic expansion of nonviolent demonstrations for specific reforms, and we intend to build militant nonviolent actions until that government moves against poverty."[66] Socially, the activists worked hard to bridge differences; create a coalition among various groups; and involve actors from the federal government, religious institutions, and community organizations. The structure of Resurrection City, as a spatially condensed fabric, helped develop trust and communication practices among the participants.

The city's spatial manifestation, order, and social dynamics mirror the power structures of this initiative. As a whole, the SCLC supervised, promoted, and monitored the campaign. Within the campaign, the SCLC differentiated between the organization that supervised and promoted the event and the masses that were supposed to occupy Resurrection City as demonstrators (i.e., poor people claiming their rights). Additionally, before the actual settlement, the organizers were divided into two groups of decision makers. First, the General Services Administration (GSA) was responsible for registering and identifying Resurrection City's residents.[67] The GSA also included professional committees, such as Structures, Food, Services and Administration; Child Care; and Workshops and Mass Meetings. Second, a more distant SCLC leadership was responsible for major decisions, mainly managing the campaign's finances.[68] This complex and rather hierarchical organization also prepared itself for unexpected scenarios.[69]

As they were monitoring and planning the event, the organizers established two key rules: no racism and no violence. They were conscious that "violence by the Campaigners will make the Congressmen and the middle-class Americans think the money should be spent in defense against the poor instead of in helping them. This will defeat the Campaign."[70] Thus, the participants were asked to follow a set of rules, which included the following: "Pray for guidance and commit yourselves to complete non-violence in word and action. . . . In all things, observe ordinary rules of courtesy and good behavior. . . . If cursed, do not curse back. If pushed, do not push back. If struck, do not strike back, but evidence love and goodwill at all times. . . . If arrested, do not resist or go limp. Do not argue or 'talk back' at the police, but go to jail with quiet dignity as a protest against America's treatment of the poor. Unless there are compelling reasons why you must be released, refuse bail and help fill up the jails with protesters."[71] Furthermore, the participants were warned that if they were caught violating Resurrection City's regulations, they would be brought to the community's director of security (or the person acting for him), who would turn them over to the District of Columbia Police or would handle the problem on-site.[72] In addition to this central organization within the city, there were efforts to form a council. Community groups formed their own local leadership, settling as groups in specific areas around the city's compound.[73] In this sense, the SCLC established the rules and a platform that allowed local initiatives to emerge and develop while order was regulated and maintained by leaders.

Importantly, the campaign was led by religious people with a worldview that envisioned the relationship between God and the state as a clear and well-defined hierarchy: "From a religious point of view, there are two types of laws: man-made laws and the higher law of God. This higher law holds that all men are equal and have the right to equality and a decent life. Worship of the state, or government, is wrong because the state is composed of mortal men and their laws. It is our duty under God to express our true loyalty by exposing the evils in our society and government and working to change them."[74] In terms of the political dynamic, two points should be emphasized. First, the campaign was led by a concentrated leadership that had a clear hierarchy between leaders and activists. The central leadership's approval was clearly needed for every detail. This approach also influenced the strict ways in which communication and regulation were practiced and used as a mechanism to create behavioral codes, thereby providing a degree of homogeneity. Second, the leadership was constantly in dialogue regarding their demands. This dialogue occurred between the leadership (who presented their demands) and cabinet-level departments (who responded to these demands). In essence, this dialogue was about reducing the distance between the poor and the government, as noted by one of the reporters: "Probably for the first time, in American history, nameless poor persons faced high-ranking cabinet officers and told them what they thought was wrong with this nation."[75]

Resurrection City existed for forty-three days. In late May and early June, the area was flooded. A storm began, and the "rainfall swelled the Potomac River, made a muddy morass of the Poor People's Campaign's Resurrection City."[76] At its peak, some 2,800 residents occupied the city, but that number dropped drastically after the rainfall, with only 500 people remaining. The city's life span should be seen in the context of the campaign and the process that led to it. Although those who stayed attempted to revive the city, the government gave the organizers a deadline to leave by June 23 at 8:00 p.m.—some six weeks after the city was constructed.[77] The final residents were evicted by the police. All the structures were removed and sold to a contractor, and the area was returned to its original purpose as a park.[78] The agreed-upon distance was reestablished.

In sum, isolated within the city, Resurrection City was developed as an abstract idea, and the initial program was developed prior to the approval of the site. The organizers used urban planners to design the city and recruited and supported its inhabitants. However, despite being geographically distant, this island of dissent on the Mall challenged the agreed-upon dynamics between national power and citizens, making the needs of the poor concrete. In other words, Resurrection City was a spatial message and a staging action that challenged the agreed-upon distance manifested on the Mall, offering an alternative symbolic array of a city and a place that was less grand and less formal.

Distance

City design is a grand tactic that is based on imagining a new event-place as a representation of an alternative ideology. This tactic involves creating a detailed project that supports daily life and evolves over time. As huge endeavors, city-design protests suit large-scale events or national campaigns in which all the key actors and participants are aware of their roles and support an agreed-upon imagined space. The protest's physicality is central, and the conceptualization of the new place, that is, the space's urban plan, has a major influence on the ways in which the distance among participants is defined and implemented. In other words, physical and social distance is mediated by the object; thus, various plans will create different configurations of distance. In this type of protest, the body is creative; responding to the space's physicality, as in the case of cities, is part of its imagination and place-making. Institutionalized organizations make this tactic possible; to fulfill its objectives, this tactic requires coordination between participants and authorities and the creation of coalitions with many different sectors. At its core, then, the city-design protest involves the construction of a utopian island of dissent that aims to bridge social and political distance through the place-making process.

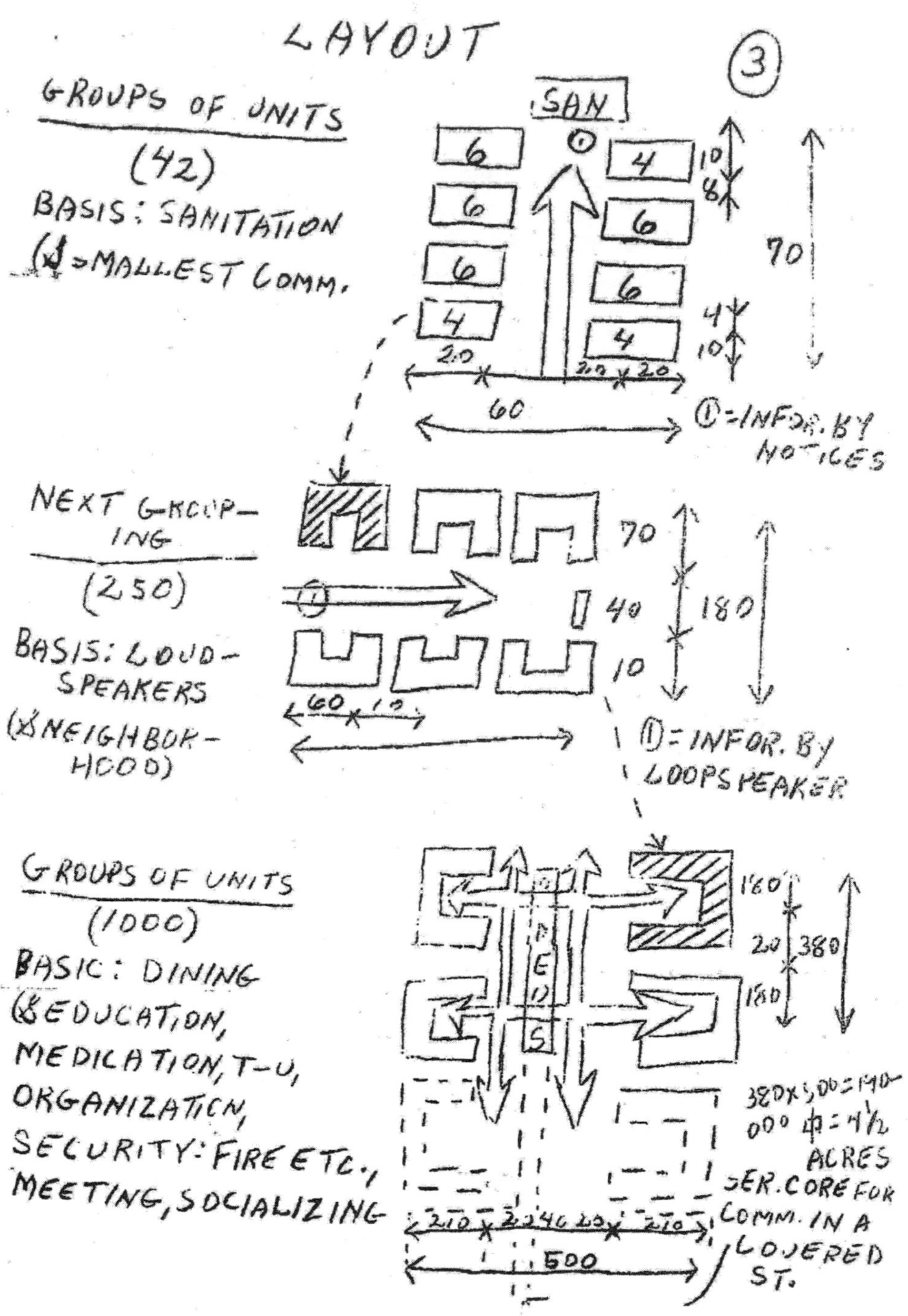

Figure 8.7. The layout of Resurrection City, Washington, DC. Source: "Minutes of the Shelters (& Site) Committees," Library of Congress, SCLC (4), March 10, 1968: reel 395, 28.

CITY DESIGN | Washington DC, National Mall
May 13–June 24, 1968

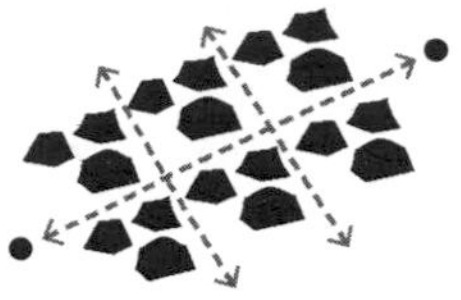

ATTRIBUTES

- Power Display
- Territorial Claiming
- Holistic System

Figure 8.8. Most construction took place on-site with the protesters. Resurrection City, Washington, DC, 1968. Photo by Tunney Lee.

Figure 8.9. *Left*: The Reflecting Pool, Washington Mall, 2007. *Right*: A pedestrian path along the Reflecting Pool and the location of Resurrection City (to the left side of the path). Photos by author.

Key Features	National Mall
Location	National Mall, downtown Washington, D.C.
Buildings/activities	Government/national structures, symbolic monuments, recreation
Space	~915,000 sq. meters
Key value/concern	Symbolic, leisure
Spatial definition within the city	A national multipurpose park

Table 8.3. Key Features and Spatial Attributes.

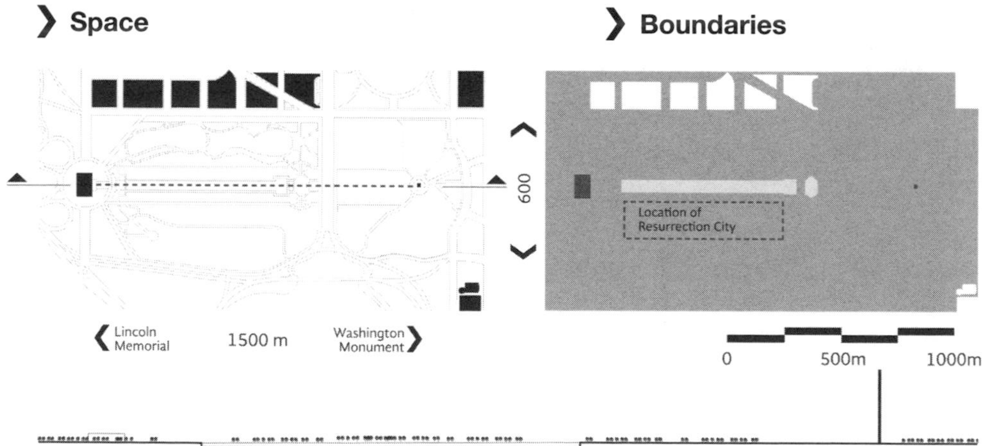

Figure 8.10. National Mall: Built form and space. Illustration by author.

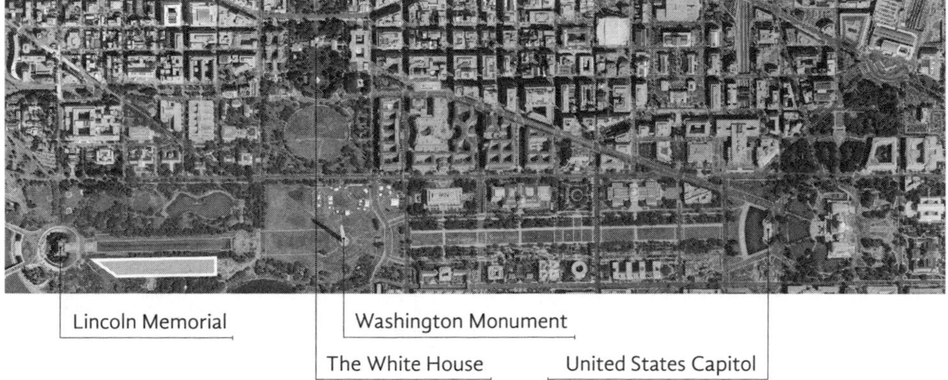

Figure 8.11. National Mall: Urban context and space of gathering. Illustration by author.

Distance	Geography	A distant island of dissent and a staging platform, from which actions take place beyond its physical boundaries
	Physical	Planned distance in the physical array of the encampment
	Meaning	Aiming to reduce (communicative) distance between national powers and citizens

Table 8.4. Event and the Conceptualization of Distance.

Figure 8.12. Resurrection City organizational structure. Source: Poor People's Campaign fact sheet, security system, 1968, Library of Congress, SCLC 886-12 (2).

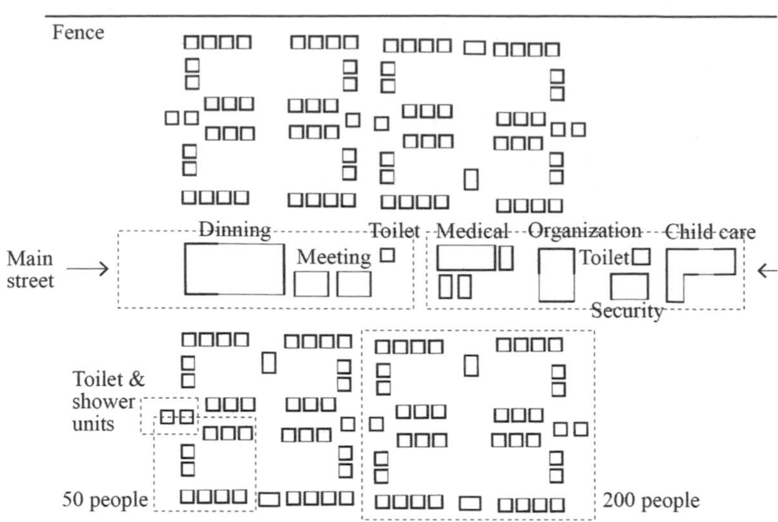

Figure 8.13. General scheme of Resurrection City, 1968. According to the plan, the city was to include larger structures for services and smaller ones for living, with a main street that would serve as a central community area to both functionally and symbolically unite diverse elements. Illustration by author based on a drawing prepared by John Wiebenson in "Planning and Using Resurrection City."

Figure 8.14. Demonstrators took an active part in community life through a variety of roles. Resurrection City in the mud, May 24, 1968. Photo by Marion S. Trikosko and Thomas J. O'Halloran, Library of Congress, Washington, DC.

NARRATIVE | NEW YORK, ZUCCOTTI PARK, SEPTEMBER 17–NOVEMBER 15, 2011

> As one people, united, we acknowledge the reality: that the future of the human race requires the cooperation of its members; that our system must protect our rights, and upon corruption of that system, it is up to the individuals to protect their own rights, and those of their neighbors; that a democratic government derives its just power from the people, but corporations do not seek consent to extract wealth from the people and the Earth; and that no true democracy is attainable when the process is determined by economic power. We come to you at a time when corporations, which place profit over people, self-interest over justice, and oppression over equality, run our governments. We have peaceably assembled here, as is our right, to let these facts be known.
>
> Declaration of the Occupation of New York City, September 29, 2011[79]

The narrative is a spatial choreography that aims to enhance people's feelings of empathy by telling a simple or even generic story that is popular and easy to digest. The narrative is understood to be generated by "the people," and its focus is society. It is often structured as an open-ended story, with a simple and direct message. Although it has a fixed core, the narrative is loose enough to be further elaborated and developed by whoever wishes to contribute to it. These qualities are significant for the recruiting actors and for the spread of the action to other venues. Thus, objects, placards, or any other physical means are often ready-made and instant, and they can be found or designed by the protesters. Usually, this tactic does not seek to control or unify the design of the actions, which are regarded as rolling events.

This approach's power lies in its minimal physical design preparation. The narrative's development and evolution is accumulative in both time and space, and predicting or calculating the boundaries or definitions of the event(s) is difficult. This spatial approach allows activists to tentatively initiate actions, to change or add new locations to their map of dissent, and to be flexible in terms of their participation and growth. In that respect, the narrative is often used as a unified means of simultaneously supporting a web of events in multiple venues. ICTs are an important tool for spreading the narrative and for developing spatial alliances that extend beyond the event's contextual (geographical, political, and spatial) boundaries. Social media, such as Facebook, YouTube, and Twitter, are used as the primary means of communication. The best way to describe this type of communication is as a cloud where a set of ingredients enabling mobilization coexist: identities, narratives, frames and meanings, know-how, and other "soft" resources.[80] This tactic is fundamentally different from the "old" prepackaged ideals and ideologically charged beliefs because it can be customized by and for individuals.[81] According to Jeffrey Juris, this network/cloud logic is based on four key principles: (1) building horizontal ties and connections among diverse, autonomous groups; (2) using the free and open circulation of information; (3) collaborating via decentralized coordination and direct democratic decision making; and (4) enabling self-directed networking.[82]

This approach mirrors political leadership, which tends to be diffuse. No distance or hierarchies exist among participants; instead, individual cells operate independently but maintain links to the movement through the circulation of information. Most importantly, this tactic can be regarded as "clouds of struggle" that change the ways in which scale is addressed and perceived, enhancing global-local relationships through social media and reconfiguring the relationships between places. However, although social networking tools allow activists to rapidly circulate information and to coordinate physical movements across space, they are perhaps most effective in recruiting large numbers of individuals to converge at particular physical locations for protests. Rather than generating organizational networks, this tactic primarily creates interpersonal networks, as seen in 2011, when outraged masses were shouting "We are the 99 percent," demonstrating against the inequalities engendered by global capitalism. The Occupy movement is an international protest movement directed toward social and economic inequality. Although the movement is an amalgam of different local groups with different foci, they all share the principal claim that large corporations control the global financial world, which disproportionately benefits a minority and thus undermines democracy. Its 2011 protest was highly visible, particularly after Anonymous, an internet hacker group, called on protesters to flood into lower Manhattan; set up tents, kitchens, and peaceful barricades; and occupy Wall Street for a few months.

Context

"Are you ready for a Tahrir moment?[83] On September 17, flood into lower Manhattan, set up tents, kitchens, peaceful barricades and occupy Wall Street." Inspired by the unrest in the Arab world, this call was published by the online journal *AdBusters* on July 13, 2011.[84] Two thousand people attended the first rally and marched on Wall Street in downtown Manhattan, and nearly two hundred camped out that night in Zuccotti Park.[85] The occupation continued to build over the next few days and weeks, partly because of the viral spread of images and police violence via the media. Without a clear strategic campaign outline, the movement mainly motivated responders to address rising inequality, unemployment, and the corporate influence over electoral politics. Protesters would gather in public places in a manner similar to their rallies in the online world of social networking. This spatial tactic of physically occupying public spaces had various goals, including a symbolic function, an educational purpose, a "glue" function, and an activation function.[86] Overall, the narrative and demonstrations under the banner of Occupy Wall Street resonated with many people and expressed a widespread sense of economic injustice and a desire for better political representation, as was manifested in their declaration:

> To the people of the world, We, the New York City General Assembly occupying Wall Street in Liberty Square, urge you to assert your power. Exercise your right to peaceably assemble; occupy public space; create a process to address the problems we face, and generate solutions accessible to everyone. To all communities that take action and form groups in the spirit of direct democracy, we offer support, documentation, and all of the resources at our disposal. Join us and make your voices heard![87]

The Occupy Wall Street campaign can be regarded as an evolving project that attempted to challenge the distance between global powers and the people. In this case, the action's spatial manifestation reflects the social and political power structures of the actors that initiated it. Spatially, the Occupy Wall Street campaign should be viewed as an autonomous, self-managed group of individuals who established an evolving platform that was characterized by the on-site development of various institutions, such as media, a newspaper, a library, and even spaces for meditation and worship.[88] With no legal permission, individuals united through the viral flows of social media, and the participants used occupation as a means of highlighting this symbolic struggle and as an opportunity to create a trusting space in multiple venues. The spatial evolution of these multiple encampments in different cities was based on what Jeffrey Juris calls the *logic of aggregation*. This logic helped facilitate and reinforce a widespread occupation that was considered both an effective protest tactic and a model of an alternative, directly democratic world.[89]

Place

Zuccotti Park is a three-quarter-acre site in New York's Financial District that is owned and managed by a commercial real estate company; it is accessible to the public under city law. This central urban space in the downtown area was intended to serve office workers by encouraging passive recreation, including resting, eating lunch, and playing chess.[90] The park's internal design is based on a skewed grid, with a long diagonal axis that crosses the two ends of the site. Pink granite pavers, benches, fixed two-seat tables, honey locust trees, and some five hundred inset uplighting strips have been laid along the grid to provide shade and light, while outlets in the tree wells and two spigots deliver power and water, respectively. The site's internal design and details (its long diagonal axis, benches, trees, and tables) had to be considered in the spatial organization of the occupation.

The decision to occupy Zuccotti Park was a pragmatic one, made possible by ambiguities in the regulation system of privately owned public spaces, which has created places in which the city government must negotiate its authority with corporate owners and site occupants. More specifically, "Zuccotti Park owes its existence to an incentive zoning transaction memorialized in a 1968 Special Permit that traded zoning concessions other than a floor area bonus in return for this public space."[91] As Jerold Kayden explains, "Unlike most other outdoor privately owned public spaces in New York City, Zuccotti Park is a one-off. . . . The nature of permissible public use, including the legal authority of the owner to impose its own rules to govern the conduct of those within the space, is undefined." Under existing law, the owner could not legally dislodge Occupy Wall Street or even apply for authorization from the city for a nighttime closing. According to one reading of the law, doing so is impossible.[92] The organizers knew that, while the city was tightly controlling public spaces and requiring permits for public gatherings, this privately owned place could be home to signs, megaphones, sleeping bags, tents, and blankets. Furthermore, the site's proximity to the United Federation of Teachers' headquarters, restaurants, and businesses allowed the participants to use their amenities (e.g., gathering places and toilets). The following weeks showed that the state would use police control to assert its hegemony over the terms of public assembly and discourse. When protesters crossed the border of Liberty Plaza onto city streets or squares, they encountered "order maintenance policing," a euphemistic directive that empowers New York police to intervene in public events, irrespective of criminal action.[93] Beyond the regulatory issues, the space is physically enclosed, a pause within or an extension of the city's network. Its defined boundaries and its human scale facilitated the participants' efforts to challenge distance and increased the sense of ritual and solidarity.[94] Here, the residential encampment of the protest site was connected to the rest of the city through periodic efforts to be visible to Wall Street and other actions.

Event

Although it spread quickly, this instantaneous framework found creating inclusive alliances difficult. Thus, as the encampment established itself and evolved, differences and divisions in the lived experiences of those inhabiting the park bubbled to the surface. As one group noted, "Though the distinctions were not hard and fast, the west end often felt quite distinct, even to the casual visitor. In general, it seemed that the eastern end of the park accommodated the more reform-orientated and middle class of the movement's supporters, while the western end housed more working-class and politically uncompromising activists."[95] Although Occupy Wall

Street sought to be a diverse and inclusive action, the movement increasingly had to confront decisions that permeated the wider society, as class-related and other differences became apparent. However, this spatial tactic succeeded in three main ways: (1) a physical, intimate, and immediate platform of interaction modeled an alternative community and generated intense feelings of solidarity;[96] (2) the development of a local-global platform of spatial alliances enhanced the spread of alternative communities; and (3) media coverage of the spread of alternative communities contributed to the debate over the consequences of inequality and unemployment beyond its geographic boundaries.[97]

Accordingly, in terms of space, the activists were supporting a web of events whereby dissent occurred in multiple venues simultaneously, with Zuccotti Park serving as a staging ground.[98] This strategy allowed the activists to tentatively initiate actions, to change or add new locations to their map of dissent, and to be flexible in terms of their participation and growth. Flexibility was also supported by social media, such as Facebook, YouTube, and Twitter, which were used as the primary means of communication within the Occupy movement. These means represent a new type of social mobilization, the opposite of defined hierarchies or definitions of distance. In this respect, the ready-made tent represents this flexibility and the event's nomadic character. However, although the occupation tactic was successfully adopted in other cities, scholars began highlighting the limitations of this approach even during the campaign. In particular, they issued concerns about the defense of a specific space's permanent and round-the-clock occupancy, which could lead to the fetishization of that space and make its defense the movement's overwhelming goal at the expense of actions that would further the broader goals that the space was occupied to advance.

Although this progressive, egalitarian, and radically democratic grassroots struggle aimed to mobilize all the sectors of US society, some have argued that it failed to represent the diversity of the 99%, being skewed toward the upper end of the spectrum of socioeconomic power and privilege (i.e., 81% of the protesters were white; 62% were male; 64% were young [only 1.3% were black/African American, and only 7.7% were Hispanic]).[99] The campaign's demographic portrait was very much influenced by social media practices (e.g., "bring a friend"), thus limiting the campaign in terms of diversity. Therefore, in terms of social dynamics, the Occupy movement activists aimed to be inclusive and to accept a plurality of actors, visions, and positions.[100] Accepting differences refers both to identity and to ideological positioning, with groups limiting and expanding their membership to suit their goals. Either way, this approach to social dynamics accepts differences as an underlying value that can not only expand the scope and scale of events but also give rise to conflicts among participants or result in a diffuse message. This acceptance influences social communication and the dynamics of the protest, with participants developing trust and solidarity on-site (if at all).

One of the key characteristics of the Occupy movement versus more top-down campaigns was the self-organization and consensus-based assemblies that involved hundreds of people in deliberations and decision making. These groups were powerful expressions of direct democracy in action.[101] As noted in their declaration of autonomy,

> Occupy Wall Street is a people's movement. It is party-less, leaderless, by the people and for the people. It is not a business, a political party, an advertising campaign or a brand. It is not for sale. . . . The people who are working together to create this movement are its sole and mutual caretakers. If you have chosen to devote resources to building this movement, especially your time and labor, then it is yours.[102]

Prior to September 17, participants planned to launch a major anti–Wall Street protest. In anticipation of this event, new committees formed, including a Food Committee, which raised $1,000 for supplies; a Student Committee; an Outreach Committee; Internet Working Groups; the Art and Culture Working Group; and the Tactical Committee.[103] The Tactical Committee had the greatest impact; this group "determined the time and place for the first General Assembly to happen and everything that would need to be done in order for that to happen."[104] In addition to the various committees that continued to act during the days of encampment, the movement developed a dynamic for participatory assemblies and horizontal collaboration. The General Assembly (GA), usually held at 7:00 p.m. in the shadow of the large red statue at the east end of Zuccotti Park, was a nightly display of consensual democracy, which soon became one of the defining experiences of Occupy Wall Street. Formally, the GA served a prosaic function as the campaign's decision-making body and the forum through which organizers ensured that the participants' needs were met. The GA also served as a platform for venting grievances.[105] However, the GA did not always run smoothly. Its proceedings could easily be derailed by people making unnecessary calls for the microphone or requesting superfluous information.[106] Moreover, the meetings were held publicly, were open to anyone who cared to attend, and were intended to give voice to anyone present who wished to speak, which posed multiple problems. Continuing debates focused on how to refine and develop this process and pondered whether the GA model could maintain its democratic character.[107]

The Occupy movement camps existed for nearly two months. Police forcibly removed protesters from their encampments in Denver, Portland, Salt Lake City, Oakland, Zurich, and New York City. Overnight, New York City police officers moved into Zuccotti Park, handing out fliers that told protesters that they had to leave or face arrest. At 1:00 a.m. on November 15, the police fenced off the park, and no one was allowed past the barricades. This forced eviction of the occupiers took place, even though the Supreme Court had signed a temporary restraining order that permitted protesters to return to Zuccotti Park. Ignoring this decision, New York City officials kept the park clear, reopening it at 5:00 p.m. after receiving a more favorable court ruling that banned tents and sleeping bags from the park.[108] Mayor Bloomberg claimed victory for the principles of obedience and respect for the status quo and emphasized that the eviction resulted from the collective effort of eighteen mayors in major US cities in conjunction with federal authorities. The collective effort of this national coalition of mayors can be regarded as a mirror image of the coalition among the different activist groups in the US. Importantly, the extreme political and ideological distance between the local governments and protesters contributed to the latter's abrupt eviction.

In sum, located in a central yet constrained place in the city, the Occupy movement was characterized as an evolving, dynamic process that developed on-site. Participants were recruited through social media following cloud logic, with little control over those who chose to participate, which was ultimately reflected demographically. However, although geographically central, this island of dissent in Zuccotti Park aimed to challenge the agreed-upon dynamics between "global powers" and "the 99%," which were both rather abstract categories. Wall Street served more as a reference point than as the core of the protesters' agenda. In other words, located in the here and now, in a concrete private space, the Occupy movement successfully created a narrative, which manifested itself as a dense occupation that displayed private struggles and anxieties in abstract terms.

Distance

The narrative concerns the here and now. Physically, these types of actions take place in spaces that are part of, or relate to, the narrative. In the case of an "economic" global struggle, the narrative will take place in sites that represent its power; a narrative that focuses on an "economic" struggle related to national issues might take place in a different space. All narrative tactics involve developing a story or a message that is popular and easy to digest as a means of assembling as many actors as possible—the more universal, open-ended, and direct the narrative is, the more participants it will attract. Thus, the power of the narrative's spatial choreography lies in its immediate geographical spread to distant locations. Political leadership, which tends to be diffuse, is the primary means of both reducing social distance among participants and enhancing the growth of the movement. Paradoxically, the more universal/global the claims of participants are, the greater the distance between actors and governments will be. A call to action needs an address. The universal simultaneously applies to everyone and no one, and it allows governments to disassociate themselves from grievances. However, the narrative is not a weak spatial choreography; in fact, it has many advantages: it is instantaneous and does not require long preparation or considerable funding, a real advantage in the context of ICTs. However, durability, the challenge of all protests, is a particularly complex task in the case of the narrative, which is based on the ad hoc development of social ties. Consequently, the narrative's potential to create an impressive visual impact, which publicly displays private struggles, is both its strength and its weakness.

NARRATIVE | New York, Zuccotti Park, September 17–November 15, 2011

| Of the people,
by the people,
for the people |

ATTRIBUTES

- Of the People
- Illustrative Object
- Accumulative Story

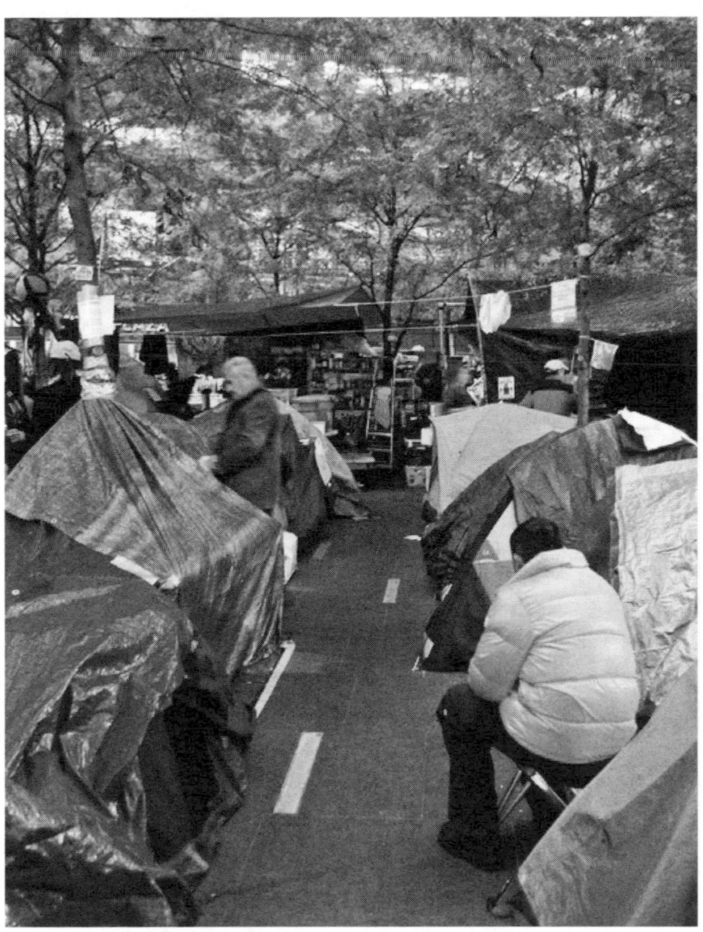

Figure 8.15. The Occupy movement created a narrative that manifested as a dense occupation that displayed private struggles and anxieties. Zuccotti Park, New York, 2011. Photo by David Shankbone.

Key Features	National Mall
Location	Financial District, downtown New York City
Buildings/activities	Meeting place
Space	~3,800 sq. meters
Key value/concern	Leisure
Spatial definition within the city	An urban block designed as a park

Table 8.5. Key Features and Spatial Attributes.

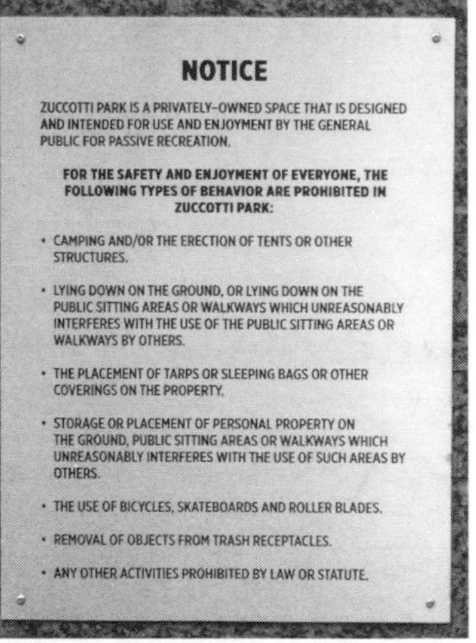

Figure 8.16. A placard declaring the ambiguities in the regulation system of privately owned public spaces in New York City. Photo by Chris Rhie.

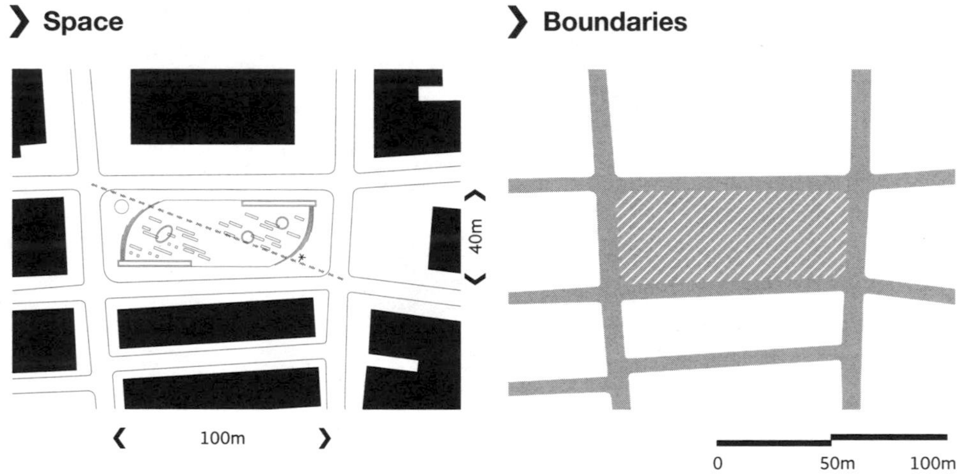

Figure 8.17. Zuccotti Park: Built form and space. Illustration by author.

Distance	Geography	A central island of dissent and staging platform, from which actions take place beyond its physical boundaries
	Physical	Unplanned distance, dense occupation, and arbitrariness
	Meaning	Aiming to reduce the distance between global/economic powers and the people (communicative channel does not exist)

Table 8.6. Event and the Conceptualization of Distance.

Figure 8.18. Zuccotti Park: Urban context and space of gathering. Illustration by author.

Figure 8.19. This central urban space was intended to serve office workers by encouraging passive recreation, including resting, sitting for lunch, and playing chess. Photo by Chris Rhie.

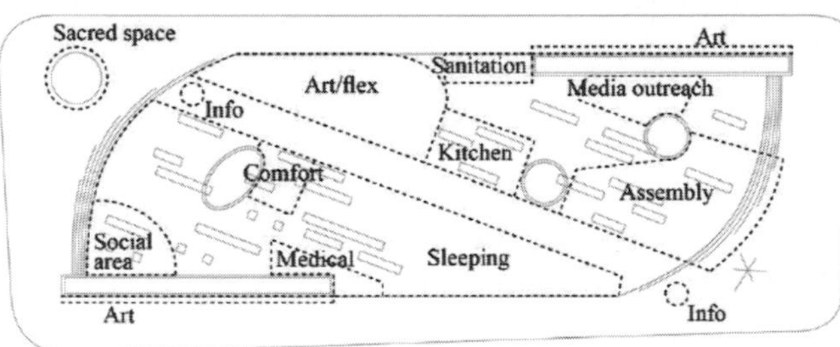

Figure 8.20. General scheme of spatial array in Zuccotti Park, New York, 2011. The activists were supporting a web of events, whereby dissent occurred in multiple venues simultaneously, with Zuccotti Park serving as a staging ground. Illustration by author based on a drawing prepared by Jonathan Massey and Brett Snyder in "Mapping Liberty Plaza."

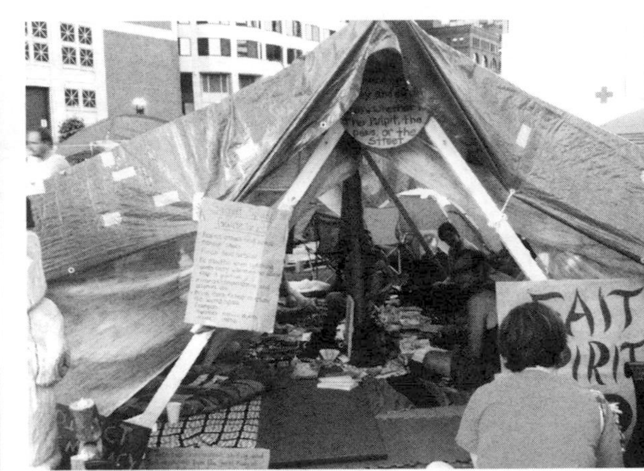

Figure 8.21. *Above*: Occupy movement, Boston, 2011. Photos by Anna Muessig. *Below*: Space of Info, Occupy movement, Zuccotti Park, New York, 2011. Photo by David Shankbone.

PART III

Continuum

ר אלים
יך להשפט

9
Performing Protestability

Previous page: Ethiopian Israelis clash with police during a Tel Aviv protest. Photo by Yaira Yasmin.

CHAPTER 9

Performing Protestability

> Any politics which acknowledge the openness of the future (otherwise, there could be no realm of political) entails a radically open time-space, a space which is always being made.
>
> Doreen Massey, *For Space*

Each era is different in terms of the ways in which distances are conceptualized and protests are performed and controlled. Thus far, the twenty-first century marks an era of the sophisticated crowd, which is determined to participate in the decision-making process. Different from the crowds of Sigmund Freud or Gustav Le Bon,[1] contemporary crowds are *conscious* about their power in advocating for a change. Whether political upheaval, symbolic transformation, social alteration, or all of the above, social change is a key goal in any protest.[2] To achieve this goal, activists carefully and strategically plan their actions in hopes of realizing change. This process of planning is about designing a direction for how to effect the desired change. As Charles Tilly argues, the planning of the event is influenced by the context and the setting at a particular time in history, which has a significant impact on the ways that protesters see and organize themselves.[3] With contextual variations, people in the twenty-first century have become more active and responsive to political dynamics and have learned how to translate this *responsiveness* into communicative action. Not all protests aim to achieve radical change; most protests can be regarded as a form of "spatial dialogue" or "public negotiation" over a contested matter, which is displayed physically and publicly. These spatial dialogues are supported by communication technology that contributes significantly to this process, not only as a means of communication but also as a means of exposure. However, communication technologies are merely the means; protests are fueled by the people's will to respond, discuss, negotiate, debate, and resist political dynamics and their ability to reimagine spaces. This will is growing stronger. In contemporary times, this will is the very basic tool that people can use to temporarily *break free of individualist constraints* by constructing temporary collectives that suggest counter positions to the social status quo.

Figure 9.1. Protest in Tahrir Square, Cairo, Egypt, July 2011. Young Egyptians call for investigations into the killing of protesters by police officers in one of the earlier protests of the Egyptian revolution. Photo by Yaira Yasmin.

Figure 9.2. The protest in Rabin Square was part of the summer social justice protests and the tent cities protest during summer 2011. Protesters in Rabin Square, Tel Aviv, Israel, May 2011. Photo by Yaira Yasmin.

In a world of social and political fragmentation, in which all sense of community has been "lost," protest events are bolstering the illusion of "togetherness." Participation in collective actions is a social process that creates organizational bonds and affective ties with fellow members and participants, which facilitate the creation of shared solidarities and identities.[4] Indeed, as Elias Canetti argues, during a protest, the people "who suddenly feel equal have not really become equal; nor will they feel equal forever"; instead, they "return to their separate houses, they lie down on their own beds, they keep their own possessions and their names."[5] They maintain their distance from one another. Nevertheless, although activists are aware of this gloomy prospect, physical protests remain a method of political partnership and a tactic for maintaining or changing places. Thus, the *civilian consciousness* of the capacity to act, *the responsiveness of the public* to political dynamics, and the need to temporarily *break free of individualist constraints* have dramatically changed and influenced the dynamics and choreographies of protests.

Moreover, the performance of contemporary protest events can be better understood in the context of two major conceptual changes associated with: (1) the concept of deliberative democracy and (2) the politics of scale. First, in understanding contemporary forms of participation, it is helpful to question the canonic ideas about the state and democracy (as suggested in the writings of John Rawls and Jürgen Habermas,[6] who advocate for practical rationality as the foundation of consensus) and adopt the more recent ideas of Chantal Mouffe regarding democracy. Mouffe argues that (national) consensus is not necessarily a desirable or achievable aim. Instead, political contestation, the experience of conflict, and the reality of exclusion make up a central part of contemporary life, which should be understood as "agonistic" engagement.[7] This conflictual dialogue is seen to be a vital component of democracy. Following this rationale, she argues, democracy should attempt to create practices and institutions that allow conflict to emerge and take an agonistic form, "a form of adversarial confrontation instead of antagonism between enemies."[8] Thus, as agonistic engagements, contemporary protests should not be seen as struggles between adversaries but as part of the agonistic order that characterizes contemporary democracy, which is more receptive to a multitude of voices, the struggles in pluralist societies, and the complexity of their power structure. Undeniably, contemporary protesters do not aspire to a harmonistic idea of democracy or to an accessible public sphere with equal positions for all citizens; rather, they perceive the public sphere as an arena of conflict, with protest events manifesting desires and demands that might affect the field of politics.

Second, our particular time in history should be understood through the lens of the dramatic change in the conceptualization of the politics of scale.[9] The discourse about scale is debated, with scholars suggesting three trajectories for its understanding.[10] The first affirms the hierarchical conceptualization of scale. Verticality suggests a three-scale map, which includes the microscale of the urban as the domain of experience, the mesoscale of the nation-state as the sphere of ideology, and the macroscale of the global as the scale derived from the materialist's position (centered on the world of economy).[11] The second approach develops a hybrid concept of vertical–horizontal models for addressing social processes.[12] This approach celebrates flow and mobility, focusing on network relations and emphasizing the global–local scale.[13] The third abandons scale entirely, suggesting instead a flat ontology that focuses on the notion of event-spaces and event-reactions to avoid the predetermination of hierarchies and boundaries. This sea change in the conceptualization and politics of scale is also apparent in contemporary protests, which present a complex scale's (not systematic) morphology and through which actors construct spaces of change. In that sense, it is not the ICTs that dramatically changed the dynamic of contemporary protests. It is how people understand the politics of scale and how they learn to use it in their claims for change. Worldwide protests against the invasion of Iraq (2003), the Occupy movement (2011), and the Women's March (2017) are all actions associated with this awareness of scale and the concrete and symbolic roles of urban spaces in a globalized world.

These agonistic engagements, with multiple actors and voices, and the awareness of the politics of scale have resulted in the supremacy of synchronicity as a choreography.[14] Protests are based on a network of national movements and ad hoc connections among people from more than one country, who mobilize around a common concern. Synchronicity uses the "network" concept and escapes hierarchical leadership, relying significantly on ICTs. A prominent example of this choreography is the Women's March on Washington (January 21, 2017, at 10:00 a.m.). A day after the inauguration of the forty-fifth president of the United States of America, a women's march coursed through main streets of the capital city. This march was a carefully planned and organized performance, starting at the intersection of Independence Avenue and Third Street SW near the US Capitol; an additional five entry points were spread along the march route (located on both sides of Independence Avenue), which ended at the National Mall.

The event followed four key principles that can be seen in numerous current protests. *Tolerating difference* based on the acceptance of a plurality of actors, visions, and instruments for social transformation, with groups limiting and expanding their membership in ways that suit their goals. For example, the Women's March on Washington wanted to be seen as an inclusive act that would be the first step in what the organizers hoped would spark a social movement. The chant of "Women's Rights are Human Rights, and Human Rights are Women's Rights" extends to a wide range of civil rights: reproductive rights, LGBTQIA rights, labor rights, rights for those with disabilities, immigrant rights, and environmental justice. In fact, organizers declared the following:

> We support the advocacy and resistance movements that reflect our multiple and intersecting identities. We call on all defenders of human rights to join us. This march is the first step towards unifying our communities,

> grounded in new relationships, to create change from the grassroots level up. We will not rest until women have parity and equity at all levels of leadership in society. We work peacefully while recognizing there is no true peace without justice and equity for all.[15]

Another principle, *organizational decentralization*, is not concentrated but diffuse, often restricting itself to specific goals. In the case of the Women's March, which was open to different groups and individuals, no leadership was claimed. Often, the organizational structure also translates into a geographical logic of *multiplicity*. Instead of a megascale event in a city center, many actions take place in multiple venues simultaneously. Each act is organized by its respective local group, which allows activists a degree of flexibility in changing/adding new locations to their map of dissent and in increasing participation. This *informal dynamic* can be seen in the map of the Women's March, with an estimated 440,000 participants in Washington, DC, and approximately 4 to 5 million participants in different locations worldwide. Spatially, the use of urban space is direct in this type of action, and the event's repertoire is basic, often a procession that ends at a known central point. Most of these protests took to the streets, public parks, and squares—in front of national and municipal buildings and US embassies. Social media significantly contributed to the spread and scale of this event. A dedicated website was installed; under the "resources" page, forty different online tools were listed, including a map of the march route, a printable guide for the day of the protest, digital security for protesters, an outline of protesters' legal rights, ways of commuting, volunteer opportunities, and the unity of goals, which helped participants before, during, and after the main event. Protesters were asked not to engage in any illegal actions and to obey local and federal law enforcement officers. The march was meticulously planned and cooperated with the local authorities, with over one thousand marshals providing directions to the marchers. A private security firm was also hired; some professional security workers were identified, but some did not accompany the participants throughout the entire march. Law enforcement officers were committed to not arresting any undocumented immigrants who were participating in the march, and a legal team for immigrant rights was available at the event.

The Women's March on Washington was broadcast online on Facebook and Twitter, and national and international mass media provided extensive coverage of the march. Nurturing connectivity and solidarity among different protest groups in different locations around the world as a means of constructing an orchestrated spectacle on a global scale, the march was based on some key agreed-upon design elements, including (1) the action repertoire; (2) unified slogans, which could be downloaded from a dedicated website; and (3) the simultaneous timing of the protests. The peaceful nature of the march and the image created with the help of the "pussy hat project" created a collective visual statement and a memorable and distinct image. However, although this spatial choreography was quite photogenic, enabling demonstrators to reach a wider constituency and to capture the public's imagination, this type of action is often seen to be about objecting to something rather than standing for something, which is why governments or elites tend to tolerate and even support these types of events and thus contribute further to their normalization.

This spatial choreography is becoming popular, enjoying the strength of social media in defining the spatial choreography of the event; however, it is limited in terms of how it redefines: (1) social distances and (2) spatial distance. With regard to the former, ICTs help bring many actors to the event, but they do not help bridge differences; in other words, they are unable to recruit from multiple sectors, such as religious communities, the federal government, and social organizations, under an agreed-upon message, a process that might increase trust and allow participants, even temporarily, to feel that they belong to an imagined society. Paradoxically, contemporary protests present a social profile of participants that is not sufficiently diverse, and messages are varied, triggering fragmentation. With regard to the latter, the planning process of events predominantly focuses on logistics and the impact of the media in producing a memorable image. However, this primacy of sight over content results in a lack of new meanings attached to public spaces or a lack of new futures.

Furthermore, the choreography of contemporary protests raises new questions about the relationships between the diffuse, open system suggested by activists and the structural (often bounded) system of political power. How are these two systems correlated? Can their different conceptualizations of space coexist? A pessimistic reply would point to the miscorrelation between the two and the difficulties associated with bridging the gap between them. This perspective would help explain violence toward activists and the need for a geography of domination to keep a system stable (i.e., the state). An optimistic reply would argue that protests are platforms that can help fortify a knowledge-based agonistic and democratic dialogue, which is built on the free exchange of dissenting ideas. A pragmatic response would argue that this process cannot be stopped; thus, both the state and people in democratic and nondemocratic regimes need to immerse themselves in a mutually reformative adaptation process that considers the juxtaposed spheres in which we exist and act. After all, in a global world of thought, we can find new ideas through acts of dissent, which can be presented, assessed, and debated. Engaging in this process, people must also consider themselves part of a larger whole and refuse to retreat to the isolation of the private sphere. To counteract discrepancies, imagination may be the only tool at their disposal.

CHALLENGING DISTANCE IN FUTURE PROTESTS

In perceiving protests as dynamic political and sociospatial practices, the key questions are as follows: How do contemporary choreographies of protest enhance or limit change? How can we use the choreography of protest to go beyond public displays of suffering and distress and instead make such suffering and distress a public concern? How can we conceptualize social and political distance in a new way that will effect change? What are the contemporary challenges of protests, and how might they affect future manifestations?

Contemporary activists clearly face numerous challenges, but, paying particular attention to the concept of distance, four such challenges are outlined here: First, the dynamics between the citizens/residents, municipalities, and state and global powers have dramatically changed, and their relationships cannot be seen as linear or hierarchical. This change dramatically affects not only the target of protests (i.e., the address of protests) but also the choreography of protest as a whole. If activists in the past were expressing their local grievances to the municipality and their national concerns to the government, many of the local concerns today stem from global dynamics. *The hierarchy is broken*; the scale is flattened. The narrative choreography is often applied in protests that address trade agreements, which respond to global dynamics. However, as previously stated, the more universal/global the participants' claims are, as examined in the case of the Occupy movement, the greater is the distance between the protesters and the governments, which might also result in violence toward activists. This distance, stemming from protesters addressing anomalies of global concern, allows governments to disassociate themselves from public grievances.

A second, related challenge is the "normalization" of protests. Protests are not rare or unique events anymore; they instead represent a "normal" communicative practice. This process of normalization changes the social configuration of protests and attracts more first-timers and more diverse crowds.[16] Moreover, the more protests become an accepted means of participation, the more they will attract social movements that defend mainstream issues, which represent and attract more heterogeneous crowds.[17] This process of normalization will most likely continue in the future, as it is seemingly a self-reinforcing process. However, this normalization allows those in power to address protests as habitual occurrences, as acts that do not challenge power or endanger those in power; thus, protesters' messages can be ignored. In that respect, normalization does not challenge political distance but instead acts within the existing boundaries.

Another related challenge is the emergence of the "post-political city," that is, "managing the spatial distribution and circulation of things and people within a consensually agreed neo-liberal arrangement."[18] Cities are often represented as cohesive and inclusive places where division, conflict, and polemics are being marginalized. In particular, consumption practices supported by technological platforms have enhanced the shrinkage of social space. As Eric Swyngedouw argues, "The social space is increasingly colonised or sutured by consensual neo-liberal techo-managerial policies."[19] This social colonization process is tightly linked to the dramatic increase in surveillance practices and the personal use of technological devices. Surveillance practices are used in many cities that have installed technological means to monitor and control public spaces to diminish fear and anxiety among inhabitants. Ideas and projects such as

"Safe City," "City without Violence," and "Smart City," which have been implemented worldwide (in large cities and small towns in democratic and nondemocratic regimes), propose to "protect" people in urban spaces by monitoring and observing individuals and tracking people's locations and activities to "optimize services." However, municipalities or governments are not the only ones to modify behavioral patterns in public spaces; the personal use of technological devices, particularly location-aware technologies, also influences patterns of mobility throughout cities and people's relationships with places,[20] dramatically changing the forms of public exchange. This state of affairs, which blurs the distinction between the real and the virtual, modifies through consumption and surveillance practices the social sphere and its politics.

Finally, another related challenge is the power of social and traditional media, which enhances the supremacy of images, of sight and visibility over text, meaning, and processes. Sight and visibility have always been key categories for understanding the dynamics at work in public spaces. However, with the development of social media and the significant role of images, sight and visibility have become central when examining the means through which people project themselves and, at least partially, manage their behaviors in public. Visibility—or, as Andrea Mubi Brighenti argues, the practice of "seeing and being seen"—constitutes forms of noticing, managing attention, and determining the significance of events and subjects. "Visibility lies at the intersection of aesthetics (relations of perception) and politics (relations of power)."[21] These relationships are central in media technologies, which function as extensions of the corporeal senses and "contribute to selectively enhance a certain type of sensory perception and establish a 'ratio' among the senses, a hierarchical ranking."[22] This observation regarding the ways in which media technologies have modified visibility practices is linked to the choreography of contemporary protests, which prioritizes the image of the event over other components, particularly social distance and the role of trust and solidarity in cultivating change.

› HOW CONTEMPORARY CHOREOGRAPHY OF PROTESTS ENHANCES OR LIMITS CHANGE

Key Principles of Current Protests	··›	Key Challenges of Future Protests
- Tolerating Difference - Multiplicity Logic - Organizational Decentralization - Informal Dynamic		**Political**: Post-political city, consensual neoliberal techo-managerial policies **Social**: "Normalization" of protests **Spatial**: Supremacy of technology and visualization, prioritizing the image of the event over other components

Figure 9.3. The challenges of future protests.

Figure 9.4. Protests are not rare or unique events anymore; they instead represent a "normal" communicative practice. Shown are protests across Israel against the Natural Gas Deal, Tel Aviv, November 2015. Photos by Yonatan Gat.

These dramatic changes in the conceptualization of the politics of scale—the normalization of protests, the emergence of the postpolitical city, and the supremacy of technology and visualization—define new links between observing, knowing, and acting for both governments and individuals. However, the key question is ultimately more profound. Acknowledging that we live in a technology-based society and that individuals have more tools with which to manage and "show" themselves in public, the question becomes how these practices—both data collection through CCTV and the sharing of information through location-aware technologies—change public spaces and collective actions. The question is not so much whether public spaces, as experienced and monitored today, are still public but rather what opportunities such spaces provide. Today, individuals in public spaces are (willingly or unwillingly) becoming identifiable subjects. This visibility raises critical questions about some of the key categories in the literature associated with protests, such as the "crowd," the "front," and "distance." In addition, are these categories emptied of their meaning now that virtual spaces are considered the "front," especially when this new "front" is a platform through which identifiable subjects communicate? This condition, nurtured by both agencies and subjects, suggests that the idea of urban public spaces as places that provide relative anonymity is increasingly inaccurate. What are the future configurations of public spaces? How might these configurations affect future public protests and spatial choreographies? Predicting the configuration of future protests is impossible. However, it is to be assumed that the new norms surrounding visibility practices and data sharing will alter the ways in which people perceive public spaces and protestability. In an age characterized by blurry boundaries between people, places, and spaces, further scrutiny of the dynamic notion of distance and proximity might be helpful.

PERFORMING PROTESTABILITY AS AN ETHICAL TASK

Challenging distance as an act of protest, which might violate order and stability, involves agency. Protesters are well-informed actors who engage with the details of spatial choreography, including the manipulation of symbols and their communication to the public at large. This process is critical in materializing the political battle and in challenging the prescribed and agreed-upon political and social meanings of a place.[23] As argued by James Mayo, the designer of a protest event "must manipulate symbols to direct participant activity." This process of manipulation, which is very much necessary to recruit an audience for the cause, also raises ethical issues. This manipulation process is the basis of any protest. Therefore, instead of questioning whether symbols are manipulated, we need to ask to what degree they are manipulated, how they are manipulated, and for what purpose.[24] The successful articulation of a protest design is not only about the visualization of ideological ideas but also about the creation of an "aesthetic environment which induces directed behaviour."[25]

This link between protest design and participants' behavior is vital, and it is further enhanced when the political organization increases its demands for participants' costumes and the arena's decorations. In other words, when political actors require greater control over participants' behavior, the need for design coordination increases. Public gatherings that adopt this approach can be regarded as overdesigned events. That is, careful attention is given to every detail in the physical setting and the details of the protest to create a holistic image with limited flexibility for subjective interpretations. This control over the image and meaning of the protest, which implies a high level of control over participants' behavior, raises an ethical paradox. On the one hand, control is needed to define the event's boundaries and meanings; on the other hand, control is a seductive and coercive power, which conflicts with the ideas underlying protest and free speech.[26]

This dialectic between design and control relates to the awareness and will to control people's consciousness and behavior in a particular setting rather than to a specific type of gathering (the spectacle, the procession, or place-making) or a particular spatial choreography. This ethical dialectic is also relevant to state-organized events. Public gatherings initiated by the state often seek to enhance consensus regarding a sociospatial configuration and, in turn, to achieve solidarity and national unity. Although the state and protesters might have different aims, their methods for action show many similarities. For example, conventional processions share many form-related and historical similarities with the military parade; they proceed in a disciplined fashion and with collective determination, conveying an aesthetic image and a threat of force. These aesthetics apply to spatial events and protests and to politics in general. Walter Benjamin has noted this phenomenon by referring to the Nazi Party, which was fully aware of the effects of the aesthetics of politics. This awareness was particularly evident in the 1934 Zeppelin Field event masterminded by architect Albert Speer, which relied on carefully contrived architectural orchestration and lighting. Speer directed a battery of 130 antiaircraft searchlights into the night sky to create his famous "cathedral of light." This event was not only a display of acoustic and visual power, with a planned rhythm that signified an imagined, unified order, but also an architectural spectacle. Neil Leach argues that by developing the sublime in Nazi Germany, architecture set the stage for an aesthetic celebration of the violence that underpinned fascist thinking, thereby enlisting architectural aesthetics to serve political power and to increase the tension between ideologies and ethics.[27] However, although extreme examples of symbolic manipulation in processions tend to be associated with the Nazi regime, sovereign displays do not merely serve dictatorships; they can also be found in most official ceremonies of democratic states.

This connection between protests and the design of urban spaces elucidates the importance of urban designers and architects as active agents in the spheres in which people and states negotiate with one another. However, as noted, design alone does not determine exactly how people will interact with one another; it instead offers possibilities for or restrictions on spatial interactions. Thus, unsurprisingly, architects and planners, equipped as "readers" and "designers" of cities, have participated as agents in protests.[28] However, their participation is infrequent. Echoing Antonio Gramsci,[29] most architects and planners, operating independently or within institutions, do not see themselves as reformers and perceive their actions as detached from politics. By contrast, at the margins, one can find an organic architect/planner who participates in the sociopolitical struggle and recognizes knowledge as a key component of modern power and as a condition that is critical to the creation and mobilization of society. However, although professionals might help materialize protestability, their participation is not obligatory. To a certain extent, during protests, each protester becomes an insurgent architect,

Figure 9.5. The supremacy of technology and visualization defines new links among observing, knowing, and acting for both governments and individuals. Hundreds of Ethiopian Israelis clash with police during a Tel Aviv protest. Demonstrators protest "police racism" and deride the decision to close a criminal investigation into a police officer who manhandled an Ethiopian-Israeli soldier, June 2015. Photo by Yaira Yasmin.

a translator, who helps shape society. He thinks strategically and tactically about what to change and where, about how to change things, and about what tools to use to enact such change—though still somehow continuing to live in this world. In the words of David Harvey:

> To insist on the personal as political is to confront the question of the person and the body as an irreducible moment (defined as a particular spatiotemporal scale) for the grounding of all politics and social action. But the individual, the body, the self, the person (or whatever term we wish to use) is a fluid construct rather than some absolute and immutable entity fixed in concrete.[30]

Embedded in a material context and in social and mental life, our body, the self, is integral to the craft of a spatial choreography, which makes it is a subtle ethical task. But political struggles are often judged not only according to their intrinsic ethical status but also according to their visual appeal and outward appearance.[31] A protest's choreography, its design, may fall prey to aesthetic corruption. Thus, while advocating for change, the protest's design must not only be sensitive to the event's spatial and political qualities and its overall aesthetics but also reflect a profound understanding of its ethical meaning with regard to society.[32]

Notes

CHAPTER 1. CHALLENGING DISTANCE

1. Historically, obedience was seen as a virtue, whereas disobedience was considered a sin. The historical reason for this belief was simple: a minority ruled the majority. Resources were divided unequally; thus, obedience was how the ruler obtained and maintained some of his resources. In terms of order, people wanted to obey, and the power was then seen as omniscient and good. In this case, obedience is good, and disobedience is evil. Fromm, *On Disobedience*, 26.
2. Ibid.
3. Canetti, *Crowds and Power*, x.
4. Birnhack, *Merchav Prati*, 123–124.
5. For further reading on the relationships between the design of place, national identity, and power, see Dovey, *Framing Places*; Leach, *The Anaesthetics of Architecture*; Torre, "Claiming the Public Space"; and Vale, *Architecture, Power and National Identity*.
6. For a discussion of the psychological approach to distance and the ways in which it affects the perception of events, see Liberman and Trope, "The Psychology of Transcending," 1201.
7. Tilly, *Politics of Collective Violence*, 197.
8. Davis, "The Power of Distance," 619.
9. Canetti, *Crowds and Power*, 20.
10. Hatuka, "Civilian Consciousness," 348.
11. In addressing contemporary protests, much attention has been given to the role of communication technologies and their impact on the relationships between activists. For further reading on how communication technologies influence dialogical dynamics in daily life and during protests, see, for example, D'Arcus, *Boundaries of Dissent*; Juris, *Networking Futures* and "The New Digital Media"; McCaughey and Ayers, *Cyberactivism*; Souza e Silva and Frith, *Mobile Interfaces*.
12. Goffman, *Behavior in Public Places,* 13–32.
13. Collins, "Private/Public Divide," 437–438.
14. Souza e Silva and Frith, *Mobile Interfaces*, 51.
15. Dovey, *Framing Places*, 11.
16. Edelman, *From Art to Politics*, 76.
17. For further reading, see Loukaitou-Sideris and Ehrenfeucht, *Sidewalks*; Low and Smith, *The Politics of Public Space*; and Zukin, *The Cultures of Cities.*
18. See, for example, Gershuny, "Web Use and Net Nerds"; Pfaff, "Mobile Phone Geographies"; and Ratti et al., "Mobile Landscapes."
19. Sarjakoski, "Networked GIS for Public Participation."
20. Brighenti, "New Media and Urban Motilities," 411; Manovich, *The Language of New Media*.

21. Sheller, "Mobile Publics"; Young, *The Exclusive Society*; Wacquant, "Territorial Stigmatization."
22. Sennett, *The Fall of Public Man*.
23. Putnam, *Bowling Alone*.
24. Turkle, *Alone Together*.
25. Bauman, *In Search of Politics*, 65; see also Slavoj Žižek's remarks to the activists of the Occupy movement: "There is a danger. Don't fall in love with yourselves. We have a nice time here. But remember, carnivals come cheap. What matters is the day after, when we will have to return to normal lives. Will there be any changes then?" Žižek, "Occupy Wall Street."
26. Giddens and Pierson, *Conversations with Anthony Giddens*, 94–150.
27. Arendt defines action as a human being's exercise of freedom, which is a combination of "I will" and "I can": the will and the ability "to take an initiative, to begin, to set something into motion." In the Arendtian scheme of the private/public dichotomy, action occurs when someone for whom the necessities of life have been satisfied in the private realm enters the public realm. For Arendt, public space results only from people's action—it is not a given. Arendt, *The Human Condition*, 177, and *What Is Freedom?*, 160.
28. Edelman, *Symbolic Uses of Politics*, 95.
29. Ibid., 101.
30. Lofland, *Protest*, 1–6.
31. Turner, "The Public Perception of Protest," 816.
32. Giddens and Pierson, *Conversations with Anthony Giddens*, 98; Henning, "Distanciation and Disembedding," 1188–1189.
33. Davis, "The Power of Distance," 602–603.
34. Liberman and Trope, "Construal-Level Theory," 440–463.
35. McCrea, Wieber, and Myers, "Construal Level Mind-sets," 51–68.
36. Liberman and Trope, "Construal-Level Theory," 118–134.
37. De Certeau, *The Practice of Everyday Life*, xix.
38. See, for example, Giddens, *Modernity and Self-Identity* and *The Constitution of Society.*
39. De Certeau, *The Practice of Everyday Life*.
40. Ibid., 29–42.
41. Ibid., 36–37.
42. Ibid., 37.
43. Holston, "Spaces of Insurgent Citizenship," 167.
44. Society is "organized around regimes of visibility that contribute to the definition and management of power, representations, public opinion, conflict, and social control." Brighenti, *The Publicness of Public Space*, 53.
45. This control of sight—of what is visible to various agencies (e.g., governmental and commercial agencies)—is associated with the surveillance and monitoring of the actors' activities to generate personal data. The increased collection of individual information was initially linked to more intensive forms of state policing. However, in the contemporary context of liberal democracies, states' interests in their citizens have gradually shifted from the maintenance of the power implied in state policing to a desire to ensure "national" improvement and progress. See Graham, "Spaces of Surveillant Simulation."

46. Massey, *For Space*, 148.
47. Ibid.
48. See Hardt and Negri, "The Fight for 'Real Democracy'"; Maeckelbergh, *The Will of the Many*; J. Smith, *Social Movements for Global Democracy*.
49. Castells, *Networks of Outrage and Hope*, 9.

CHAPTER 2. CHOOSING A PLACE

1. Knox, "Symbolism, Styles and Settings," 7.
2. Edelman, *Symbolic Uses of Politics*, 96.
3. Differing from military or police institutions, which exercise power and perpetrate violence in the name of the state, political settings are symbolic representations that are built for the public as reminders of authority and power
4. Vale, *Architecture, Power and National Identity*, xii.
5. Edelman, *From Art to Politics*, 77.
6. D'Arcus, *Boundaries of Dissent*, 20.
7. Edelman, *From Art to Politics*, 90.
8. Goffman, *Relations in Public*.
9. Goffman, *Behavior in Public Places*, 199.
10. Carmona et al., *Public Places, Urban Spaces*, 61.
11. Ibid., 68.
12. See, for example, Madanipour, *Public and Private Spaces of the City*; Putnam, *Bowling Alone*; Sennett, *The Fall of Public Man*.
13. Lofland, *Protest*.
14. Edelman, *Symbolic Uses of Politics*, 95–113.
15. Parkinson, *Democracy and Public Space*, 202.
16. Edelman, *From Art to Politics*, 90.
17. Carmona et al., *Public Places, Urban Spaces*, 142.
18. Krier, *Urban Space*, 19–20.
19. For further reading, see Loukaitou-Sideris and Ehrenfeucht's *Sidewalks* and Mehta's *The Street.*
20. Carmona et al., *Public Places, Urban Spaces*, 146.
21. The Azadi March was a public protest that was held in Pakistan from August 14, 2014, to December 17, 2014. The Pakistan Tehreek-e-Insaf Party organized this protest against Prime Minister Nawaz Sharif, claiming systematic rigging by the Pakistan Muslim League-Nawaz (PML-N) in the 2013 general election. Marches traversed many regions of Pakistan, including Lahore, Islamabad, Karachi, Multan, Mianwali, Sargodha, Gujrat, Rahim Yar Khan, Nankana Sahib, Sahiwal, Jhelum, Larkana, and Gujranwala. For further reading, see the Global Nonviolent Action Database, http://nvdatabase.swarthmore.edu/.
22. The goal of this protest in the streets of Lima was to condemn President Alberto Fujimori's illegal third reelection and to remove him from power. About 20,000 demonstrators from the

four corners of Peru, many of whom traveled by bus for several days to participate, peacefully marched down the streets of Lima to protest against Fujimori's illegal election to a third term.

23. For further reading, see Low, Taplin, and Scheld, *Rethinking Urban Parks*; Forsyth and Musacchio, *Designing Small Parks*.
24. In Turkey, for example, the equivalent to the square is the *meydan*, a mundane space, a junction of axes that joins structures and spaces that were not *intentionally* designed to define an integrated spatial entity. Thus, the scale, form, and style of buildings in the *meydan* are often not correlated with one another. Moreover, the *meydan* concerns the flow of both people and space, as opposed to the notion of control that is reflected in the square. However, this flexibility also makes the *meydan* changeable. The intentional planning of *meydan*s in neighborhoods did not exist in Ottoman and Islamic cities (excluding eighteenth-century neighborhood fountains, which functionally created squares around them); instead, large mosque courtyards in the proximity of marketplaces were the gathering places of the masses, as was the case with the Roman forum. Baykan and Hatuka, "Politics and Culture."
25. For further reading, see Halbwachs, *On Collective Memory*; Olick, "Collective Memory," 7–8.
26. This idea led to a better understanding of the role of memory in the creation of political identities, as discussed in the work of Pierre Nora (*Realms of Memory*), who examines the making of the French national memory in the creation of political identity; the work of Eric Hobsbawm and Terence Ranger (*The Invention of Tradition*), who explore the political utility of tradition in the construction of collective identity; and the work of Benedict Anderson (*Imagined Communities*), who studies the ways in which "imagined communities" are constructed as public memories to concretely affirm otherwise abstract ideals (Hutton, "Memory," 1418–1422).
27. Yiftachel, "Planning and Social Control."
28. This approach is prominent in the discourse on agency in everyday life. Hatuka and D'Hooghe, "After Postmodernism"; de Certeau, *The Practice of Everyday Life*; Lefebvre, *Everyday Life in the Modern World*; Chase, Crawford, and Kaliski, *Everyday Urbanism*.
29. Davis and Hatuka, "The Right to Vision."
30. Huyssen, *Present Pasts*, 2.
31. Ibid., 4.
32. Beginning with the discussion of the public and publicness, one can identify four key lines of thought: (1) a liberal-economic model, in which the public is defined by the state and administrative functions; (2) a republican virtue model, in which the public sphere is conceptualized as pertaining to the community, the polity, and citizens; (3) a model rooted in practices of sociability, in which the public refers to symbolic displays and self-representation; and (4) a Marxist-feminist model, in which "public" refers to the state and economy. Weintraub, "Theory and Politics of the Public/Private Distinction," 1–42.
33. Madanipour, *Whose Public Space?*, 3.
34. Boyer, "Cities for Sale"; Mitchell, "The End of Public Space?"
35. Watson, *City Publics*.
36. Madanipour, *Whose Public Space?*, 5.
37. Balibar, "Europe as Borderland," 201.

CHAPTER 3. ENHANCING THE IMPACT

1. Massey, *For Space*, 195.
2. Here I build on the use of the term "resistance" suggested by Nigel Thrift in his essay "The Still Point." He later developed this approach in his book *Non-Representational Theory*.
3. This principle can be applied, with some contextual modifications, to many of the protests in the Arab world in 2011 (i.e., the Arab Spring), to Israeli social justice protests in the summer of 2011, and to the Occupy Wall Street protests in the United States in the autumn of 2011.
4. For example, see Cresswell, *In Place/Out of Place*; Irazábal, *Ordinary Places, Extraordinary Events*; Mitchell, *The Right to the City*; Sibley, *Geographies of Exclusion*; Soja, *Postmodern Geographies*.
5. Castells, *The City and the Grassroots*; Harvey, *Justice, Nature, and the Geography of Difference*.
6. This assumption has been vastly challenged; see, for example, Sharp et al., *Entanglements of Power*, and Allen, *Lost Geographies of Power*.
7. This process of appropriating and transforming space has become a focal issue in much of the literature on politics and space and on the ways in which societies negotiate their identities and claims by modifying their modes of operation. See, for example, Agnew, *Place and Politics*; Cosgrove and Daniels, *The Iconography of Landscape*; Mitchell, "Iconography and Locational Conflict"; Routledge, "Backstreets, Barricades, and Blackouts" and "Critical Geopolitics and Terrains of Resistance."
8. Following the debate on the notion of scalarity, I suggest that scale, rather than a linear division, is a polymorphous dynamic that works in association with particular scales and across scales. For further discussion, see Jessop, Brenner, and Jones, "Theorizing Sociospatial Relations."
9. Melucci, *Challenging Codes*, 115.
10. Ibid.
11. Handelman, *Models and Mirrors*.
12. Though the groups analyzed here have been studied over the last decade, particularly within the context of women's grassroots movements, none of the studies has *comparatively* examined the groups' dissent strategies and spatial manifestations. For more on WIB, see, for example, Baum, "Women in Black and Men in Pink"; Benski, "Breaching Events"; Blumen and Halevi, "Staging Peace"; and Helman and Rapoport, "Women in Black." For more on *Machsom Watch*, see, for example, Hallward, "Negotiating Boundaries, Narrating Checkpoints"; Halperin, "Between the Lines"; Levy and Mizrahi, "Alternative Politics"; and Kaufman, "Resisting Occupation or Institutionalizing Control?" For more on AATW actions in Bil'in, see Hallward, "Creative Responses to Separation."
13. Participant observation notes, MW shift, West Bank, September 2, 2010. The participant observation notes cited here and elsewhere can be found in my personal archive.
14. Gordon, "The Israeli Peace Camp in Dark Times."
15. Newman and Hermann, "A Comparative Study of Gush Emunim and Peace Now."
16. Arieli and Sfard, *Wall and Omission*.

17. Ibid., 21.
18. Yiftachel and Yacobi, “Barriers, Walls and Dialectics,” 154–155.
19. Methodologically, the empirical study of these groups is part of a larger research project that examines the dissent strategies of peace activists worldwide. As a researcher, I was in the position of an observer. Before I took on the role of an observer, I did not have any personal familiarity with any of my contacts in these groups. However, in studying these groups, I aimed to build trusting relationships. Once I had gained their trust, the activists were generous in sharing data, as they viewed data sharing as a means of spreading their ideas. From October 2009 to January 2011, the study of these three groups was based on identical sets of interview questions (focusing on space, organization, symbols, and actions), participants' observations during acts of dissent, activists' private archival resources (e.g., documents from group meetings and photos), and newspaper reports.
20. As has been argued by Kathleen M. Kirby, patterns of belonging and exclusion may initially divide a conceptual space, but they ultimately operate materially, structuring physical space and discursively defining political operative laws to material effect. Kirby, *Indifferent Boundaries*, 13. On the relationships between the law and dissent, see Mitchell, *The Right to the City*, 161–194; D'Arcus, *Boundaries of Dissent*, 27–30.
21. Lasting from 1987 to 1993 (though it weakened significantly in 1991), the First Intifada (“uprising”) was a Palestinian uprising against the occupation of the West Bank and the Gaza Strip, which Israel repressed.
22. See the map of locations (map 3.1), which is based on their activities in May 1990.
23. According to an estimate made by Helman and Rapoport, “Women in Black,” 698.
24. Alia Strauss, Women in Black activist, interview with the author, December 24, 2009, Tel Aviv.
25. Today, the Jerusalem vigil still uses these signs, along with a sign calling for an end to the siege of Gaza. The Tel Aviv vigil now carries different signs, which relate to ongoing events. Participant observation notes, WIB shift, Tel Aviv, December 25, 2009.
26. A radical example is the July 1989 assault on the Jerusalem vigil by a group of Meir David Kahane supporters. Following this event, the Jerusalem group met and decided on three rules of conduct: “1. Women participants only; 2. Wearing black; 3. ‘Stop the Occupation’ sign.” Quotation from the minutes of a meeting held on July 12, 1989, Women in Black archive of Daphna Kaminer.
27. Participant observation notes, WIB shift, Jerusalem, January 22, 2010.
28. WIB Jerusalem leaflet, March 1991.
29. Ibid.
30. Ibid.
31. The development of the vigils was rather spontaneous. According to one activist, “Somebody decided to start, or a couple of women met and decided to start, and started inviting their friends, people they knew. At that time, there weren't computers like there are today; very few people had computers then, but it went by word of mouth, and telephone calls and inviting friends, and then I showed up there, and they said ‘Oh good, lovely,’ and then I was part of the group.” Alia Straus, Women in Black activist, interview with author, December 24, 2009.

32. The Second Intifada, also known as the al-Aqsa Intifada, refers to the second Palestinian uprising, which began in September 2000. Palestinian tactics ranged from carrying out mass protests and general strikes (as in the First Intifada [1987–1993]) to mounting suicide bombing attacks and firing Qassam rockets into Israeli residential areas. Israeli tactics ranged from creating checkpoints and constructing the West Bank barrier to making arrests and conducting targeted attacks on terrorist leaders. During the Chomat Magen (Defensive Shield) operation in 2002, the Israeli army reoccupied parts of the West Bank that had previously been relinquished.
33. The checkpoints have been in place since 1991, when Israel started monitoring the movement of the Palestinian population and bringing in cheap foreign labor from developing countries. During the Oslo years, more checkpoints were established, and all Palestinian residents of the West Bank and Gaza were required to obtain permits to enter Israel. See also Naaman, "The Silenced Outcry," 168–180. For more information, see http://www.machsomwatch.org/en.
34. Yehudit Elkana, Machsom Watch activist, interview with the author, December 31, 2009, Jerusalem.
35. From the "About Us" section at http://www.machsomwatch.org/en.
36. The constant dynamic of changing and lifting internal barriers pushes the organization, especially its Tel Aviv branch, to search for new directions. For example, some activists, who were originally associated with MW, have formed another human rights volunteer organization: Yesh Din (There Is a Law). This group has been working to assist Palestinians with legal tools since 2005. For more information, see Yesh Din's website: http://www.yesh-din.org.
37. Kotef and Amir, "(En)Gendering Checkpoints," 987.
38. Map 3.1 is based on a map sent by the group in October 2010, which shows the general activity from 2001 to 2010. Day-to-day events and political decisions influence any changes in activity.
39. http://www.machsomwatch.org/.
40. http://www.flickr.com/photos/8116065@N08/sets.
41. https://www.facebook.com/machsomwatch/. In July 2017, the page had 4,697 followers and 4,792 likes.
42. Shay Carmeli Polak, interview with the author, January 18, 2010, Tel Aviv.
43. Ibid.
44. http://www.awalls.org/about_aatw.
45. Map 3.1 is based on data from the AATW website in October 2010.
46. AATW leaflet.
47. Parallel to the activity on the ground, the village also won an appeal to the Israeli high court of justice to change the wall's current path (2006).
48. On the aesthetics and politics, see Roei, "Molding Resistance."
49. https://www.facebook.com/%D7%90%D7%A0%D7%A8%D7%9B%D7%99%D7%A1%D7%98%D7%99%D7%9D-%D7%A0%D7%92%D7%93%D7%94%D7%92%D7%93%D7%A8-Anarchists-Against-The-Wall-184879698210917. In July 2017, the page had 5,807 followers and 5,875 likes.

50. Yehudit Elkana, interview with the author, December 31, 2009, Jerusalem.
51. Ibid.
52. Participant observation notes, MW shift, December 28, 2009; participant observation notes: MW shift, September 2, 2010.
53. Anarchists against the Wall, "About," 2009. http://www.awalls.org/about_aatw.
54. AATW activist, interview with the author, January 18, 2010. While we cannot validate this statement with regard to the current reality on the ground, it is in line with a news report from 2007 (Sharon interview with the author, 2007).
55. Palestine News Network, "Crossing the Line: Inside the Israeli Anarchists against the Wall," November 28, 2010. http://english.pnn.ps/index.php?option=com_content&task=view&id=9201.
56. AATW activist, interview with the author, January 18, 2010; Anarchists against the Wall, "About," 2009. http://www.awalls.org/about_aatw.
57. Sasson-Levi and Rapoport, "Body, Gender, and Knowledge," 398.
58. On aesthetics and politics, see Roei, "Molding Resistance."
59. Hallward, "Creative Responses to Separation," 548.
60. Rafael, "The Cell Phone and the Crowd," 405.
61. Graham, "Software-sorted geographies," 99.
62. Referring to cities in general, they suggest that what we see here is how the public realms in cities and essential publicness are rapidly being "mass customized," unbundled, commodified, individualized, and coordinated through networked technologies that link the body to a global scale. Amin and Thrift, *Cities*, 128.

CHAPTER 4. BARGAINING POWER

1. However, even when organizations that speak for ethnic, religious, or racial categories have a legitimate right to exist, some organizations will gain recognition as valid representatives of their ethnic, religious, or racial categories only through struggles. Ibid., 34.
2. Goffman, *The Presentation of Self in Everyday Life*.
3. Salter, "Places Everyone!"
4. Hatuka, "Civilian Consciousness," 348.
5. Agnew, "The Territorial Trap"; Amin, "Regions Unbound"; Rumford, "Theorizing Borders."
6. The conventional distinction lies between formal and substantive aspects of citizenship. The formal refers to membership in a nation-state, and the substantive refers to the civil, political, socioeconomic, and cultural rights that people possess and exercise. However, "formal membership in the nation-state is increasingly neither a necessary nor a sufficient condition for substantive citizenship." Holston and Appadurai, "Introduction: Cities and Citizenship," 4.
7. Although one essential nation-building project has been to dismantle the historic primacy of urban citizenship and to replace it with national primacy, cities are still strategic arenas for the development of citizenship. Holston and Appadurai, "Introduction: Cities and Citizenship," 2.

8. According to Charles Tilly, no demonstration took place anywhere in the world before the 1760s, and the term "demonstration" was first used by the British Whigs in the 1830s. Demonstrations became common in Western Europe and in North America before they spread to the rest of the world. See Tilly, *The Politics of Collective Violence*, 33 and 202.
9. Shafir, *The Citizenship Debates*, 1-28.
10. Rawls, *Political Liberalism*; Kymlicka, *Multicultural Odysseys*; Young, *Inclusion and Democracy* and *Justice and the Politics of Difference.*
11. See, for example, the Israeli-Palestinian conflict and its effect on citizenship and borders. Allegra, "Citizenship in Palestine."
12. See, for example, the following works, which respond to current dynamics and refer to the paradigmatic limitations of contemporary concepts of citizenship: Isin, *Being Political*; Toal, "Being Geopolitical"; Archibugi, *The Global Commonwealth of Citizens*; Beck and Cronin, *Cosmopolitan Vision*; Nussbaum, "Toward a Globally Sensitive Patriotism"; and Sassen, "Incompleteness and the Possibility of Making."
13. Nield, "On the Border as Theatrical Space."
14. Balibar, "Europe as Borderland"; Paasi, "Bounded Spaces in a 'Borderless World.'"
15. Butler, *Gender Trouble*; Salter, "Places Everyone!," 66–67.
16. Hatuka, *Violent Acts and Urban Space*, 165–169.
17. Della Porta and Reiter, *Policing Protest*, 13.
18. Ibid.
19. The prospects of governments that do not exercise significant control are not high, but even extreme fascist regimes have never come close to absolute control.
20. However, nondemocratic states with high governmental capacities (e.g., Iran or China) will limit the space for claim making.
21. Davis, "The Power of Distance," 601.
22. Oberschall, *Social Conflict and Social Movements*.
23. Lohmann, "The Dynamics of Informational Cascades," 49.
24. Ibid., 55.
25. Woito, "Nonviolence, Principled," 357.
26. Others believe that democracy is the political system that can best absorb nonviolent actions; in many cases, this principle has been successful in democratic regimes. Ibid., 358.
27. Sharp, *The Politics of Nonviolent Action* (3 vols.).
28. Sharp's list is a mix of protests and noncooperation, including legal and illegal acts (McCarthy, "Methods of Nonviolent Actions," 321); however, it helps visualize the physical protests occurring in space within a wider context of dissent.
29. According to Mitchell, early federal interventions in speech and assembly cases were "not concerned either with protecting the right to dissent or with creating the boundaries in which dissent was possible, but rather with controlling the public *behavior* of the working class." Mitchell, *The Right to the City*, 54.
30. Ibid., 13.
31. Tilly, *The Politics of Collective Violence*, 6.

32. Ibid., 207.
33. Negotiation processes are (sometimes) exposed by the media, which tends to result in more tolerant policing. In particular, since the 1970s, the daily press has seemingly been more critical of "tough" police interventions and more diverse in its coverage. Della Porta and Reiter, *Policing Protest*, 18.
34. Tilly, *The Politics of Collective Violence*, 16. See also 196–197.
35. See Örs, "Genie in the Bottle," 491 and 496.
36. Cammaerts, "Mediation of Insurrectionary Symbolic Damage," 544.
37. Mitchell, *The Right to the City*, 53; emphasis in original.
38. Anderson, *Imagined Communities*.
39. This development outside the city wall is characteristic of the modern urbanization of medieval cities worldwide. For further discussion on Jaffa's urbanization, see Kark, *Jaffa: A City in Evolution*.
40. On the formal decision on April 8, 1921, see *Yediot Iriat Tel Aviv*, Tel Aviv Historical Archive, 1921.
41. For further reading on protests in Tel Aviv before and after the establishment of the Israeli state, see Hatuka and Kallus, "The Architecture of Repeated Rituals."
42. The rapid influx of Jews into Palestine in the years after 1917 was also in response to their widespread persecution in Central Europe.
43. The 1933 protests took place in Jerusalem, Jaffa, Haifa, and Nablus. The first protest in Jerusalem took place on October 13; the Jaffa and Nablus protests occurred on October 27; the Haifa protest lasted from October 27 to October 28; and the Jerusalem protest took place on October 28 and 29. Unlike those in 1920, 1921, and 1929, these demonstrations were directed against the mandatory government, which was accused of tilting the balance against the Arabs in administering the mandate, not against the Jews.
44. In British documents, Palestinian Arabs are called "Arabs"; to avoid confusion, I have used "Palestinian Arab community" and "Palestinian Jewish community" throughout the book.
45. On October 9, 1933, Mr. Hall, the administrative officer of the government, sent for Musa Kazim Pasha, noting that no political procession had been allowed since the disturbances of 1929 and that the government would not allow a procession in Jerusalem. Mr. Hall advised Pasha to have the Executive's resolution cancelled. The administrator also stated that Pasha's group should apply to hold a protest through the legal channels. *Palestine Gazette*, November 16, 1933, Faraday Collection, Box 2, File 2(1), 90, Middle-East Center Archive (MECA), St. Anthony College, Oxford.
46. Ibid., 92.
47. For example, see Khalidi, *Palestinian Identity*; C. D. Smith, *Palestine and the Arab-Israeli Conflict*.
48. The original date was October 20, 1933, but the date was apparently changed to October 27 because one of the leaders was very interested in a lawn tennis tournament in Jaffa on October 20. *Palestine Gazette*, November 16, 1933, Faraday Collection, Box 2, File 2(1), 93, Middle-East Center Archive (MECA), St. Anthony College, Oxford.
49. Ibid.
50. As Elias Canetti says, "The destruction of representational images is the destruction of a hierarchy which is no longer recognized. It is a violation of generally established and universally visible and valid distances." Canetti, *Crowds and Power*, 19.

51. Ibid., 16.
52. *Palestine Gazette*, November 16, 1933, Faraday Collection, Box 2, File 2(1), 90, 94, Middle East Center Archive (MECA), St. Anthony College, Oxford.
53. Wright, *Crowds and Riots*, 95.
54. *Palestine Gazette*, November 16, 1933, 95.
55. District Police Headquarters, Police Dispositions for Friday, October 27, 1933; October 25, 1933, *Faraday Collection* Box 1, File 1, MECA.
56. Canetti, *Crowds and Power*, 23.
57. Police Dispositions for Friday, October 27, 1933; October 25, 1933, Faraday Collection, Box 1, file 1, MECA.
58. Ibid.
59. *Palestine Gazette*, November 16, 1933, 95.
60. Canetti, *Crowds and Power*, 23.
61. "The Arab demonstrations," *Near East and India Journal* (newspaper), February 1, 1934. *Faraday Collection*, Box 2, File 2, MECA.
62. Tilly, *The Politics of Collective Violence*, 194–220.
63. Žižek, *The Ticklish Subject*, 171–244.
64. Beck, "World Risk Society and Manufactured Uncertainties," 292.

CHAPTER 5. STAGING THE ACTION

1. Wright, "Disciplining the Body"; Foucault, *Power/Knowledge*, 55–62.
2. According to the writings of Giddens, Lefebvre, and de Certeau, agency is possible in everyday life (see discussion in chapter 1), but spatial practices are generally subject to rules and norms.
3. Canetti, *Crowds and Power*, 29.
4. Foster, "Choreographies of Protest," 412.
5. Butler and Athanasiou, *Dispossession*, 178.
6. Ibid. On approaching the body as articulate matter and the central role that physicality plays in constructing both individual agency and sociality, see Foster, "Choreographies of Protests."
7. Foster, "Choreographies of Protest," 396.
8. Canetti, *Crowds and Power*, 388.
9. Ibid., 393.
10. Ibid.
11. Butler and Athanasiou, *Dispossession*, 180.
12. Ibid., 196.
13. Foster, "Choreographies of Protest," 412.
14. Handelman, *Models and Mirrors*, 16.
15. Swyngedouw, "'Every Revolution Has Its Square,'" 25.
16. Arendt defines action as a human being's exercise of freedom, which is a combination of "I will" and "I can": the will and the ability "to take an initiative, to begin, to set something

into motion." In the Arendtian scheme of the private–public dichotomy, action occurs when someone for whom the necessities of life have been satisfied in the private realm enters the public realm. For Arendt, public space results only from people's action; it is not a given. Arendt, *The Human Condition*, 177; and "What Is Freedom?," 160.

CHAPTER 6. SPECTACLES

1. Sennett, *The Spaces of Democracy*, 15–21.
2. Canetti, *Crowds and Power*, 36.
3. For further reading on the Oslo Accords, see Grinberg, *Imagined Peace, Discourse of War*.
4. The plan, which was based on the 1925 (Patrick) Geddes report, was approved by the British Mandate in 1927, was amended in 1938, and is still the official plan of the city. For further details on the Geddes Plan and its implementation, see Kallus, "Patrick Geddes and the Evolution of a Housing Type in Tel-Aviv."
5. For the protocols for the city's engineering suggestions, see Tel Aviv Council, "5th Protocol of the Planning Committee," Tel Aviv Historical Archive, 1945, File 4–2615; Tel Aviv Council, "4th Protocol of the Planning Committee," Tel Aviv Historical Archive, 1945, File 4–2615.
6. Ombudsman, "Memorandum," Tel Aviv Historical Archive, 1975, File 4–1350.
7. Sennett, *The Spaces of Democracy*, 15–21.
8. The empty space at the site of the future square was used for public political gatherings of the Jewish community, voicing itself mainly in front of the British Mandate as early as the 1930s. In those years, the gatherings had an informal character, and the area of the square, though important, wasn't the only arena for political processions or events. With the establishment of the state of Israel (1948), it was developed as a space for national and municipal gatherings. However, from the late 1970s on, the square became a national focal point for dissent and protest. Hatuka and Kallus, "The Architecture of Repeated Rituals."
9. Yitzhak Arzi, *To the Council Members*, Tel Aviv Historical Archive, 1977, file 25, folder 2532.
10. Horowitz and Lissak, *Trouble in Utopia*.
11. It was known as "the Protest of the 400,000" because of the estimated number of participants. Maya Michaeli, "The State Square," *Tel Aviv* (weekly newspaper), October 26, 2001.
12. On September 16, 1982, a group of Lebanese Christian Phalangists entered the Palestinian refugee camps of Sabra and Shatila (near Beirut). They massacred between 800 (according to Israeli official reports) and 3,500 (according to the Israeli journalist Kapeliouk) people, including women and children. The day before, the Israeli army had entered this area of the city, sealed the camps from the outside world, and passively observed the events of September 16–18.
13. "The street was flooded with right-wing people demonstrating against the agreement," Shlomo Lahat, testimony written to the author by his wife, August 23, 2010, in author's personal archive.
14. Eli Eshet, interview with the author, September 3, 2010, Tel Aviv. Eshet was the director general of Tel Aviv under Shlomo Lahat from 1983 to 1993. He was approached by Shlomo Lahat to help organize and manage the rally.

15. The Peace and Security Association "was established in 1988 by a group of reserve officers led by the late General Aharon Yariv, who was the founder and Head of the Jaffe Center for Strategic Studies at Tel Aviv University (today named the Institute for National Security Studies) and prior to that the Head of the Israel Defense Forces Intelligence Branch. . . . The Peace and Security Association is a non-profit, non-partisan, voluntary membership-based organization engaging over hundreds of high-ranking members from the security and diplomacy establishments. The association supports a viable and sustainable peaceful resolution to the conflict in the Middle East as a necessary step towards ensuring Israel's security and social resilience under any agreement and maintaining its democratic foundation in the long-term." http://www.peace-security.org.il/page/79/About.aspx.
16. Jean Friedman, a French Jewish Zionist, established an organization under the name Efshar ("Possible" in Hebrew), which aimed to support acts advancing the peace agreements. Friedman asked Shlomo Lahat to lead the organization. Shlomo Lahat, testimony written to the author by his wife, August 23, 2010, in author's personal archive.
17. Eli Eshet, interview with the author, September 3, 2010, Tel Aviv.
18. Ibid.
19. Ibid.
20. See the BBC report, "1995: Israeli PM shot," November 4, 1995. http://news.bbc.co.uk/onthisday/hi/dates/stories/november/4/newsid_2514000/2514437.stm.
21. Eli Eshet, interview with the author, September 3, 2010, Tel Aviv.
22. Azaryahu, "Spontaneous Formation of Memorial Space"; Vinitzky-Seroussi, "Jerusalem Assassinated Rabin."
23. Diani, "Structural Bases of Protest Events." 66.
24. Canetti, *Crowds and Power*, 73.
25. Diani, "Structural Bases of Protest Events."
26. Taylor, "Making a Spectacle," 97.
27. Romero, "History of Argentina in the Twentieth Century," 215.
28. Initially, those who were abducted were subjected to systematic and prolonged torture. The most common forms of torture were electric prod; the so-called "submarine," a practice in which the tortured individual's head was submerged under water to the point of unconsciousness; and sexual abuse. Ibid., 218.
29. Torre, "Claiming the Public Space," 143.
30. Fisher, *Mothers of the Disappeared*, 22.
31. Bouvard, *Revolutionizing Motherhood*, 67.
32. Aida de Suárez testimony in Fisher, *Mothers of the Disappeared*, 29.
33. Bouvard, *Revolutionizing Motherhood*, 69.
34. Fisher, *Mothers of the Disappeared*, 53.
35. Ibid., 1; Torre, "Claiming the Public Space," 143.
36. Taylor, "Making a Spectacle," 106.
37. Torre, "Claiming the Public Space," 142–143.
38. Aida Sarti, interview with the author, September 4, 2006, Buenos Aires.

39. Taylor, "Making a Spectacle."
40. Maria del Rosario testimony in Fisher, *Mothers of the Disappeared*, 54.
41. Taylor, "Making a Spectacle," 100.
42. Aida Sarti testimony in Fisher, *Mothers of the Disappeared,* 54.
43. Bouvard, *Revolutionizing Motherhood*, 70–72; Aida Sarti, interview with the author, September 4, 2006, Buenos Aires.
44. Taylor, "Making a Spectacle," 102.
45. Bouvard, *Revolutionizing Motherhood*, 70. After the split in the movement, the weekly march became separated into two groups of women, marching separately but at the same time.
46. The white kerchiefs were adopted from the cloth diapers that a few of the Mothers had worn on their heads in a pilgrimage to the Virgin of Luján's sanctuary. The diapers were those of their missing children, whose names were embroidered on them, which became the headgear that differentiated the Mothers from the multitude of other women in the kerchiefs on that religious march. In latter demonstrations, the Mothers constructed full-size cardboard silhouettes representing their missing children and husbands, shielding their bodies with the ghostly shapes of the "disappeared," a custom evolved from the Mother's pilgrimage to the Virgin of Luján's sanctuary in 1977. Aida Sarti, interview with the author, September 4, 2006, Buenos Aires.
47. Ibid.
48. Bosco, "The Madres de Plaza de Mayo," 354.
49. Taylor, "Making a Spectacle," 107.
50. LaCapra, *Writing History, Writing Trauma*, 65–70.
51. Fisher, *Mothers of the Disappeared*, 90–125.
52. Bouvard, *Revolutionizing Motherhood*, 65.
53. Ibid., 2; Fisher, *Mothers of the Disappeared*, 91–93.
54. Fisher, *Mothers of the Disappeared*, 99–100.
55. Bouvard, *Revolutionizing Motherhood*, 2.
56. Fisher, *Mothers of the Disappeared*, 125.
57. Aida Sarti, interview with the author, September 4, 2006, Buenos Aires.
58. The goals are based on a quotation in Fisher, *Mothers of the Disappeared*, 91–92.
59. Bouvard, *Revolutionizing Motherhood*, 112 and 123. Aida Sarti, interview with the author, September 4, 2006, Buenos Aires.
60. According to an estimate made by Helman and Rapoport in "Women in Black," 698.
61. Alia Strauss, Women in Black activist, interview with the author, December 24, 2009, Tel Aviv.
62. Today, the Jerusalem vigil maintains these signs, and also includes a sign calling for the lifting of the siege of Gaza. The Tel Aviv vigil now carries different signs, which relate to ongoing events. Participant observation notes, WIB shift, Tel Aviv, December 25, 2009.
63. Alia Strauss, Women in Black activist, interview with the author, December 24, 2009, Tel Aviv.
64. Shadmi, "Between Resistance and Compliance," 27.
65. Social discourse is built on male conceptions, such as power, competition, oppression, and aggression. Such a culture does not allow women free expression unless they adopt male norms. Shadmi, "Between Resistance and Compliance," 27.

66. Participant observation notes, WIB shift, Jerusalem, January 22, 2010.
67. An exception is a women's demonstration held in December 1989 by various women's organizations walking from west to east Jerusalem. Yossi Levi, Maariv, December 31, 1989.
68. It is also worth noting that supportive tourists sometimes join the vigils and are welcomed by the women when they do. For current information, see participant observation notes, from a vigil held in Jerusalem on January 22, 2010. For earlier years, regarding the Jerusalem vigil, see Helman and Rapoport, "Women in Black," 683.
69. Alia Strauss, Women in Black activist, interview with the author, December 24, 2009, Tel Aviv.
70. Kaminer, *The Politics of Protest;* Jacobi, *Women in Zones of Conflict*. Kaminer emphasizes the role of WIB in this process, while Jacoby recognizes the importance and visibility of WIB but does not necessarily give it a leading role.
71. Kaminer, *The Politics of Protest*, 82–83; Chazan, "Israeli Women and Peace Activism," 153.
72. The role of gender in WIB activities is key to understanding the movement, and three points should be emphasized. First, not all the activists have (or had) a conscious feminist agenda, and, more importantly, such agendas do not specifically express themselves in the movement's leaflets, which should be understood in the context of the movement's democratic and inclusive character, which also enables vigils today to be open to the participation of men. Notably, while the Jerusalem vigil banned men from joining the vigils, a step taken following a physical assault on the activists, the Nachshon Junction vigil reported in the same month that they were opening their vigil to men (internal document of the Jerusalem vigil, July 14, 1989, summarizing a meeting held after the event; fax report from a Nachshon Junction activist, July 19 1989, Dafna Kaminer personal archive). Second, the movement outspokenly identified with feminist issues on numerous occasions. Third, while the level of feminist consciousness and outspokenness among the activists might differ, many of the outspoken and hostile responses directed at WIB were undoubtedly of a sexist nature. For further reading on the relationships between gender and WIB, see Blumen and Halevi, "Staging Peace through a Gendered Demonstration"; Gabriel, "Grief and Rage"; Helman and Rapoport, "Women in Black"; Sasson-Levi and Rapoport, "Body, Gender, and Knowledge"; Shadmi, "Between Resistance and Compliance"; and Svirsky, *Standing for Peace*.
73. Halevi and Blumen, "What a Difference a Place Makes," 394.
74. Alia Strauss, Women in Black activist, interview with the author, December 24, 2009, Tel Aviv.
75. Shadmi, "Between Resistance and Compliance," 27.
76. A large fountain was located in the middle of the square until the mid-1990s, when it was replaced by a sculpture with a smaller fountain. Another change in the design of the square was the addition of high flower beds on its perimeter.
77. "Women in Black—Jerusalem" leaflet, dated March 1991, Dafna Kaminer personal archive.
78. Different signs, mostly ones that relate more specifically to the ongoing situation, can also be carried based on each vigil's decisions. The Tel Aviv vigil, for example, posts a copy of the 2002 Arab Peace Initiative on a board (according to participant observations on December 25, 2009); for the Jerusalem vigil, a few women hold a large sign protesting against the Israeli siege in the Gaza Strip (according to participant observations on January 10, 2010).

79. Our observations and conversations with participants reveal that the vigils are usually not completely silent, and they have seemingly been less silent in recent years than in the past; participants can talk to pedestrians and definitely among themselves. Notably, in this context, older women participating in the Tel Aviv vigil have recently changed positions, sitting on portable chairs rather than standing (participant observations in Tel Aviv and Jerusalem, December 25, 2009, and January 10, 2010).
80. Internal document from July 14, 1989; in author's personal archive.
81. Ibid.
82. This description is based on participant observations from the Jerusalem vigil (January 10, 2010).
83. Alia Strauss, Women in Black activist, interview with the author, December 24, 2009, Tel Aviv.
84. McAdam, "Micro-mobilization Contexts and Recruitment to Activism."
85. Canetti, *Crowds and Power*, 17.

CHAPTER 7. PROCESSIONS

1. People had great difficulty escaping from the crowd, which caused panic deaths. The numbers of dead are not definitive and range from thirty-four to thirty-six, as one or two people died from their injuries. Thus, for example, Mehmet Karaca mentioned thirty-four deaths. See the interview with the author and written narrative by Karaca, July 30, 2006, Tel Aviv.
2. Çeçen, *Taksim ve Hamidiye Suları*, 16.
3. Kubilay, "Topçu Kıslası," 274.
4. Baykan and Robertson, "Spatializing Turkey."
5. Tekeli and Okyay, "Case Study of a Relocated Capital: Ankara"; Bozdogan, *Modernism and Nation Building*.
6. Tanyeli, "1950'lerden Bu Yana Mimari Paradigmaların Degişimi ve 'Reel Mimarlık.'"
7. By the end of World War I, Istanbul's population was close to one million. After the war, the non-Muslim population left the city in large numbers. However, Istanbul's cosmopolitan character, as the seat of the Sultanate, the Caliphate, and Western economic and cultural powers, decreased the new regime's willingness to promote the city. Furthermore, apart from Taksim Square, no open space in Istanbul represented the new democracy, and the new nation needed a space that was not previously marked by monuments of empire. Western ideas defined the cosmopolitan character of Beyoglu and Taksim. After all, nationalism derives from Western ideas, and it has been appropriated to express a particular essence. Chatterjee, *Nationalist Thought and the Colonial World*.
8. Kuruyazıcı, "Cumhuriyetin Istanbul'daki Simgesi," 92.
9. Ibid., 93.
10. Prost, *Istanbul Hakkında Notlar*, 70.
11. Ibid., 41.
12. Tanyeli, "1950'lerden Bu Yana Mimari Paradigmaların Degişimi ve 'Reel Mimarlık'"; Tekeli, "Turkiye'de Cumhuriyet Döneminde Kentsel Gelişme ve Kent Planlaması."

13. Istanbul was named the European Capital of Culture in 2010. Among the preparations for application for this title, the water reservoir was renovated as a museum of the Turkish Republic. The museum seems an ironic statement in the face of current liberal and globalization policies that appropriate this space.
14. For a discussion of the square's inclusiveness and significance, especially in the context of the global economy, see Abbas and Yigit, "Scenes from Gezi Park."
15. See, for example, protests in Gezi Park: Gül, Dee, and Cünük, "Istanbul's Taksim Square and Gezi Park"; Örs, "Genie in the Bottle"; Örs and Turan, "The Manner of Contention."
16. Kuruyazıcı, "Istanbul'da Beyazıt Meydanı," 759–772.
17. Silier, "The Significance of Banned May Day Demonstrations."
18. In 1976–1978, demonstrations in Istanbul were organized under the aegis of DISK.
19. Until May 1 in 1976 and 1977, meetings in Istanbul, beginning with those of political parties, took place in Taksim Square. Other meeting places were Saraçhane Square and the Hurriyeti Ebediye Tepesi (Eternal Freedom Hill). In 1961, for example, there was a great labor meeting in Saraçhane Square, which has an important place in the history of the labor union movement.
20. Mehmet Karaca, interview with the author and written narrative by Karaca, July 30, 2006, Istanbul. Karaca was Secretary-General of DISK from 1976 to 1977.
21. Mehmet Karaca, interview with the author and written narrative by Karaca, July 30, 2006, Istanbul.
22. Lefebvre, *The Production of Space*, 224–225.
23. Whether correlated or not to the demonstration, on May 13, 1977, the government's National Front coalition proposed the construction of a mosque in Taksim Square behind the reservoir, which spurred ample public debate. The mosque was not being constructed at that time, but the debate was rekindled during the rule of a coalition of two right-wing parties in the 1990s, with the initiation of an architectural competition for a design of the mosque. The proposal encountered strong resistance from civic and professional organizations, and, once again, the mosque was not built. Ekinci, *Bütün Yönleriyle Taksim Camisi Belgeseli*.
24. To date, Istanbul is often under a security lockdown in anticipation of the Labor Day protests. The police tend to block off roads into the city center, and public transport is closed "to keep the peace." In 2015, for example, Turkish police fired tear gas and water cannons at hundreds of stone-throwing May Day protesters on Friday after they defied a ban and attempted to march on Istanbul's Taksim Square. Humeyra Pamuk and Nick Tattersall, "Turkish Police Fire Tear Gas, Water Cannon at May Day Protesters, May 1, 2015." http://www.reuters.com/article/us-may-day-turkey-idUSKBN0NM3FO20150501.
25. Canetti, *Crowds and Power*, 28.
26. For further reading on the Statsi, see Gieseke, *The History of the Stasi*; Macrakis, *Seduced by Secrets*.
27. The people's reality included the health consequences of industrial pollution, stagnation in the standard of living, and the decrepit state of the industrial structure. They were also aware of the economic differences between the East and the West. Lohmann, "The Dynamics of Informational Cascades," 59.

28. Pfaff, *Exit-Voice Dynamics and the Collapse of East Germany*, 94–95.
29. On the status of the church in the socialist regime, see ibid., 82–84.
30. Pastor Christian Führer, author interview, January 17, 2007, Rectory, Leipzig.
31. Rainer Müller also talks about exceptions: "There were a few exceptions, for example, one bishop of the eight bishops, namely, Forck of Berlin-Brandenburg, who was on our side. . . . There were a few superintendents and a few pastors on our side, for example, in Saalfeld, Thüringen, Jena, Leipzig, and Dresden." Rainer Müller, author interview, January 24, 2007, Archiv Bürgerbewegung, Leipzig.
32. On June 17, 1953, 500,000 workers participated in strikes, and approximately 400,000 took part in demonstrations. The protest in Berlin dissipated, but the activities continued in the provinces until June 23–24. The suppression of the events with the help of the Soviet military resulted in fifty-two deaths. This incident triggered a mass exodus of citizens to West Berlin, which damaged the reputation of the regime and threated its economy. On August 12, 1961, the borders to the West were closed. Lohmann, "The Dynamics of Informational Cascades," 62–63.
33. Kuran, "Sparks and Prairie Fires."
34. Rainer Müller, author interview, January 24, 2007, Archiv Bürgerbewegung, Leipzig.
35. Lohmann, "The Dynamics of Informational Cascades," 67.
36. Ibid.
37. The history of the square starts in 1785, when it was a site within the city walls that was designed by city architect Johann Carl Friedrich Dauthe. It was renamed Augustusplatz in 1839 to honor Frederick Augustus, the first king of Saxony. In 1928, the social-democratic city government renamed it Karl-Marx-Platz, though this name proved unpopular and was ignored, even in newspaper articles and town plans. In 1933, the National Socialists renamed it Augustusplatz; in 1953, it became Karl-Marx-Platz again; and, in 1990 (on the day of German reunification), it returned to its current name of Augustusplatz.
38. From 1996 to 1998, an underground parking lot was built under the Augustusplatz with many entrances and ventilation shafts leading onto the square, the construction of which proved controversial. In particular, the parking lot's eight illuminated glass cylinders that house the stairwells have been mocked—nicknamed "Milchtöpfe," or milk bottles. The Augustusplatz was mostly redesigned using the plans of the architect Erick van Egeraat.
39. Rainer Müller, author interview, January 24, 2007, Archiv Bürgerbewegung, Leipzig.
40. Ibid.
41. Ibid.
42. The protests should be seen in the context of other influential events, such as Mikhail Gorbachev's reforms in the Soviet Union. In the summer of 1989, some countries in Eastern Europe opened their borders to the West, and when East German professionals emigrated to the West, the GDR economy was severely affected. The leadership of the Socialist Unity Party of Germany (SED) defended the bloody June 1989 massacre of Chinese democracy at Tiananmen Square. On October 6, 1989, Gorbachev warned Erich Honecker that life would punish latecomers. Many people interpreted this statement as a signal that Soviet military forces would not intervene if the people took to the streets and demanded political reforms. Lohmann, "The Dynamics of Informational Cascades," 64–74.

43. Castells, *Networks of Outrage and Hope,* 10.
44. Fisher et al., "How Do Organizations Matter?," 104.
45. Diani, "The Structural Bases of Protest Events," 65.
46. Walgrave and Verhulst, "Government Stance and Internal Diversity of Protest," 457.
47. O'Neill, "Transnational Protest," 239.
48. Ibid., 240.
49. Fisher et al., "How Do Organizations Matter?," 104.
50. Verhulst, "February 15, 2003," 1. For detailed information regarding variation in the level of mobilization in different locations, see also pages 17–18.
51. Ibid., 13; for an elaborate discussion on the framing of the opposition, which includes a report on the written materials used, see Rucht and Verhulst, "The Framing of Opposition to the War on Iraq," 239–260.
52. Verhulst, "February 15, 2003," 5–8.
53. At the Florence meeting, the idea was still confined to Europe, as is evident from the statement released at the end of the Forum's meeting: it was addressed to "all citizens of Europe," calling on "movements and citizens of Europe to start continent-wide resistance to war." The quotations are taken from the call published at the end of the meeting. The full text can be found in Verhulst, "February 15, 2003," 9.
54. Tarrow, "Transnational Politics," 11.
55. Ibid.
56. Ailsa Gunson, participant in the protest, interview with the author, January 1, 2007, London.
57. For details on the coalitions and organizations involved, see Simonson, "The Anti-War Movement."
58. Verhulst, "February 15, 2003," 12.
59. Ibid., 8–13.
60. Ailsa Gunson, participant in the protest, interview with the author, January 1, 2007, London.
61. If no first-timer crowds would be participating in the protest, the normalization process would be stopped and even reversed. Walgrave and Verhulst, "Government Stance and Internal Diversity of Protest," 457.
62. Ailsa Gunson, participant in the protest, interview with the author, January 1, 2007, London.
63. Stop the War Coalition website on September 13, 2010, http://stopwar.org.uk/content/blogcategory/24/41/.
64. Simonson elaborates on the agenda of each of the varied coalitions involved. Simonson, "The Anti-War Movement."
65. However, finding a correlation between the level of mobilization and the character of participants is possible. The large demonstrations in the Western world especially attracted attention for the diversity of their participants, while other, smaller demonstrations might have had much more homogeneous crowds. Verhulst, "February 15, 2003," 2.
66. Some of the slogans are mentioned in Rucht and Verhulst, "The Framing of Opposition to the War on Iraq," 246; other slogans and the signs handed out by the Stop the War Coalition can be viewed on this private video available online: http://il.youtube.com/watch?v=bttncKzmmtI&feature=related.
67. Ailsa Gunson, participant in the protest, interview with the author, January 1, 2007, London.

68. Sassen, "Local Actors in Global Politics"; Tarrow, "Transnational Politics."
69. Large rallies also took place in the United States (750,000), Spain (800,000), and Italy (3,000,000). The protest in Italy was also associated with the return of Silvio Berlusconi to power in 2001. Diani, "The Structural Bases of Protest Events," 69.
70. BBC report, "Million March against Iraq War," Sunday, February 16, 2003; accessed at http://news.bbc.co.uk/2/hi/2765041.stm on September 18, 2015.
71. Ailsa Gunson, participant in the protest, interview with the author, January 1, 2007, London.
72. Ibid.
73. Ibid.
74. Walgrave and Verhulst, "Government Stance and Internal Diversity of Protest," 1377–1379.
75. Ibid.
76. As argued by Elizabeth Grosz, becoming is not a capacity inherited by life, an evolutionary outcome or consequence; it is instead "the very principle of matter itself, with its possibilities of linkage with the living, with its possibilities of mutual transformation, with its inherent and unstable volatility." Grosz, "Bergson, Deleuze and the Becoming of Unbecoming," 10. For additional reading on becoming, see Dovey, *Becoming Places*; Thrift, *Non Representational Theory*.
77. Canetti, *Crowds and Power*, 20.
78. Marston, Jones, and Woodward, "Human Geography without Scale," 422–426.
79. McCormack, "Becoming," 281.
80. Negrón, "Caracas of Latin America," 15–16.
81. With nationwide jurisdiction, the CNU completed the Regulating Plan of Caracas in 1951. Ibid., 17.
82. With the recovery of democracy in 1958, Caracas, with over one million inhabitants, strove to recover its own institution for city planning. As a result, in 1960, the Municipal Office for Urban Planning of the Federal District was created, which was associated with the municipal council. Ibid., 17.
83. In the 1970s and 1980s, several projects and proposals aimed to tackle this issue by focusing mainly on housing and transportation. In 1983, the metro of the state-owned Caracas Subway Company opened the first section of the city's underground mass transportation system. Ibid., 18.
84. "Assemblage—whether as an idea, an analytic, a descriptive lens or an orientation—is increasingly used in social science research, generally to connote indeterminacy, emergence, becoming, processuality, turbulence and the sociomateriality of phenomena. In short, it is an attempt to describe relationalities of composition—relationalities of near/far and social/material. Rather than focusing on cities as resultant formations, assemblage thinking is interested in emergence and process, and in multiple temporalities and possibilities." McFarlane, "Assemblage and Critical Urbanism," 206.
85. Ibid.
86. Over the past few decades, the public sector's actions with regard to city planning, except for the construction of new subway lines, has been nonexistent. In the 1990s, there was an initiative to develop a strategic plan (for the municipality and the metropolitan region

of Caracas). One of the plan's key goals related to the city's governance problems, which derived from its political-administrative fragmentation. Since 1989, the municipalities in the region have enjoyed autonomy, and their mayors have been directly elected, unlike the mayor of the Federal District, who was appointed by the president of the republic. This fragmentation made achieving objectives on behalf of the city as a whole difficult. The ambitions of modernity could not guarantee the well-being of the poorest sectors of the population. Negrón, "Caracas of Latin America," 20–25.

87. Teodoro Petkoff Malec, interview by Fabiola López-Durán, June 14, 2007, Caracas. Petkoff is a Venezuelan politician, ex-guerrilla, journalist, and economist. One of the most prominent leftist politicians in Venezuela, Petkoff began as a communist but gravitated toward liberalism in the 1990s. As Minister of Planning, he oversaw President Rafael Caldera's adoption of neoliberal economic policies in the mid-1990s. He has been a prominent critic of President Chávez.
88. Ibid.
89. McFarlane, "Assemblage and Critical Urbanism," 208.
90. From 1998 to 1999, 1 of every 25 protests was repressed; from 2000 to 2001, 1 of every 28 protests was repressed; and, from 2002 to 2003, 1 of every 36 protests was repressed. The use of the army to police public demonstrations continued to decrease, and it was ultimately prohibited in the 1999 Constitution. López Maya, Lander, and Parker, "Popular Protest in Venezuela," 98.
91. Ibid., 94–95.
92. The essential struggle epitomized by the differing views in April 2002 was a continuation of the historically opposed visions of Venezuela, which date back to colonial times, of the Creoles (whites), on the one hand, and the *pardos* (mixed race) and slaves (blacks) on the other. Although the Creoles sought to liberate themselves from Spain to perpetuate and deepen the colonial occupation and exploitation of Venezuela, the *pardos* and slaves sought their own physical, social, and economic liberation. Cannon, "Venezuela, April 2002: Coup or Popular Rebellion?," 287.
93. From the very beginning, Venezuelan society has been polarized regarding conceptions of civilization and barbarism, knowledge and ignorance, and the rich and the poor. Ibid., 286.
94. Different from the perspectives of John Rawls (*A Theory of Justice*) and Jorgen Habermas (*The Theory of Communicative Action*), who argue that the aim of a democratic society is to create consensus and that consensus is possible if people are able to put aside their personal interests and think as rational beings, agonism, as advocated by Chantal Mouffe, had a different agenda. Mouffe argues that, while we want an end to conflict, if we want people to be free, we must always allow for the possibility that conflict will arise and provide an arena in which differences can be communicated and acknowledged. For further reading, see Mouffe, *The Democratic Paradox*.
95. López Maya, Lander, and Parker, "Popular Protest in Venezuela," 97.
96. Teodoro Petkoff Malec, López-Durán interview, June 14, 2007, Caracas.
97. López Maya, Lander, and Parker, "Popular Protest in Venezuela," 107.
98. Teodoro Petkoff Malec, López-Durán interview, June 14, 2007, Caracas.

99. Cannon, "Venezuela, April 2002: Coup or Popular Rebellion?," 294.
100. Teodoro Petkoff Malec, López-Durán interview, June 14, 2007, Caracas.
101. Hellinger, "Political Overview," 49.
102. Teodoro Petkoff Malec, López-Durán interview, June 14, 2007, Caracas.
103. Ibid.
104. Petkoff explains in the interview that Chávez's acts were based on a revolutionary ideology, according to which contradictions must be deepened. "The revolution does not give way; it is intransigent; the revolution is them; and therefore whoever opposes them is counter-revolutionary. The revolutionary, by definition, feels himself to be the representative of history, progress, justice, and truth, such that, of course, everyone who opposes him is the enemy of justice, progress, history, and truth and therefore must be denied the most basic things. This moral supremacism is very characteristic of the extreme left and the extreme right; that is, Bush does whatever he feels like out of this idea of moral supremacy, and, on the left, it's like this as well, as in all extreme sectors, where the idea of isolating your opponents in an urban ghetto is fitting for those who feel themselves to be the representatives of truth and history. So, it's clear that they must deny civil rights to their adversaries." Ibid.
105. Cannon, "Venezuela, April 2002: Coup or Popular Rebellion?," 297.
106. Ibid.
107. See, for example, Rawls, *A Theory of Justice*, and Habermas, *The Theory of Communicative Action*.
108. Mouffe, "A Vibrant Democracy Needs Agonistic Confrontation," http://www.citsee.eu/interview/vibrant-democracy-needs-agonistic-confrontation-interview-chantal-mouffe.

CHAPTER 8. PLACE-MAKING

1. Hung, *Remaking Beijing*, 46.
2. In general, semiotic approaches to architecture emphasize the symbolic aspects of architectural features and the ways in which they encode and communicate meaning. For further reading, see Eco, "Function and Sign," 182–201.
3. Spivak, "Can the Subaltern Speak?," 217–313.
4. Tiananmen Gate was located inside the Imperial City and opened onto a secluded palace square, where public access was forbidden. In addition, the gate was not regarded as the "gate of the nation" in Imperial China. The "gate of the nation," which was situated midway between Tiananmen Gate and the Front Gate, was the main entrance to the Imperial City. This gate was called Great Qing Gate in the Qing dynasty and the Chinese Gate in republican China. Dong, *Republican Beijing*, 27.
5. Dovey, *Framing Places*, 81.
6. Hung, *Remaking Beijing*, 34.
7. Dovey, *Framing Places*, 72.
8. Lefebvre, *The Production of Space*, 221.

9. Lee, "How Is a Political Public Space Made?"
10. The May Fourth Incident can be regarded as the first time the space in front of Tiananmen Gate was used for a large-scale mass protest. On November 29, 1919, 30,000 students from thirty-four schools in Beijing gathered at the gate to protest against Japanese militaristic activity in Fujian Province. A rally was held after the assembly. On December 7, a citizens' meeting with more than 100,000 participants was held to protest the Fujian Incident. Other similar events held in the republican period include the rally against the May Thirtieth Incident in June 1925 and the demonstration on March 18, 1926. Lee, "How Is a Political Public Space Made?" See also Chow, *The May Fourth Movement*, 109–110.
11. In imperial times, the most scenic and spacious places in the city were either royal gardens or temples. Only a few scenic areas were accessible to the public. However, in the late Qing dynasty and the early republican period, Beijing's municipal administrators paid greater attention to improving the standard of living of city dwellers. Lee, "How Is a Political Public Space Made?"
12. Hung, *Remaking Beijing*, 59–60.
13. Lee, "How Is a Political Public Space Made?"
14. Hung, *Remaking Beijing*, 18 and 23.
15. Hershkovitz, "Tiananmen Square and the Politics of Place," 399.
16. Dovey, *Framing Places*, 71.
17. Hung, *Remaking Beijing*, 35–36.
18. Guthrie, "Political Theater," 438; Hung, *Remaking Beijing,* 15; Lee, "How Is a Political Public Space Made?," 32.
19. Zhao, *The Power of Tiananmen*, 123 and 128.
20. Ibid., 136.
21. Ibid., 149–150.
22. Ibid., 150–155.
23. This demonstration did not have a well-defined goal, but seven demands were developed during the event. Zhao, *The Power of Tiananmen*, 148–149. In addition, scholars argued that the student demand for democracy was not carefully analyzed. The student movement declared itself a pro-democracy campaign, but the Beijing students' conception of democracy differed greatly from Western standards of democracy. Most of the students associated democracy with economic principles, thus aiming to achieve specific short-term reforms rather than to restructure the entire Chinese political system, as the Western media assumed. Lui, "Looking Back at Tiananmen Square," 142.
24. Guthrie, "Political Theater," 421 and 426.
25. Ibid.; Zhao, *The Power of Tiananmen*, 146–147, 154–155.
26. Zhao, *The Power of Tiananmen*, 147.
27. Ibid., 148.
28. Guthrie, "Political Theater," 427.
29. Hung, *Remaking Beijing*, 43; Zhao, *The Power of Tiananmen*, 199.
30. Hung, *Remaking Beijing*, 43.
31. Ibid., 16–17, 42–43.

32. According to Guthrie, the hunger strike carried a message of commitment (by the intellectuals) to the cause of all the people of China. Guthrie, "Political Theater," 439–440.
33. Ibid., 163, 181, 187.
34. Zhao, *The Power of Tiananmen*, 199–200.
35. To read about the pitching of tents during the last days of the protest, see Zhao, *The Power of Tiananmen*, 197.
36. Beijing University is perceived as one of the most prestigious universities in China. Scholars have argued that the students in Tiananmen Square had an elite class consciousness, as demonstrated by reports of students calling soldiers and police "peasants." Reports have shown that many students believed that they deserved better lives than other social groups as well as a stronger voice in determining the course of China's reforms. The Chinese government and other officials also believed that the intellectuals only wanted for a better standard of living. Lui, "Looking Back at Tiananmen Square," 141.
37. Ibid., 140.
38. Tilly, *The Politics of Collective Violence*, 196.
39. The only public government report, entitled "Report on Checking the Turmoil and Quelling the Counterrevolutionary Rebellion," released on July 6, 1989, is vague on casualties. Thus, since Beijing authorities have never made public a full accounting of the dead and injured, numbers vary significantly. Human rights organizations' estimate of the dead range from several hundred to more than two thousand. See, for example, Seth Faisonjune, "The Persistent Mystery: How Many Died in 1989?," *New York Times*, June 4, 1999. For further reading on the event dynamic, see Zhao, *The Power of Tiananmen*, 200–207.
40. Palmowski, "Tiananmen Square."
41. Zhao, *The Power of Tiananmen*, 400.
42. Fager, *Uncertain Resurrection*, 15–17.
43. Poor People's Campaign News, "Dr. King Touring Nation in Poor People's Campaign," Library of Congress, SCLC (4), March (1968): reel 28, 185.
44. King wanted a multiracial movement and thus chose to call it the Poor People's Campaign rather than identifying it with the civil rights movement, which could have been seen to exclusively focus on expanding opportunities for blacks. Garrow, *Protest at Selma*; Tunney Lee, interview with the author, May 4, 2004, Cambridge, MA.
45. Poor People's Campaign News, "Dr. Abernathy Announces Timetable for Memphis March, Mule Train, Shanty Town and Mass Movement on Washington in Poor People's Campaign," Library of Congress, SCLC (3), April (1968): reel 54.
46. Poor People's Campaign News, "Questions & Answers about the Washington Campaign, for SCLC Staff Only," Library of Congress, SCLC (4), January (1968): reel 28, 24.
47. These resources include the Washington Monument, the Thomas Jefferson Memorial, the Lincoln Memorial, the Franklin Delano Roosevelt Memorial, the DC War Memorial (WWI), the World War II Memorial, the Korean War Veterans Memorial, the Vietnam Veterans Memorial, the Martin Luther King Jr. Memorial, the George Mason Memorial, Pennsylvania Avenue from the Capitol to the White House, and numerous other historic sites, memorials,

and parklands. For additional details, visit the official website, http://www.nps.gov/nama/index.htm.

48. For the history of the planning process, see Longstreth, *The Mall in Washington*.
49. See this website: http://www.nps.gov/nama/historyculture/index.htm.
50. Ibid.
51. Capitol Hill is the only area where the Washington Mall abuts the city's ordinary fabric in any way. Although the Mall provides a superb site for special occasions, most of its expanse is not easily integrated with the life of the city. See Longstreth, *The Mall in Washington*, 31.
52. See "Minutes of the Shelters (& Site) Committees," Library of Congress, SCLC (4), March 10, 1968: reel 28, 395.
53. See ibid. and an interview conducted with Tunney Lee, one of the planners on the team, in which other options were mentioned, including Rock Creek Park and the National Airport. The airport had many advantages because of the asphalt, toilets, and restaurants. Lee and Vale, "Resurrection City," 113–114.
54. For further reading on the City Beautiful movement and the McMillan Plan, see Hines, "The Imperial Mall."
55. The particular significance of the Lincoln Memorial comes from Lincoln's legacy of preserving the Union, ending slavery, and promoting economic and financial modernization.
56. Poor People's Campaign News, "Questions & Answers," 24.
57. James Goodell (then at Urban America), Kenneth Jadin (Department of Architecture, Howard University), Tunney Lee (architect and planner from Washington, DC), and John Wiebenson (School of Architecture, University of Maryland) were members of the Shelters (& Site) Committee. See the "Minutes of the Shelters (& Site) Committees," Library of Congress, SCLC (4); Wiebenson, "Planning and Using Resurrection City," 58–68.
58. "Administrative Units of Resurrection City in Fact Sheet, General Services Administration," Library of Congress, SCLC (4), 1968: reel 27, 517.
59. Ibid.
60. Tunney Lee, interview with the author, May 4, 2004, Cambridge, MA.
61. See "Minutes of the Shelters (& Site) Committees," Library of Congress, SCLC (4); Wiebenson, "Planning and Using Resurrection City."
62. Tunney Lee, interview with the author, May 4, 2004, Cambridge, MA.
63. Ibid.
64. See "Administrative Units of Resurrection City in Fact Sheet, General Services Administration," Library of Congress, SCLC (4).
65. Tunney Lee, interview with the author, May 4, 2004, Cambridge, MA.
66. "Statement by Martin Luther King, Jr.—Southern Christian Leadership Conference," Library of Congress, SCLC (4), December 4, 1967: reel 27, 705.
67. "Administrative Units of Resurrection City in Fact Sheet, General Services Administration," Library of Congress, SCLC (4)
68. Wiebenson, "Planning and Using Resurrection City," 58–68.
69. See, for example, the considerations for exploring alternate housing and transportation: "To

develop alternate housing arrangements in the Washington Metropolitan area (e.g., private homes, churches, gymnasiums, and hotel facilities) in case the participants are unable to live in New City. To develop resources (e.g., buses, cabs, and private cars) for transporting participants without expense to various campaign activities in the Washington Metropolitan area." "Poor People's Campaign Committees," Library of Congress, SCLC (4), 1968: reel 28, 298–299.

70. "Nonviolent Action," Library of Congress, SCLC (2), 1968: reel 12, 779.
71. Ibid.
72. "Administrative Units of Resurrection City in Fact Sheet, General Services Administration," Library of Congress, SCLC (4).
73. Wiebenson, "Planning and Using Resurrection City."
74. Poor People's Campaign News, "Questions & Answers."
75. Paul W. Valentine, "Confusion Obscures Poor People's Specific Demands," *Washington Post*, June 11, 1968.
76. Martin Weil, "Persistent Rain Causes Area Flooding," *Washington Post*, May 29, 1968.
77. Paul W. Valentine, "Poor People Get Extension of One Week," *Washington Post*, June 1, 1968.
78. Wiebenson, "Planning and Using Resurrection City."
79. Declaration of the Occupation of New York City. This document was accepted by the NYC General Assembly on September 29, 2011. http://occupywallstreet.net/policy/declaration-occupation-new-york-city.
80. Milan, "From Social Movements to Cloud Protesting," 893.
81. Ibid.
82. Juris, "Reflections on #Occupy Everywhere," 266.
83. Tahrir Square, located in the center of Cairo, was the key space for protests during the 2011 protests in Egypt. The space became a symbol of megascale dissent, not only for the Egyptians but also universally.
84. Writers for the 99% (Group), *Occupying Wall Street*.
85. Graeber, "On Playing by the Rules."
86. Marcuse, "The Purpose of the Occupation Movement."
87. Declaration of the Occupation of New York City, New York City General Assembly Condensed Documents, September 29, 2011. http://occupywallstreet.net/learn.
88. Juris, "Reflections on #Occupy Everywhere."
89. Marcuse, "The Purpose of the Occupation Movement."
90. Zuccotti Park was damaged by the 2001 terrorist attacks on the World Trade Center and redesigned in 2006 by Cooper, Robertson and Partners. For a further spatial analysis of the park and details regarding the physicality of the event, see Massey and Snyder, "Occupying Wall Street."
91. Kayden, "Occupying Wall Street at the Public-Private Frontier."
92. Ibid.
93. Massey and Snyder, "Occupying Wall Street."
94. See Massey and Snyder, "Mapping Liberty Plaza."
95. Writers for the 99% (Group), *Occupying Wall Street*, 63.

96. Juris, "Reflections on #Occupy Everywhere."
97. Marcuse, "The Purpose of the Occupation Movement."
98. Deleuze and Guattari, *A Thousand Plateaus*.
99. Cordero-Guzman, "Main Stream Support for a Mainstream Movement."
100. Hardt and Negri, "The Fight for 'Real Democracy'"; Maeckelbergh, *The Will of the Many;* N. Smith, "Contours of a Spatialized Politics."
101. Graeber, "On Playing by the Rules"; Juris, *Networking Futures*; Nugent, "Commentary"; Polletta, *Freedom Is an Endless Meeting*.
102. Statement of Autonomy, http://occupywallstreet.net/policy/statement-autonomy.
103. Writers for the 99% (Group), *Occupying Wall Street*, 11.
104. Ibid., 12.
105. Ibid., 27.
106. Ibid., 31.
107. Ibid., 32.
108. Ibid., 187.

CHAPTER 9. PERFORMING PROTESTABILITY

1. The idea of the crowd in the mid-nineteenth century focused on interrelated historical and psychological perspectives. In general, the crowd—or, at worst, the mob—was seen as a threat to government. For example, Hippolyte Taine's *Origins de la France contemporaine*, appearing in 1875, portrays hysterical crowds as the gravediggers of the old monarchy, a potent weapon in the hands of political extremists during the French Revolution. Gustave le Bon's book (1895) emerged in this context, presenting the psychology of the crowd as a scientific problem, challenging the discourse of the elite by expanding the scope of "the crowd" to include all kinds of collective phenomena. Le Bon argued that being part of a crowd does not require physical proximity; it is instead a mentality. Le Bon's ideas were challenged by Sigmund Freud, who rejected the idea that crowds are dominated by a "group mind," claiming that a relationship of frustration exists between crowd members and their leaders. According to Freud, if an individual cannot "have" a desired object, then he or she tries to be the same as that "object." Since the 1960s, crowd theories have attempted to evade dichotomies (e.g., rational vs. irrational and "normal" vs. pathological), which has been conducive to an expanded approach to crowd analysis with regard to at least three interrelated key issues. Focus has shifted from the crowd as a phenomenon to the act of crowding, which, in turn, has led to fewer deterministic connections between crowd violence and the social order. Freud, *Group Psychology and the Analysis of the Ego*; Le Bon, *The Crowd: A Study of the Popular Mind*.
2. Lofland, *Protest*.
3. Tilly, *The Politics of Collective Violence*.
4. Walgrave and Verhulst, "Government Stance and Internal Diversity of Protest," 457.
5. Canetti, *Crowds and Power*, 18.
6. Rawls, *A Theory of Justice*; Habermas, "Three Normative Models of Democracy."

7. Mouffe, *Deliberative Democracy or Agonistic Pluralism?*
8. Mouffe, "A Vibrant Democracy Needs Agonistic Confrontation."
9. Brenner, "The Limits to Scale?"; Cox, "Spaces of Dependence, Spaces of Engagement"; Marston, "The Social Construction of Scale"; Marston, Jones, and Woodward, "Human Geography without Scale"; J. Smith, *Social Movements for Global Democracy*.
10. Marston, Jones, and Woodward, "Human Geography without Scale."
11. P. Taylor, "A Materialist Framework for Political Geography." These scales by Taylor were expanded to include the body and home (Harvey, "Pattern, Process, and the Scale Problem in Geographical Research"; N. Smith, "Homeless/Global").
12. Brenner, "Global, Fragmented, Hierarchical."
13. For example, Doreen Massey perceives global-local relationships through the scale of connectivity and the politics of connectivity, which create what she calls "power geometries." Massey suggests enhancing agency as a means of better understanding the impact of globalization and its effect on the relationships between places. Massey, *Space, Place, and Gender* and *For Space*.
14. See the key attributes and further explanation in chapter 7.
15. See the organizers' website: https://www.womensmarch.com/mission/.
16. Indeed, to some degree, the site of protest normalization, protest participation, and conventional participation remains the privilege of well-educated and more affluent individuals. Walgrave and Verhulst, "Government Stance and Internal Diversity of Protest," 457.
17. Ibid.
18. Swyngedouw, "'Every Revolution Has Its Square,'" 23.
19. Ibid.
20. Souza and Frith, *Mobile Interfaces in Public Spaces*, 138.
21. Brighenti, "Visibility," 324.
22. Ibid., 325.
23. Noa Roei explores the role of art in the act of protest and the ways it creates distance and challenges agreed-upon symbols and boundaries between the oppressed and the oppressors. Roei, "Molding Resistance."
24. James Mayo explains this dynamic and the role of design in collective gatherings in his illuminating text "Propaganda with Design: Environmental Dramaturgy in the Political Rally," 25.
25. Ibid.
26. For further reading on the question of ethics and protests, see Bourg, *From Revolution to Ethics*; May, *Contemporary Political Movements and the Thought of Jacques Rancière*; and Rancière, *Disagreement: Politics and Philosophy*.
27. Leach, *The Anaesthetics of Architecture*, 17–32.
28. In particular, see the cases of Resurrection City and the Occupy movement.
29. For further reading, see the work of Antonio Gramsci, including *Selections from the Prison Notebooks*.
30. Harvey, *Spaces of Hope*, 236.
31. Leach, *The Anaesthetics of Architecture,* 19.
32. Mayo, "Propaganda with Design," 27.

Bibliography

Abbas, Tahir, and Ismail Hakki Yigit. "Scenes from Gezi Park: Localisation, Nationalism and Globalisation in Turkey." *City* 19, no. 1 (2015): 61–76. doi:10.1080/13604813.2014.969070.

Agnew, John A. *Place and Politics: The Geographical Mediation of State and Society*. Boston: Allen and Unwin, 1987.

———. "The Territorial Trap: The Geographical Assumptions of International Relations Theory." *Review of International Political Economy* 1, no. 1 (1994): 53–80.

Allegra, Marco. "Citizenship in Palestine: A Fractured Geography." *Citizenship Studies* 13, no. 6 (2009): 553–573.

Allen, John. *Lost Geographies of Power*. Malden, MA: Wiley-Blackwell, 2003.

Allmark, Panizza. "Framing Plaza de Mayo: Photographs of Protest." *Continuum: Journal of Media and Cultural Studies* 22, no. 6 (2008): 839–848. doi:10.1080/10304310802484605.

Amin, Ash. "Regions Unbound: Towards a New Politics of Place." *Geografiska Annaler Series B: Human Geography* 86, no. 1 (2004): 33–44.

Amin, Ash, and Nigel Thrift. *Cities: Reimagining the Urban*. Cambridge, UK: Polity, 2002.

Anderson, Benedict R. *Imagined Communities: Reflections on the Origin and Spread of Nationalism*. London: Verso, 1991.

Archibugi, Daniele. *The Global Commonwealth of Citizens: Toward Cosmopolitan Democracy*. Princeton, NJ: Princeton University Press, 2008.

Arditti, Rita. *Searching for Life: The Grandmothers of the Plaza de Mayo and the Disappeared Children of Argentina*. Berkeley: University of California Press, 1999.

Arendt, Hanna. *The Human Condition*. Chicago: University of Chicago Press, 1998.

———. "What Is Freedom?" In *Between Past and Future: Eight Exercises in Political Thought*, 142–169. New York: Viking Press, 1968.

Arieli, Shaul, and Michael Sfard. *Wall and Omission: The Separation Barrier—Safety or Greediness?* [in Hebrew]. Tel Aviv: Yediot Ahronot, 2008.

Azaryahu, Maoz. "The Spontaneous Formation of Memorial Space: The Case of Kikar Rabin, Tel Aviv." *Area* 28, no. 4 (1996): 501–513. http://www.jstor.org/stable/20003735.

Balibar, Etienne. "Europe as Borderland." *Environment and Planning D: Society and Space* 27, no. 2 (2009): 190–215. doi:10.1068/d13008.

Bartee, Wayne C. *A Time to Speak Out: The Leipzig Citizen Protests and the Fall of East Germany*. London: Praeger, 2000.

Baum, Dalit. "Women in Black and Men in Pink: Protesting Against the Israeli Occupation." *Social Identities: Journal for the Study of Race, Nation and Culture* 12, no. 5 (2006): 563–574. doi:10.1080/13504630600920274.

Bauman, Zygmunt. *Community: Seeking Safety in an Insecure World*. Cambridge, UK: Polity; Malden, MA: Blackwell, 2001.

———. *In Search of Politics*. Cambridge, UK: Polity, 1999.

Baykan, Aysegul, and Tali Hatuka. "Politics and Culture in the Making of Public Space: Taksim Square, 1 May 1977, Istanbul." *Planning Perspectives* 25, no. 1 (2010): 49–68. doi:10.1080/02665430903421734.

Baykan, Aysegul, and Roland Robertson. "Spatializing Turkey." In *Identity, Culture and Globalization*, edited by Eliezer Ben-Rafael and Yitzhak Sternberg, 177–192. Leiden, Netherlands: Brill, 2001.

Beck, Ulrich. "World Risk Society and Manufactured Uncertainties." *IRIS* 1, no. 2 (2009): 291–299. http://www.fupress.net/index.php/iris/article/view/3304.

Beck, Ulrich, and Ciaran Cronin. *Cosmopolitan Vision*. Cambridge, UK: Polity Press, 2006.

Benski, Tova. "Breaching Events and the Emotional Reactions of the Public: Women in Black in Israel." In *Emotions and Social Movements*, edited by Helena Flam and Debra King, 57–78. New York: Routledge, 2005.

Birnhack, Michael. *Merchav Prati* [Private space: The right to privacy, law and technology (Hebrew)]. Tel Aviv: Bar Ilan and Nevo, 2010.

Bloor, David. "Sociology of Knowledge." In *Routledge Encyclopedia of Philosophy: Sociology of Knowledge*. Web: Routledge, 1998. Available at doi:10.4324/9780415249126-R033-1.

Blumen, Orna, and Sharon Halevi. "Staging Peace through a Gendered Demonstration: Women in Black in Haifa, Israel." *Annals of the Association of American Geographers* 99, no. 5 (2009): 977–985. doi:10.1080/00045600903202848.

Bodnar, Judit. "Reclaiming Public Space." *Urban Studies* 52, no. 2 (2015): 1–15. doi:10.1177/0042098015583626.

Bosco, Fernando J. "The Madres de Plaza de Mayo and Three Decades of Human Rights' Activism: Embeddedness, Emotions, and Social Movements." *Annals of the Association of American Geographers* 96, no. 2 (2006): 342–365. doi:10.1111/j.1467–8306.2006.00481.x.

Bourg, Julian. *From Revolution to Ethics*. Quebec: McGill-Queens University Press, 2007.

Bouvard, Marguerite Guzman. *Revolutionizing Motherhood: The Mothers of the Plaza de Mayo*. Wilmington, DE: Scholarly Resources, 1997.

Boyer, M. Christine. "Cities for Sale: Merchandising History at South Street Seaport." In *Variations on a Theme Park: The New American City and the End of Public Space*, edited by Michael Sorkin, 181–204. New York: Hill and Wang, 1992.

Bozdogan, Sibel. *Modernism and Nation Building: Turkish Architectural Culture in the Early Republic*. Seattle: University of Washington Press, 2001.

Brenner, Neil. "Global, Fragmented, Hierarchical: Henri Lefebvre's Geographies of Globalization." *Public Culture* 10, no. 1 (1997): 135–167.

———. "The Limits to Scale? Methodological Reflections on Scalar Structuration." *Progress in Human Geography* 25, no. 4 (2001): 591–614. doi:https://doi.org/10.1191/030913201682688959.

Brenner, Neil, David J. Madden, and David Wachsmuth. "Assemblage Urbanism and the Challenges of Critical Urban Theory." *City* 15, no. 2 (2011): 225–240. doi:10.1080/13604813.2011.568717.

Brighenti, Andrea Mubi. "New Media and Urban Motilities: A Territoriologic Point of View." *Urban*

Studies 49, no. 2 (2012): 399–414. doi:10.1177/0042098011400771.

———."The Publicness of Public Space: On the Public Domain." *Quaderni* (Dipartimento di Sociologia e Ricerca Sociale, Università di Trento) 49 (2010): 1–56. http://web.unitn.it/files/quad49.pdf.

———."Visibility: A Category for the Social Sciences." *Current Sociology* 55, no. 3 (2007): 323–342. doi:10.1177/0011392107076079.

Butler, Judith. *Gender Trouble: Feminism and the Subversion of Identity*. New York: Routledge, 1990.

Butler, Judith, and Athena Athanasiou. *Dispossession: The Performative in the Political*. Cambridge, UK: Polity, 2013.

Callon, Michel, Pierre Lascoumes, and Yannick Barthe. *Acting in an Uncertain World: An Essay on Technical Democracy (Inside Technology)*. Translated by Graham Burchell and edited by Wiebe E. Bijker, W. Bernard Carlson, and Trevor Pinch. Cambridge, MA: MIT Press, 2009.

Cammaerts, Bart. "The Mediation of Insurrectionary Symbolic Damage." *The International Journal of Press/Politics* 18, no. 4 (2013): 525–548.

Campbell, Tim. *Beyond Smart Cities: How Cities Network, Learn and Innovate*. New York: Routledge, 2012.

Canetti, Elias. *Crowds and Power*. Translated by Carol Stewart. New York: Viking Press, 1962.

Cannon, Barry. "Venezuela, April 2002: Coup or Popular Rebellion? The Myth of a United Venezuela." *Bulletin of Latin American Research* 23, no. 3 (2004): 285–302. doi:10.1111/j.0261–3050.2004.00109.x

Carmona, Matthew, Tim Heath, Taner Oc, and Steve Tiesdell. *Public Places, Urban Spaces: The Dimensions of Urban Design*. Amsterdam and Boston: Architectural Press/Elsevier, 2010.

Castells, Manuel. *The City and the Grassroots: A Cross-Cultural Theory of Urban Social Movements*. London: E. Arnold, 1983.

———. *The Informational City: Information Technology, Economic Restructuring, and the Urban-Regional Process*. Oxford: Basil Blackwell, 1989.

———. *Networks of Outrage and Hope: Social Movements in the Internet Age*. Cambridge, UK: Polity Press, 2013.

———. *The Rise of the Network Society*. Oxford: Blackwell, 1996.

Çeçen, Kazim. *Taksim ve Hamidiye Suları* [The waters of Taksim and Hamidiye (Turkish)]. Istanbul: ISKI Yay, 2002.

Chase, John, Margaret Crawford, and John Kaliski, eds. *Everyday Urbanism*. New York: Monacelli Press, 1999.

Chatterjee, Partha. *Nationalist Thought and the Colonial World: A Derivative Discourse*. Minneapolis: University of Minnesota Press,1993.

Chazan, Naomi. "Israeli Women and Peace Activism." In *Calling the Equality Bluff: Women in Israel*, edited by Barbara Swirski and Marilyn P. Safir, 152–161. New York: Pergamon Press, 1991.

Chow, Tse-Tsung. *The May Fourth Movement: Intellectual Revolution in Modern China*. Cambridge, MA: Harvard University Press, 1960.

Collins, Damian. "Private/Public Divide." In *International Encyclopedia of Human Geography*, edited by Rob Kitchin and Nigel Thrift, 437–441. Oxford, UK: Elsevier, 2009. https://doi.org/10.1016/B978-008044910-4.00989-5.

Cordero-Guzman, R. Hector. "Main Stream Support for a Mainstream Movement: The 99% Movement Comes from and Looks Like the 99%." Retrieved from occupywallst. org/media/pdf/OWS-profile1-10-18-11-sent-v2-HRCG.pdf.

Cosgrove, Dennis, and Stephan Daniels, eds. *The Iconography of Landscape: Essays on the Symbolic Representation, Design, and Use of Past Environments*. Cambridge: Cambridge University Press, 1988.

Cox, Kevin. "Spaces of Dependence, Spaces of Engagement and the Politics of Scale, or: Looking for Local Politics." *Political Geography* 17, no. 1 (1998): 1–23. doi:10.1016/S0962–6298(97)00048–6.

Cresswell, Tim. *In Place/Out of Place: Geography, Ideology, and Transgression*. Minneapolis: University of Minnesota Press, 1996.

D'Arcus, Bruce. *Boundaries of Dissent: Protest and State Power in the Media Age*. New York: Routledge, 2006.

Davis, Diane E. "The Power of Distance: Re-Theorizing Social Movements in Latin America." *Theory and Society* 28, no. 4 (1999): 585–638. doi:10.1023/A:1007026620394.

Davis, Diane, and Tali Hatuka. "The Right to Vision: A New Planning Praxis for Conflict Cities." *Journal of Planning Education and Research* 31, no. 3 (2011): 241–257.

Deakin, Mark, and Husam Al Waer, eds. *From Intelligent to Smart Cities*. London: Routledge, 2014.

de Certeau, Michel. *The Practice of Everyday Life*. Berkeley: University of California Press, 1984.

De Landa, Manuel. *A Thousand Years of Nonlinear History*. New York: Swerve Editions, 2000.

Della Porta, Donatella, and Herbert Reiter, eds. *Policing Protest: The Control of Mass Demonstrations in Western Democracies*. Minneapolis: University of Minnesota Press, 1998.

Deleuze, Gill, and Felix Guattari. *A Thousand Plateaus: Capitalism and Schizophrenia*. London: Athlone, 1987.

Diani, Mario. "The Structural Bases of Protest Events: Multiple Memberships and Civil Society Networks in the 15 February 2003 Anti-War Demonstrations." *Acta Sociologica* 52, no. 1 (2009): 63–83. doi:10.1177/0001699308100634.

Dodge, Martin, and Rob Kitchin. "Codes of Life: Identification Codes and the Machine-Readable World." *Environment and Planning D: Society and Space* 23 (2005): 851–881.

Dong, Madeleine Yue. *Republican Beijing: The City and Its Histories*. Berkeley: University of California Press, 2003.

Dovey, Kim. *Becoming Places: Urbanism/Architecture/Identity/ Power*. New York: Routledge, 2010.

———. *Framing Places: Mediating Power in Built Form*. London: Routledge, 1999.

Eco, Umberto. "Function and Sign: The Semiotics of Architecture." In *Rethinking Architecture*, edited by Neil Leach, 182–202. London: Routledge, 1997.

Edelman, Murray. *From Art to Politics: How Artistic Creations Shape Political Conceptions*. Chicago: University of Chicago Press, 1995.

———. *The Symbolic Uses of Politics*. Urbana: University of Illinois Press, 1964.

Eisinger, Peter K. "Protest Behavior and the Integration of Urban Political Systems." *The Journal of Politics* 33, no. 4 (1971): 980–1007. doi:http://dx.doi.org/10.2307/2128419.

Ekinci, Oktay O. *Bütün Yönleriyle Taksim Camisi Belgeseli* [Documentation on the Taksim Mosque from all perspectives (Turkish)]. Istanbul: Çagda Yayınları, 1997.

Engler Mira. "A Living Memorial: Commemorating Yitzhak Rabin in the Tel Aviv Square." *Places* 12, no. 2, (1999): 1–4. http://escholarship.org/uc/item/6fg2j06d.

Fager, Charles. *Uncertain Resurrection: The Poor People's Washington Campaign*. Grand Rapids, MI: William B. Eerdmans, 1969.

Farías, Ignacio. "The Politics of Urban Assemblages." *City* 15, no. 3–4 (2011): 365–374. doi:10.1080/13604813.2011.595110.

Fisher, Dana R., Kevin Stanley, David Berman, and Gina Neff. "How Do Organizations Matter: Mobilization and Support for Participants at Five Globalization Protests." *Social Problems* 52, no. 1 (2005): 102–121.

Fisher, Jo. *Mothers of the Disappeared*. Boston: South End Press, 1989.

Forsyth, Ann, and Laura Musacchio. *Designing Small Parks: A Manual for Addressing Social and Ecological Concerns*. Hoboken, NJ: John Wiley and Sons, 2005.

Foster, Susan Leigh. "Choreographies of Protest." *Theatre Journal* 55, no. 3 (2003): 395–412. doi:10.1353/tj.2003.0111.

Foucault, Michel. *Power/Knowledge: Selected Interviews and Other Writings 1972–1977*. Edited by Colin Gordon. New York: Pantheon Books, 1980.

Freud, Sigmund. *Group Psychology and the Analysis of the Ego*. New York: W. W. Norton, 1959.

Fromm, Erich. *On Disobedience: Why Freedom Means Saying "No" to Power*. New York: Harper Perennial and Modern Thought, 2010.

Gabriel, Ayala H. "Grief and Rage: Collective Emotions in the Politics of Peace and the Politics of Gender in Israel." *Culture Medicine and Psychiatry* 16, no. 3 (1992): 311–335. doi:10.1007/BF00052153.

Garrow, David. *Protest at Selma: Martin Luther King, Jr., and the Voting Rights Act of 1965*. New Haven: Yale University Press, 1978.

Gershuny, Jonathan. "Web Use and Net Nerds: A Neofunctionalist Analysis of the Impact of Information Technology in the Home." *Social Forces* 82, no. 1 (September 2003): 141–166. doi:10.1353/sof.2003.0086.

Giddens, Anthony. *The Constitution of Society*. Cambridge: Cambridge University Press, 1984.

———. *Modernity and Self-Identity*. Cambridge: Cambridge University Press, 1991.

Giddens, Anthony, and Christopher Pierson. *Conversations with Anthony Giddens: Making Sense of Modernity*. Cambridge, UK: Polity Press, 1998.

Gieseke, Jens. *The History of the Stasi, East Germany's Secret Police 1945–1990*. Translated by David Burnett. New York: Berghahn Books, 2014.

Goffman, Erving. *Behavior in Public Places: Notes on the Social Organization of Gatherings*. New York: The Free Press, 1963.

———. *Interaction Ritual: Essays in Face-to-Face Behavior*. New Brunswick, NJ: Aldine, 1967.

———. *The Presentation of Self in Everyday Life*. Woodstock, NY: Overlook Press, 1973. Originally published 1959.

———. *Relations in Public: Microstudies of the Public Order.* New York: Basic Books, 1971.

Goldsmith, Stephen, and Susan Crawford. *The Responsive City: Engaging Communities Through Data-Smart Governance*. San Francisco: Jossey-Bass, 2014.

Gordon, Neve. "The Israeli Peace Camp in Dark Times." *Peace Review* 15, no. 1 (2003): 39–45. http://www.academia.edu/8402859/The_Israeli_Peace_Camp_in_Dark_Times.

Graeber, David. "On Playing by the Rules—The Strange Success of #OccupyWall Street, 2011." *Naked Capitalism*. http://www.nakedcapitalism.com/2011/10/david-graeber-on-playing-by-the-rules-%E2%80%93-the-strange-success-of-occupy-wall-street.html.

Graham, Stephen. "Bridging Urban Digital Divides? Urban Polarisation and Information and Communications Technologies (ICTs)." *Urban Studies* 39, no. 1 (2002): 33–56. doi:10.1080/00420980220099050.

———. "Software-Sorted Geographies." *Progress in Human Geography* 29, no. 5 (2005): 562–580. doi:10.1191/0309132505ph568oa.

———. "Spaces of Surveillant Simulation: New Technologies, Digital Representations, and Material Geographies." *Environment and Planning D: Society and Space* 16, no. 4 (1998): 483–504. doi:10.1068/d160483.

Graham, Stephen, and David Wood. "Digitizing Surveillance: Categorization, Space, Inequality." *Critical Social Policy* 23, no. 2 (2003): 227–248. doi:10.1177/0261018303023002006.

Gramsci, Antonio. *Selections from the Prison Notebooks*. Edited and translated by Quentin Hoare and Geoffrey Nowell-Smith. London: Lawrence and Wishart, 1971.

Grinberg, Lev. *Imagined Peace, Discourse of War: The Failure of Leadership, Politics and Democracy in Israel, 1992–2006* [in Hebrew]. Tel Aviv: Resling, 2007.

Grosz, Elizabeth. "Bergson, Deleuze and the Becoming of Unbecoming." *Parallax* 11, no. 2 (2005): 4–13. doi:10.1080/13534640500058434.

Gül, Murat, John Dee, and Cahide Nur Cünük. "Istanbul's Taksim Square and Gezi Park: The Place of Protest and the Ideology of Place." *Journal of Architecture and Urbanism* 38, no. 1 (2014): 63–72. doi:10.3846/20297955.2014.902185.

Guthrie, Douglas J. "Political Theater and Student Organizations in the 1989 Chinese Movement: A Multivariate Analysis of Tiananmen." *Sociological Forum* 10, no. 3 (1995): 419–454. doi:10.1007/BF02095829.

Habermas, Jürgen. *The Theory of Communicative Action*. Vol. 1 Cambridge, UK: Polity Press, 1986–1989.

———. "Three Normative Models of Democracy." In *Democracy and Difference: Contesting the Boundaries of the Political*, edited by Seyla Benhabib, 21–30. Princeton, NJ: Princeton University Press, 1996.

Hadjar, Andreas. "Non-Violent Political Protest in East Germany in the 1980s: Protestant Church, Opposition Groups and the People." *German Politics* 12, no. 3 (2003): 107–128. doi: 10.1080/0964400032000242716.

Haggerty, Kevin, and Richard Ericson. "The Surveillant Assemblage." *The British Journal of Sociology* 51, no. 4 (2000): 605–622. doi:10.1080/00071310020015280.

Halbwachs, Maurice. *On Collective Memory*. Edited, translated, and with an introduction by Lewis A. Coser. Chicago: University of Chicago Press, 1992.

Halevi, Sharon, and Orna Blumen. "What a Difference a Place Makes: The Reflexive (Mis) management of a City's Pasts." *Journal of Urban History* 37, no. 3 (2011): 384–399. doi:10.1177/0096144211400380.

Hallward, Maia Carter. "Creative Responses to Separation: Israeli and Palestinian Joint Activism in Bil'in." *Journal of Peace Research* 46, no. 4 (2009): 541–558. doi:10.1177/0022343309334612.

———. "Negotiating Boundaries, Narrating Checkpoints: The Case of Machsom Watch." *Critique: Critical Middle Eastern Studies* 17, no. 1 (2008): 21–40. http://www.americantaskforce.org/sites/default/files/Hallward.pdf.

Halperin, Irit. "Between the Lines: The Story of Machsom Watch." *Journal of Humanistic Psychology* 47, no. 3 (2007): 333–339. doi:10.1177/0022167807301896.

Handelman, Don. *Models and Mirrors: Towards an Anthropology of Public Events*. Cambridge: Cambridge University Press, 1990.

Hardt, Michael, and Antonio Negri. "The Fight for 'Real Democracy' at the Heart of Occupy Wall Street: The Encampment in Lower Manhattan Speaks to a Failure of Representation." *Foreign Affairs*, October 11, 2011. https://www.foreignaffairs.com/articles/north-america/2011-10-11/fight-real-democracy-heart-occupy-wall-street.

Harvey, David. *Justice, Nature, and the Geography of Difference*. Cambridge, MA: Blackwell, 1996.

———. "Pattern, Process, and the Scale Problem in Geographical Research." *Transactions of the Institute of British Geographers* 45 (1968): 71–78. doi:10.2307/621393.

———. *Spaces of Hope*. Berkeley: University of California Press, 2000.

Hatuka, Tali. "The Challenge of Distance in Designing Civil Protest: The Case of Resurrection City in Washington Mall and the Occupy Movement in Zuccotti Park." *Planning Perspectives* 31, no. 2 (2016): 253–282.

———. "Civilian Consciousness of the Mutable Nature of Borders: The Power of Appearance along a Fragmented Border in Israel/Palestine." *Political Geography* 31, no. 6 (2012): 347–357. doi:10.1016/j.polgeo.2012.05.004.

———. "Negotiating Space: Analyzing Jaffa Protest Form, Intention and Violence, October 27th 1933." *Jerusalem Quarterly* 35 (Autumn 2008): 93–106.

———. "Transformative Terrains: Counter Hegemonic Tactics of Dissent in Israel." *Geopolitics* 17, no. 4 (2012): 926–951. doi:10.1080/14650045.2012.659298.

———. "Urban Absence: Everyday Practices versus Trauma Practices in Rabin Square, Tel Aviv." *Journal of Architecture and Planning Research* 26, no. 3 (2009): 198–212. http://www.jstor.org/stable/43030869.

———. *Violent Acts and Urban Space in Contemporary Tel Aviv: Revisioning Moments*. Austin: University of Texas Press, 2010.

Hatuka, Tali, and Aysegul Baykan. "Politics and Culture in the Making of Public Space: Taksim Square, 1 May 1977, Istanbul." *Planning Perspectives* 25, no. 1 (2010): 49–68. doi.org/10.1080/02665430903421734.

Hatuka, Tali, and Alexander D'Hooghe. "After Postmodernism: Readdressing the Role of Utopia in Urban Design and Planning." *Places Journal* 19, no. 2 (2007): 20–27.

Hatuka, Tali, and Rachel Kallus. "The Architecture of Repeated Rituals." *Journal of Architectural Education* 61, no. 4 (2008): 85–94. doi:10.1111/j.1531-314X.2008.00192.x.

Hatuka, Tali, and Eran Toch. "Being Visible in Public Space: The Normalization of Asymmetrical Visibility." *Urban Studies* 54, no. 4 (2016): 984–998. doi:10.1177/0042098015624384.

Hellinger, Daniel. "Political Overview: The Breakdown of *Puntofijismo* and the Rise of *Chavismo*." In *Venezuelan Politics in the Chávez Era: Class, Polarization, and Conflict*, edited by Steve Ellner and Daniele Hellinger, 27–54. Boulder, CO: Lynne Rienner, 2003.

Helman, Sara, and Tamar Rapoport. "Women in Black: Challenging Israel's Gender and Socio-Political Orders." *The British Journal of Sociology* 48, no. 4 (1997): 681–700. doi:10.2307/591603.

Henning, Christoph. "Distanciation and Disembedding." In *Blackwell Encyclopedia of Sociology*, edited by George Ritzer. Blackwell Publishing, 2007. *Blackwell Reference Online*. doi:10.1111/b.9781405124331.2007.x.

Henry, Matthew. "Surveillance." In *International Encyclopedia of Human Geography*, edited by Rob Kitchin and Nigel Thrift, 95–99. Oxford, UK: Elsevier, 2009. doi:10.1016/B978-008044910-4.01008-7.

Hershkovitz, Linda. "Tiananmen Square and the Politics of Place." *Political Geography* 12 (1993): 395–420. doi:10.1016/0962–6298(93)90010–5.

Hines, Thomas S. "The Imperial Mall: The City Beautiful Movement and the Washington Plan of 1901-1902." In *The Mall in Washington, 1791–1991*, edited by Richard Longstreth, 78–99. Studies in the History of Art, Symposium Papers XIV, vol. 30. Washington, DC: National Gallery of Art, 1991.

Hobsbawm, Eric, and Terence Ranger, eds. *The Invention of Tradition*. New York: Cambridge University Press, 1983.

Holston, James. "Spaces of Insurgent Citizenship." In *Making the Invisible Visible*, edited by Leonie Sandercock, 155–173. Berkeley: University of California Press, 1998.

Holston, James, and Arjun Appadurai. "Introduction: Cities and Citizenship." In *Cities and Citizenship*, edited by James Holston, 1–21. Durham, NC: Duke University Press, 1999.

Horowitz, Dan, and Moshe Lissak. *Trouble in Utopia: The Overburdened Polity of Israel*. Albany, NY: SUNY Press, 1989.

Hung, Wu. *Remaking Beijing: Tiananmen Square and the Creation of a Political Space*. Chicago: University of Chicago Press, 2005.

———. "Tiananmen Square: A Political History of Monuments." *Representations* 35 (1991): 84–117. doi:10.2307/2928718.

Hutton, Patrick H. "Memory." In *New Dictionary of the History of Ideas*, edited by Maryanne C. Horowitz, 1418–1422. New York: Charles Scribner's Sons, 2005.

Huyssen, Andreas. *Present Pasts: Urban Palimpsests and the Politics of Memory*. Stanford, CA: Stanford University Press, 2003.

Irazábal, Clara, ed. *Ordinary Places, Extraordinary Events: Citizenship, Democracy and Public Space in Latin America*. London: Routledge, 2008.

Isin, Engin F. *Being Political: Genealogies of Citizenship*. Minneapolis: University of Minnesota Press, 2002.

Iveson, Kurt. *Publics and the City*. Oxford, UK: Blackwell, 2007.

Jacobi, Tami Amanda. *Women in Zones of Conflict: Power and Resistance in Israel*. Montreal: McGill-Queen's University Press, 2005.

James-Chakraborty, Kathleen. *German Architecture for a Mass Audience*. London: Routledge, 2000.

Jessop, Bob, Neil Brenner, and Martin Jones. "Theorizing Sociospatial Relations." *Environment and Planning D: Society and Space* 26, no. 3 (2008): 389–401. doi:10.1068/d9107.

Juris, Jeffrey S. *Networking Futures: The Movements against Corporate Globalization*. Durham, NC: Duke University Press, 2008.

———. "The New Digital Media and Activist Networking within Anti-Corporate Globalization Movements." The *Annals of the American Academy of Political and Social Science* 597, no. 1 (2005): 189–208. doi:10.1177/0002716204270338.

———. "Reflections on #Occupy Everywhere: Social Media, Public Space, and Emerging Logics of Aggregation." *American Ethnologist* 39, no. 2 (2012): 259–279. doi:10.1111/j.1548-1425.2012.01362.x.

Kallus, Rachel. "Patrick Geddes and the Evolution of a Housing Type in Tel-Aviv." *Planning Perspectives* 12, no. 3 (1997): 281–320. doi:10.1080/026654397364663.

Kaminer, Reuven. *The Politics of Protest: The Israeli Peace Movement and the Palestinian Intifada*. Brighton, UK: Sussex Academic Press, 1996.

Kark, Ruth. *Jaffa: A City in Evolution, 1799–1917*. Translated by Gila Brand. Jerusalem: Yad Izhak Ben-Zvi Press, 1990.

Kaufman, Ilana. "Resisting Occupation or Institutionalizing Control? Israeli Women and Protest in West Bank Checkpoints." *International Journal of Peace Studies* 13, no. 1 (2008): 43–62. https://www.gmu.edu/programs/icar/ijps/vol13_1/IJPS13n1Kaufman.pdf.

Kayden, Jerold S. "Occupying Wall Street at the Public-Private Frontier." *The Architect's Newspaper*. October 12, 2011. http://www.archpaper.com/news/articles.asp?id=5691#.

Khalidi, Rashid. *Palestinian Identity: The Construction of Modern National Consciousness*. New York: Columbia University Press, 1997.

Kirby, Kathleen M. *Indifferent Boundaries: Spatial Concepts of Human Subjectivity*. New York: Guilford Press, 1996.

Knox, Paul L. "Symbolism, Styles, and Settings: The Built Environment and the Imperatives of Urbanized Capitalism." *Architecture et Comportement* 2, no. 2 (1984): 107–122.

Kotef, Hagar, and Merav Amir. "(En)Gendering Checkpoints: Checkpoint Watch and the Repercussions of Intervention." *Signs: Journal of Women in Culture and Society* 32, no. 4 (2007): 973–996. https://doi.org/10.1086/512623.

Krier, Rob. *Urban Space*. New York: Rizzoli International, 1979.

Kubilay, A. Y. "Topçu Kıslası." *Dunden Bugune Istanbul Ansiklopedisi* 7 (1994): 274.

Kuran, Timur. "Sparks and Prairie Fires: A Theory of Unanticipated Political Revolution." *Public Choice* 61 (1989): 41–74. doi:10.1007/BF00116762.

Kuruyazıcı, Hasan. "Cumhuriyetin Istanbul'daki Simgesi: Taksim Cumhuriyet Meydanı" [The symbol of the republic in Istanbul: The Taksim Republican Square]. In *75 Yılda Degişen Kent ve Mimarlık* [The changing city and architecture in 75 years (Turkish)], edited by Yıldız Sey, 89–99. Istanbul: Tarih Vakfı Yayınları, 1998.

———. "Istanbul'da Beyazıt Meydanı: Oluşumu—Gelişimi—Değişimi" [Beyazit Square in Istanbul: Constitution—development—change (Turkish)]. In *Prof. Dr. Haluk Abbasoğlu'na 65. Yaş Armağanı Euergetes Fetschrift für Prof. Dr. Haluk Abbasoğlu zum 65. Geburstag, II. Cilt*, edited by İnci Delemenö Sedef Çokay-Kepçe, Aşkım Özdizbay, and Özgür Turak, 759–772. Antalya, Turkey: Suna-İnan KıraçAkdeniz Medeniyetleri Araştırma Enstitüsü, 2008.

Kymlicka, Will. *Multicultural Odysseys: Navigating the New International Politics of Diversity*. Oxford, UK: Oxford University Press, 2007.

LaCapra, Dominick. *Writing History, Writing Trauma*. Baltimore, MD: Johns Hopkins University Press, 2001.

Leach, Neil. *The Anaesthetics of Architecture*. Cambridge, MA: MIT Press, 1999.

Le Bon, Gustav. *The Crowd: A Study of the Popular Mind*. New York: Dover Publications, 2002 [1895].

Lee, Nelson K. "How Is a Political Public Space Made? The Birth of Tiananmen Square and the May Fourth Movement." *Political Geography* 28, no. 1 (2009): 32–43. doi:10.1016/j.polgeo.2008.05.003.

Lee, Tunney, and Lawrence Vale. "Resurrection City: Washington DC, 1968." *Thresholds* 41 (2013): 112–121. http://web.mit.edu/ebj/Desktop/ebj/MacData/afs.cron/group/thresholds/www/issue/41/t41_lee_vale.pdf.

Lefebvre, Henri. *Everyday Life in the Modern World*. London: Transaction Publishers, 1984.

———. *The Production of Space*. Oxford, UK: Blackwell, 1991.

Levy, Yagil, and Shlomo Mizrahi. "Alternative Politics and the Transformation of Society-Military Relations: The Israeli Experience." *Administration and Society* 40, no. 1 (2008): 25–53. doi:10.1177/0095399707311649.

Liberman, Nira, and Yaacov Trope. "Construal-Level Theory of Psychological Distance." *Psychological Review* 117, no. 2 (2010): 440–463. doi:10.1037/a0018963.

———. "The Psychology of Transcending the Here and Now." *Science* 322 (2008): 1201–1205. doi:10.1126/science.1161958.

Lievrouw, Leah. *Alternative and Activist New Media*. Cambridge, UK: Polity Press, 2011.

Liu, Alan P. L. "Symbols and Repression at Tiananmen Square, April–June 1989." *Political Psychology* 13, no. 1 (1992): 45–60. http://www.jstor.org/stable/3791423.

Lofland, John. *Protest: Studies of Collective Behavior and Social Movements*. New Brunswick, NJ: Transaction Books, 1985.

Lofland, Lyn H. *The Public Realm: Exploring the City's Quintessential Social Territory*. New York: Aldine De Gruyter, 1998.

Lohmann, Susanne. "The Dynamics of Informational Cascades: The Monday Demonstrations in Leipzig, East Germany, 1989–91." *World Politics* 47, no. 1 (1994): 42–101. doi:10.2307/2950679.

Longstreth, Richard, ed. *The Mall in Washington, 1791–1991*. 2nd ed. Washington, DC: National Gallery of Art, 2002.

López Maya, Margarita, Luis Lander, and Dick Parker. "Popular Protest in Venezuela: Novelties and Continuities." *Latin American Perspectives* 32, no. 2 (2005): 92–180. http://www.jstor.org/stable/30040278.

Loukaitou-Sideris, Anastasia, and Renia Ehrenfeucht. *Sidewalks: Conflict and Negotiation over Public Space*. Cambridge, MA: MIT Press, 2009.

Low, Setha, and Neil Smith, eds. *The Politics of Public Space*. New York: Routledge, 2006.

Low, Setha, Dana Taplin, and Suzanne Scheld. *Rethinking Urban Parks: Public Space and Cultural Diversity*. Austin: University of Texas Press, 2005.

Lui, Andrew. "Looking Back at Tiananmen Square." *Peace Review* 12, no. 1 (2000): 139–145. doi:10.1080/104026500113935.

Lynch, Kevin. *The Image of the City*. Cambridge, MA: MIT Press, 1960.

Mace, Rodney. *Trafalgar Square: Emblem of Empire*. Cambridge: Cambridge University Press, 1976.

Macrakis, Kristie. *Seduced by Secrets: Inside the Stasi's Spy-Tech World*. New York: Cambridge University Press, 2008.

Madanipour, Ali. *Public and Private Spaces of the City*. London: Routledge, 2013.

———. *Urban Design, Space and Society*. Basingstoke, UK: Palgrave Macmillan, 2014.

———, ed. *Whose Public Space? International Case Studies in Urban Design and Development*. London: Routledge, 2010.

Maeckelbergh, Marianne. *The Will of the Many: How the Alterglobalisation Movement Is Changing the Face of Democracy*. London: Pluto Press, 2009.

Manovich, Lev. *The Language of New Media*. Cambridge, MA: MIT Press, 2001.

Marcuse, Peter. "The Purpose of the Occupation Movement and the Danger of Fetishizing Space." *Peter Marcuse's Blog*, November 15, 2011. https://pmarcuse.wordpress.com.

Marston, Sallie A. "The Social Construction of Scale." *Progress in Human Geography* 24, no. 2 (2000): 219–242.

Marston, Sallie A., John Paul Jones III, and Keith Woodward. "Human Geography without Scale." *Transactions of the Institute of British Geographers* 30 (2005): 416–432.

Marx, Gary T. "What's New about the 'New Surveillance'? Classifying for Change and Continuity." *Surveillance and Society* 1, no. 1 (2002): 9–29. doi:10.1007/BF02687074.

Massey, Doreen. *For Space*. London: Sage, 2005.

———. *Space, Place, and Gender*. Minneapolis: University of Minnesota Press, 1994.

Massey, Jonathan, and Brett Snyder. "Mapping Liberty Plaza: How Occupy Wall Street Spatially Transformed Zuccotti Park." *Places Journal*. September 2012; accessed November 25, 2014. https://placesjournal.org/article/mapping-liberty-plaza.

———. "Occupying Wall Street: Places and Spaces of Political Action." *Places Journal*. September 2012. http://placesjournal.org/article/occupying-wall-street-places-and-spaces-of-political-action.

May, Todd. *Contemporary Political Movements and the Thought of Jacques Rancière: Equality in Action*. Edinburgh: Edinburgh University Press, 2010.

Mayo, James M., Jr. "Propaganda with Design: Environmental Dramaturgy in the Political Rally." *Journal of Architectural Education* 32, no. 2 (1978): 24–27. http://www.jstor.org/stable/1424285.

McAdam, Doug. "Micro-mobilization Contexts and Recruitment to Activism." In *From Structure to Action: Social Movement Participation Across Cultures*, edited by Bert Klandermans, Hanspeter Kriesi, and Sidney Tarrow, 125–154. Greenwich, CT: JAI Press, 1988.

McCarthy, Ronald M. "Methods of Nonviolent Actions." In *Protest, Power, and Change: An Encyclopedia of Nonviolent Action from ACT-UP to Women's Suffrage*, edited by Roger S. Powers, William B. Vogele, Douglas Bond, and Christopher Kruegler, 319–328. New York: Routledge, 2011.

McCaughey, Martha, and Micahel Ayers, eds. *Cyberactivism: Online Activism in Theory and Practice*. New York: Routledge, 2003.

McClelland, John S. *The Crowd and the Mob: From Plato to Canetti*. Boston: Unwin Hyman, 1989.

McCormack, Derek P. "Becoming." In *International Encyclopedia of Human Geography*, edited by Rob Kitchin and Nigel Thrift, 277–281. Oxford, UK: Elsevier, 2009. doi:10.1016/B978–008044910–4.00922–6.

McCrea, Sean M., Frank Wieber, and Andrea L. Myers. "Construal Level Mind-sets Moderate Self- and Social Stereotyping." *Journal of Personality and Social Psychology* 102, no. 1 (2012): 51–68. http://dx.doi.org/10.1037/a0026108.

McFarlane, Colin. "Assemblage and Critical Urbanism." *City* 15, no. 2 (2011): 204–224.

Mehta, Vikas. *The Street: A Quintessential Social Public Space*. New York: Routledge, 2014.

Melucci, Alberto. *Challenging Codes: Collective Action in the Information Age*. Cambridge: Cambridge University Press, 1996.

Milan, Stefania. "From Social Movements to Cloud Protesting: The Evolution of Collective Identity." *Information, Communication and Society* 18, no. 8 (2015): 887–900.

Mitchell, Don. "The End of Public Space? People's Park, Definitions of the Public, and Democracy." *Annals of the Association of American Geographers* 85, no. 1 (1995): 108–133.

———. "Iconography and Locational Conflict from the Underside: Free Speech, People's Park, and the Politics of Homelessness in Berkeley, California." *Political Geography* 11, no. 2 (1992): 152–169. doi:10.1016/0962–6298(92)90046-V.

———. *The Right to the City: Social Justice and the Fight for Public Space*. New York: Guilford Press, 2003.

Mouffe, Chantal. *Deliberative Democracy or Agonistic Pluralism?* Political Science Series 72. Vienna: Institute of Advanced Studies, 2000.

———. *The Democratic Paradox*. London: Verso, 2000.

———. "'A Vibrant Democracy Needs Agonistic Confrontation': An Interview with Chantal Mouffe." *The Europeanisation of Citizenship in the Successor States of the Former Yugoslavia (CITSEE)*, July 7, 2013. http://www.citsee.eu/interview/vibrant-democracy-needs-agonistic-confrontation-interview-chantal-mouffe.

Namaan, Dorit. "The Silenced Outcry: A Feminist Perspective from the Israeli Checkpoints in Palestine." *NWSA Journal* 18, no. 3 (2006): 168–180.

Negrón, Marco. "Caracas of Latin America." In *Caracas Cenital*, edited by Nicola Rocco, 10–25. Caracas: Fundación para la Cultura Urbana, 2005.

Newman, David. "The Lines That Continue to Separate Us: Borders in Our 'Borderless' World." *Progress in Human Geography* 30, no. 2 (2006): 143–161.

Newman, David, and Tamar Hermann. "A Comparative Study of Gush Emunim and Peace Now." *Middle Eastern Studies* 28, no. 3 (1992): 509–530. doi:10.1080/00263209208700912.

Nield, Sophie. "On the Border as Theatrical Space: Appearance, Dis-location and the Production of the Refugee." In *Contemporary Theatres in Europe: A Critical Companion*, edited by Joe Kelleher and Nicholas Ridout, 61–72. New York: Routledge, 2006.

Nora, Pierre. *Realms of Memory: The Construction of the French Past [Les Lieux de mémoire*]. Edited and with a foreword by Lawrence D. Kritzman; translated by Arthur Goldhammer. New York: Columbia University Press, 1998.

Norris, Clive, and Gary Armstrong. *The Maximum Surveillance Society: The Rise of CCTV*. Oxford, UK: Berg, 1999.

Nugent, David. "Commentary: Democracy, Temporalities of Capitalism, and Dilemmas of Inclusion in Occupy Movements." *American Ethnologist* 39, no. 2 (2012): 280–283. doi:10.1111/j.1548-1425.2012.01363.x.

Nussbaum, Martha C. "Toward a Globally Sensitive Patriotism." *Daedalus* 137, no. 3 (2008): 78–93.

Oberschall, Anthony. *Social Conflict and Social Movements*. Englewood Cliffs, NJ: Prentice-Hall, 1973.

Olick, Jeffrey K. "Collective Memory." In *The International Encyclopedia of the Social Sciences*, edited by William A. Darity Jr., 7–8. 2nd ed. Detroit, MI: Macmillan Reference USA, 2008.

O'Neill, Kate. "Transnational Protest: States, Circuses, and Conflict at the Frontline of Global Politics." *International Studies Review* 6, no. 2 (2004): 233–251. doi:10.1111/j.1521–9488.2004.00397.x.

Opp, Karl-Dieter, and Christiane Gern. "Dissident Groups, Personal Networks, and Spontaneous Cooperation: The East German Revolution of 1989." *American Sociological Review* 58, no. 5 (1993): 659–680. http://www.jstor.org/stable/2096280.

Orleck, Annelise, and Diana Taylor, eds. *The Politics of Motherhood: Activist Voices from Left to Right*. Hanover, NH: Dartmouth College, University Press of New England, 1997.

Örs, İlay Romain. "Genie in the Bottle: Gezi Park, Taksim Square, and the Realignment of Democracy and Space in Turkey." *Philosophy and Social Criticism* 40, nos. 4–5 (2014): 489–498. doi:10.1177/0191453714525390.

Örs, İlay Romain, and Ömer Turan. "The Manner of Contention: Pluralism at Gezi." *Philosophy and Social Criticism* 41, no. 4–5 (2015): 453–463. doi:10.1177/0191453715568924.

Paasi, Anssi. "Bounded Spaces in a 'Borderless World': Border Studies, Power and the Anatomy of Territory." *Journal of Power* 2, no. 2 (2009): 213–234.

———. *Territories, Boundaries, and Consciousness: The Changing Geographies of the Finnish-Russian Boundary*. Chichester, UK: J. Wiley and Sons, 1997.

Palmowski, Jan. "Tiananmen Square." In *A Dictionary of Contemporary World History*. 3rd ed. Oxford University Press, 2008. *Oxford Reference Online*. http://www.oxfordreference.com/views/ENTRY.html?subview=Main&entry=t46.e2315.

Parker, Noel, Nick Vaughan-Williams, Luiza Bialasiewicz, Sarah Bulmer, Ben Carver, Robin Durie, et al. "Lines in the Sand? Towards an Agenda for Critical Border Studies." *Geopolitics* 14, no. 3 (2009) 582–587.

Parkinson, John R. *Democracy and Public Space: The Physical Sites of Democratic Performance*. Oxford, UK: Oxford University Press, 2012.

Pfaff, Julia. "Mobile Phone Geographies." *Geography Compass* 4, no. 10 (2010): 1433–1447. doi:10.1111/j.1749-8198.2010.00388.x

Pfaff, Steven. *Exit-Voice Dynamics and the Collapse of East Germany: The Crisis of Leninism and the Revolution of 1989*. Durham: Duke University Press, 2006.

Polletta, Francesca. *Freedom Is an Endless Meeting: Democracy in American Social Movements*. Chicago: University of Chicago Press, 2002.

Prost, Henri. *Istanbul Hakkında Notlar* [Notes on Istanbul]. Istanbul: Istanbul Belediye Matbaası, 1938.

Putnam, Robert D. *Bowling Alone: The Collapse and Revival of American Community*. New York: Simon and Schuster, 2000.

Rafael, Vicente L. "The Cell Phone and the Crowd: Messianic Politics in the Contemporary Philippines." *Public Culture* 15, no. 3 (2003): 399–425. https://muse.jhu.edu/article/47187.

Rancière, Jacques. *Disagreement: Politics and Philosophy*. Translated by Julie Rose. Minneapolis: University of Minnesota Press, 1999.

Ratti, Carl, Dennis Frenchman, Riccardo Maria Pulselli, and Sarah Williams. "Mobile Landscapes: Using Location Data from Cell Phones for Urban Analysis." *Environment and Planning B: Planning and Design* 33, no. 5 (2006): 727–748. doi:10.1068/b32047.

Rawls, John. *Political Liberalism*. New York: Columbia University Press, 1993.

———. *A Theory of Justice*. Cambridge, MA: Belknap Press of Harvard University Press, 1999.

Roei, Noa. "Molding Resistance: Aesthetics and Politics in the Struggle of Bil'in against the Wall." In *Art and Visibility in Migratory Culture: Conflict, Resistance, and Agency*, edited by Mieke Bal and Miguel Á. Hernández-Navarro, 239–256. Brill Online Books and Journals, 2011. http://www.ingentaconnect.com/content/rodopi/tham/2011/00000023/00000001/art00014.

Romero, Luis Albert. *A History of Argentina in the Twentieth Century*. Translated by James P. Brennan. University Park: Penn State University Press, 2002.

Routledge, Paul. "Backstreets, Barricades, and Blackouts: Urban Terrains of Resistance in Nepal." *Environment and Planning D: Society and Space* 12, no. 5 (1994): 559–578. doi:10.1068/d120559.

———. "Critical Geopolitics and Terrains of Resistance." *Political Geography* 15, nos. 6–7 (1996): 509–531. doi:10.1016/0962–6298(96)00029–7.

Rucht, Dieter, and Joris Verhulst. "The Framing of Opposition to the War on Iraq." Chapter 12 in *The World Says No to War: Demonstrations against the War on Iraq*, edited by Stefaan

Walgrave and Dieter Rucht, 239–260. Social Movements, Protest, and Contention, Vol. 33. New Edition. Minneapolis: University of Minnesota Press, 2010. http://www.jstor.org/stable/10.5749/j.cttts43x.

Rumford, Chris. "Theorizing Borders." *European Journal of Social Theory* 9, no. 2 (2006): 155–169.

Salter, Mark. "Places Everyone! Studying the Performativity of the Border." *Political Geography* 30, no. 2 (2011): 66–67.

Sarjakoski, Tapani. "Networked GIS for Public Participation-Emphasis on Utilizing Image Data Computers." *Environment and Urban Systems* 22, no. 4 (1998): 381–392. doi:10.1016/S0198–9715(98)00031–3.

Sassen, Saskia. "Incompleteness and the Possibility of Making: Towards Denationalized Citizenship?" In *Political Power and Social Theory*, edited by Diane E. Davis and Julian Go, 20:229–258. Bingley, UK: Emerald Group, 2009.

———. "Local Actors in Global Politics." *Current Sociology* 52, no. 4 (2004): 649–670. doi:10.1177/0011392104043495.

———. "The Topoi of E-Space: Global Cities and Global Value Chains." *Built Environment* 24, nos. 2–3 (1998): 134–141.

Sasson-Levy, Orna, and Tamar Rapoport. "Body, Gender, and Knowledge in Protest Movements: The Israeli Case." *Gender and Society* 17, no. 3 (2003): 379–403. http://vhost4.bc.edu/content/dam/files/schools/cas_sites/sociology/pdf/SassonLevy_Rapoport.pdf.

Sennett, Richard. *The Fall of Public Man*. Cambridge: Cambridge University Press, 1976.

———. *The Spaces of Democracy*. Raoul Wallenberg Lectures, 1998. Ann Arbor, MI: University of Michigan.

Shadmi, Erella. "Between Resistance and Compliance, Feminism and Nationalism: Women in Black in Israel." *Women's Studies International Forum* 23, no. 1 (2000): 23–34. doi:10.1016/S0277–5395(99)00087–4.

Shafir, Gershon, ed. *The Citizenship Debates: A Reader*. Minneapolis: University of Minnesota Press, 1998.

Sharp, Gene. *The Politics of Nonviolent Action*. 3 vols. Boston: Porter Sargent, 1973.

Sharp, Joanne P., Paul Routledge, Chris Philo, and Ronan Paddison, eds. *Entanglements of Power: Geographies of Domination/Resistance*. London: Routledge, 2000.

Sheller, Mimi. "Mobile Publics: Beyond the Network Perspective." *Environment and Planning D: Society and Space* 22, no. 1 (2004): 39–52. doi:10.1068/d324t.

Sibley, David. *Geographies of Exclusion: Society and Difference in the West*. London: Routledge, 1995.

Silier, Orhan Y. "The Significance of Banned May Day Demonstrations for the Historiography of the First of May and Worker's Movement: Some Observations and Theses Based on the Case of Turkey." In *Storie e Immagini del 1° Maggio* [History and Image of May 1st], edited by Piero Lacaita, 725–731. Rome: Universita' Degli Studi di Lecce, 1990.

Simmel, George. *Philosophy of Money*. Translated by T. Bottomore and David Frisby; edited by David Frisby. New York: Routledge, 1978. Reprint, New York: Routledge, 2003.

Simonson, Karin. "The Anti-War Movement: Waging Peace on the Brink of War." Paper prepared for the Programme on NGOs and Civil Society of the Centre for Applied Studies in International Negotiations, Geneva, March 2003. https://www.files.ethz.ch/isn/20302/03.20.

Singh, Indu B., and Joseph N. Pelton. *The Safe City: Living Free in a Dangerous World*. North Charleston, SC: CreateSpace Independent Publishing Platform, 2013.

Smith, Charles D. *Palestine and the Arab-Israeli Conflict: A History with Documents*. Boston: Bedford/St. Martin's, 2007.

Smith, Jackie. *Social Movements for Global Democracy*. Baltimore, MD: Johns Hopkins University Press, 2008.

Smith, Neil. "Contours of a Spatialized Politics: Homeless Vehicles and the Production of Geographical Scale." *Social Text* 33 (1992): 54–81. doi:10.2307/466434.

———. "Homeless/Global: Scaling Places." In *Mapping the Futures: Local Cultures, Global Change*, edited by Jon Bird, Barry Curtis, Tim Putnam, George Roberston, and Lisa Tickner, 87–119. London: Routledge, 1993.

Smith, Philip. "Ritual." In *Blackwell Encyclopedia of Sociology*, edited by George Ritzer, 3944–3946. Blackwell Publishing, 2007. *Blackwell Reference Online*.

Soja, Edward W. *Postmodern Geographies: The Reassertion of Space in Critical Social Theory*. London: Verso, 1989.

Souza e Silva, Adriana de, and Jordan Frith. *Mobile Interfaces in Public Spaces: Locational Privacy, Control, and Urban Sociability*. New York: Routledge, 2012.

Spivak, Gayatri Chakravorty. "Can the Subaltern Speak?" In *Marxism and the Interpretation of Culture*, edited by Cary Nelson and Lawrence Grossberg, 271–317. Basingstoke, UK: Macmillan Education, 1988.

Svirsky, Gila. *Standing for Peace: A History of Women in Black in Israel*. 1996. http://www.gilasvirsky.com.

Swyngedouw, Erik. "'Every Revolution Has Its Square' Politicising the Post-Political City." In *Urban Constellations*, edited by Matthew Gandy, 22–25. Berlin: Jovis, 2011.

Taine, Hippolyte. *The Origins of Contemporary France*. Translated by John Durand. New York: Holt, 1876–1894.

Tanyeli, Ugur. "1950'lerden Bu Yana Mimari Paradigmaların Degişimi ve 'Reel Mimarlık'" [Changes in architectural paradigms from the 1950s to the present]. In *75 Yılda Degişen Kent ve Mimarlık* [The changing city and architecture in 75 years (Turkish)], edited by Yıldız Sey, 25–39. Istanbul: Tarih Vakfı Yayınları, 1998.

Tarrow, Sidney. "Transnational Politics: Contention and Institutions in International Politics." *Annual Review of Political Science* 4 (2001): 1–20. doi:10.1146/annurev.polisci.4.1.1.

Taylor, Diana. "Making a Spectacle: The Mothers of the Plaza de Mayo." In *The Politics of Motherhood: Activist Voices from Left to Right*, edited by Alexis Jetter, Annelise Orleck, and Diana Taylor, 182–196. Hanover, NH: Dartmouth College, University Press of New England, 1997.

———. "Trauma and Performance: Lessons from Latin America." *PMLA: Publications of the Modern Language Association of America* 121, no. 5 (2006): 1674–1677. doi:10.1632/pmla.2006.121.5.1674.

Taylor, Peter. "A Materialist Framework for Political Geography." *Transactions of the Institute of British Geographers* 7, no. 1 (1982): 15–34.

Tekeli, Ilhan. "Türkiye'de Cumhuriyet Döneminde Kentsel Gelişme ve Kent Planlaması" [Urban growth and urban planning during the republican period in Turkey]. In *75 Yılda Degişen Kent ve Mimarlık* [The changing city and architecture in 75 years (Turkish)], edited by Yıldız Sey, 1–24. Istanbul: Tarih Vakfı Yayınları, 1998.

Tekeli, Ilhan, and Tarık Okyay. "Case Study of a Relocated Capital: Ankara." In *Urban Planning Practice in Developing Countries*, edited by John L. Taylor and David G. Williams, 123–143. Oxford, UK: Pergamon, 1982. doi:10.1016/B978-0-08-022225-7.50010-3.

Thrift, Nigel J. *Non-Representational Theory: Space, Politics, Affect*. London: Routledge, 2008.

———. "The Still Point." In *Geographies of Resistance*, edited by Steve Pile and Michael Keith, 124–151. London: Routledge 1997.

Tilly, Charles. "Collective Violence in European Perspective." In *Violence in America: Historical and Comparative Perspectives*, edited by Hugh D. Graham and Ted R. Gurr, 4–42. New York: Signet, 1969.

———. *The Politics of Collective Violence*. Cambridge: Cambridge University Press, 2003.

Tilly, Louise A., and Charles Tilly, eds. *Class Conflict and Collective Action*. Beverly Hills: Sage, 1981.

Toal, Gerard (Ó Tuathail, Gearóid). "Being Geopolitical: Comments on Engin Isin's *Being Political: Genealogies of Citizenship*." *Political Geography* 24, no. 3 (2005): 365–372.

Torre, Susanne. "Claiming the Public Space: The Mothers of Plaza de Mayo." In *Gender, Space, Architecture*, edited by Jane Rendell, Barbara Penner, and Iain Borden, 140–150. London: Routledge, 2000.

Turkle, Sherry. *Alone Together: Why We Expect More from Technology and Less from Each Other*. New York: Basic Books, 2011.

Turner, Ralph H. "The Public Perception of Protest." *American Sociological Review* 34, no. 6 (1969): 815–831. http://www.jstor.org/stable/2093084.

Turner, Victor W. *The Forest of Symbols: Aspects of Ndembu Ritual*. New York: Cornell University Press, 1967.

Vale, Lawrence J. *Architecture, Power and National Identity*. New Haven: Yale University Press, 1992.

Verhulst, Joris. "February 15, 2003: The World Says No to War." In *The World Says No to War: Demonstrations against the War on Iraq*, edited by Stefaan Walgrave and Dieter Rucht, 1–19. Minneapolis: University of Minnesota Press, 2010.

Vidler, Anthony. *The Architectural Uncanny: Essays in the Modern Unhomely*. Cambridge, MA: MIT Press, 1992.

Vinitzky-Seroussi, Vered. "Jerusalem Assassinated Rabin and Tel Aviv Commemorated Him: Rabin Memorials and the Discourse of National Identity in Israel." *City and Society* 10 (1998): 183–203. doi:10.1525/city.1998.10.1.183.

———. *Yitzhak Rabin's Assassination and the Dilemmas of Commemoration*. Albany: State University of New York Press, 2009.

Wacquant, Loïc. "Territorial Stigmatization in the Age of Advanced Marginality." *Thesis Eleven* 91, no. 1 (2007): 66–77. doi:10.1177/0725513607082003.

Walgrave, Stefaan, and Joris Verhulst. "Government Stance and Internal Diversity of Protest: A Comparative Study of Protest against the War in Iraq in Eight Countries." *Social Forces* 87, no. 3 (2009): 1355–1387. doi:10.1353/sof.0.0171.

Watson, Sophie. *City Publics: The (Dis)enchantments of Urban Encounters*. London: Routledge, 2006.

Weintraub, Jeff. "The Theory and Politics of the Public/Private Distinction." In *Public and Private in Thought and Practice: Perspectives on a Grand Dichotomy*, edited by Jeff Weintraub and Krishan Kumar, 1–42. Chicago: University of Chicago Press, 1997.

Wiebenson, John. "Planning and Using Resurrection City." *Journal of the American Institute of Planners* 35, no. 6 (1969): 405–411. doi:10.1080/01944366908977260.

Williams, Joyce E. "Social Distance." In *Blackwell Encyclopedia of Sociology*, edited by George Ritzer. Blackwell Publishing, 2007. *Blackwell Reference Online*.

Woito, Robert. "Methods of Nonviolent Actions." In *Protest, Power, and Change: An Encyclopedia of Nonviolent Action from ACT-UP to Women's Suffrage*, edited by Roger S. Powers, William B. Vogele, Douglas Bond, and Christopher Kruegler, 319–328. New York: Routledge, 2011.

———. "Nonviolence, Principled." In *Protest, Power, and Change: An Encyclopedia of Nonviolent Action from ACT-UP to Women's Suffrage*, edited by Roger S. Powers, William B. Vogele, Douglas Bond, and Christopher Kruegler, 357–364. New York: Routledge, 2011.

Wright, Jan. "Disciplining the Body: Power, Knowledge and Subjectivity in a Physical Education Lesson." In *Culture and Text*, edited by Alison Lee and Cate Poynton, 152–169. Sydney: Allen and Unwin, 2000.

Wright, Sam. *Crowds and Riots: A Study in Social Organization*. London: Sage, 1978.

Writers for the 99% (Group). *Occupying Wall Street: The Inside Story of an Action That Changed America*. Brunswick, Vic., Australia: Scribe, 2012.

Yiftachel, Oren. "Planning and Social Control: Exploring the Dark Side." *Journal of Planning Literature* 12, no. 4 (1988): 395–406.

Yiftachel, Oren, and Haim Yacobi. "Barriers, Walls and Dialectics: The Shaping of 'Creeping Apartheid' in Israel/Palestine." In *Against the Wall: Israel's Barrier to Peace*, edited by Michael Sorkin, 138–157. New York: New Press, 2005.

Young, Iris Marion. *Inclusion and Democracy*. Oxford, UK: Oxford University, 2000.

———. *Justice and the Politics of Difference*. Princeton, NJ: Princeton University Press, 1990.

Young, Jock. *The Exclusive Society: Social Exclusion, Crime and Difference in Late Modernity*. London: Sage, 1999.

Zhao, Dingxin. *The Power of Tiananmen: State-Society Relations and the 1989 Beijing Student Movement*. Chicago: University of Chicago Press, 2001.

Žižek, Slavoj. "Slavoj Žižek Speaks at Occupy Wall Street: Transcript." *Impose Magazine*, September 17, 2013. http://www.imposemagazine.com/bytes/slavoj-zizek-at-occupy-wall-street-transcript.

———. *The Ticklish Subject: The Absent Centre of Political Ontology*. London: Verso, 1999.

Zukin, Sharon. *The Cultures of Cities*. Malden, MA: Blackwell, 1995.

Index